SOMALIA AND OPERATION
RESTORE HOPE

SOMALIA

AND OPERATION RESTORE HOPE

REFLECTIONS ON PEACEMAKING AND PEACEKEEPING

John L. Hirsch
Robert B. Oakley

Foreword by Chester A. Crocker

UNITED STATES
INSTITUTE OF PEACE PRESS
Washington, D.C.

United States Institute of Peace
1550 M Street NW
Washington, DC 20005

First published 1995

Printed in the United States of America

The paper used in this publication meets the minimum requirements of American National Standard for Information Sciences—Permanence of Paper for Printed Library Materials, ANSI Z39.48-1984.

Library of Congress Cataloging-in-Publication Data
Hirsch, John L., 1936-
    Somalia and Operation Restore Hope: reflections on peacemaking and peace-keeping / John L. Hirsh, Robert B. Oakley; foreword by Chester A. Crocker.
       p. cm.
    Includes bibliographical references.
    ISBN 1-878379-41-0 (pbk.)
    1. United Nations—Armed Forces—Somalia. 2. United States—Armed Forces—Somalia. 3. Operation Restore Hope, 1992-93. 4. War victims—Somalia. I. Oakley, Robert B., 1931- . II. Title.
JX1981.P7H575 1995
341.5'8—dc20   95-8221
                                                                   CIP

Contents

Maps

Foreword

*T*he winding down of U.S. military engagement in Somalia came at a time of turmoil and confusion about the U.S. role in the post–Cold War security order. Commentators, policymakers, and scholars will look back on America's Somalia enterprise of 1992–94 as setting the tone of this transitional era. That is why this book is so important: It matters deeply what lessons we draw from Somalia precisely because each episode in this uncharted post–Cold War transition is often characterized as a huge, clearly worded road sign. But the lessons are subtler than they might first appear. To interpret them properly, it is necessary to set aside the one-liners and the op-eds long enough to listen to the story of diplomatic veterans whose careers span a range of regions, conflicts, and decades.

This book captures the essence of the Somalia experience of humanitarian intervention. Bob Oakley and John Hirsch outline the guiding assumptions behind the initial U.S.-led phase of intervention, the United Task Force (UNITAF), and compare these guidelines and resulting practices with those of the ensuing, UN-led phase of peacekeeping, the second UN Operation in Somalia, UNOSOM II. This discussion, presented with fairness and candor, will serve as a rich field for analysis by practitioners and scholars.

Some commentators look coldly at the U.S. engagement in Somalia as a costly failure of misguided internationalism. They see in it a form of media-driven, shortsighted "ad hockery" that placed our nation's most treasured assets in harm's way as an almost casual act of strategic charity. This perspective emphasizes the absence of full disclosure about how hard it can be to intervene constructively with military force in alien societies and to exit honorably with the mission accomplished. We are reminded that Somalis, like some other people emerging from the European and Soviet empires, have long traditions of factional violence and little experience of civil order. Accordingly, we are urged to narrow our strategic focus and develop greater tolerance for the humanitarian tragedies that are certain to accompany the new world disorder. Passionate adherents of this isolationist view will go further, asserting that Somalia should inoculate us against further ventures of this sort, just as it has discouraged any inclination toward deeper U.S. military involvement in Rwanda and Bosnia.

Others want to draw different lessons, believing that our difficulties in exotic Somalia have inhibited us from doing what is necessary in Bosnia. According to this interpretation, U.S. political will to lead in shaping the post–Cold War system is being sapped by public perceptions of Somalia. This view sees Somalia as an unnecessary and somehow trivial engagement whose "failure" has discredited good ideas and placed "more important" interests, engagements, and (implicitly) peoples at risk. The lesson of Somalia, in this view, is to refrain from applying global norms and standards in U.S. policy and to disengage ourselves from the world's strategic slums and other difficult places.

Still others view the Somalia episode from a more hopeful angle as the beginning of an era in which the United States will chart a humanitarian course as one hallmark of leadership for a new age. After all, this would be perfectly consistent with the notion of American exceptionalism and the U.S. tradition of seeking to do good works in our foreign policy. The decision to intervene, unilaterally if necessary, and save Somali lives in a context where "national interests"—traditionally defined—were absent would be startling only if some other nation had done it. George Bush's judgment that U.S. forces could and should stop humanitarian disaster in Somalia was, from this perspective, the very essence of leadership. Nor was there anything partisan about that decision, as President-elect Bill Clinton's enthusiastic endorsement of it made clear. Once U.S. leaders acted, they suddenly had lots of company from friends and allies in conducting the enterprise and plenty of congressional and public support at home.

Where the Somalia exercise turned sour—according to the humanitarian purists—is when the United States and the United Nations became involved in Somali politics. We erred when we moved beyond the mandate of creating a secure environment for humanitarian operations to one of helping to put Somalia back on its feet as a country and trying to impose order on its armed factions. Uninvited, armed intervention in a strife-torn country is fine, according to this doctrine, so long as it remains politically immaculate and does not entangle outsiders in the messy business of solving local political problems.

This book enables the reader to grasp the fallacies in all these interpretations. First, it makes it abundantly clear that external intervention in Somalia has not been a failure. Much has been accomplished in humanitarian terms, and a larger tragedy has been averted. Second, the Somali political landscape has been changed forever, creating the possibility for a workable political outcome designed by Somalis themselves. Media and other observers who focus narrowly on the apparent rejection of outside plans or initiatives by local parties would—as the authors remind us—be better advised to look a little deeper and stop the rush to judgment long enough to grasp what is happening. They might then recognize that outside intervention is exactly what has knocked a hideously costly, stalemated clan war off dead center and opened the field for new political initiatives worked out by Somalis themselves. Breaking up a lethal logjam is a classic function of the third party intervening in a conflict situation.

Third, this book sheds a clear light on why and how the initial humanitarian intervention gradually became something far more broadly, if somewhat naively, defined. Somalia was transformed in a matter of months from a famine-stricken backwater where heartless warlords and hopped-up teenage gangs reigned over helpless innocents into a sort of living laboratory for the new theories of UN peacekeeping then current in both the UN headquarters and the U.S. government. Perhaps, ironically, it was the impressive leadership, coherence, and dramatic success of the UNITAF phase (December 1992 to May 1993) which made it look too easy, thus encouraging the tendency toward "mission creep" that produced UNOSOM II's vast "nationbuilding" mandate. But then the unthinking slide toward some modern version of trusteeship over an ex-colonial territory triggered a violent, nationalist backlash by a powerful Somali clan faction.

There can be little doubt about the high cost of discontinuities in the leadership of the United States–United Nations effort in Somalia. The smooth, carefully delineated and coordinated operating methods of Oakley and Marine Lt. Gen. Robert Johnston (and their unusually close links to Washington) were interrupted first by the presidential transition in Washington (changing many of the policy people at the other end of the telephone), and again when the entire field leadership of the intervention was replaced before and during the handoff from UNITAF to UNOSOM II and a less decisive and disciplined UN operation replaced an essentially U.S.-managed one. When one considers the full practical impact of these changes just a few months into the operation, is it any wonder that things turned sour? Why expect a seamless transition to UN-led peace-keeping to flow from a rancorous argument between Washington and UN headquarters about whether the transfer should even take place and whether the United States had completed the initial task? How could the transition have been seamless when the previous UNITAF management and many of the vitally important U.S. combat units had left before the new UNOSOM II management was even in place in Mogadishu?

Such jolting discontinuity of leadership, tradition, doctrine, personal chemistry, operating procedures, policy instincts, and bureaucratic systems was bound to disrupt the effectiveness and credibility of the external military presence. These factors, combined with the sweeping new mandate authorizing UNOSOM II, could only raise Somali doubts about the new UN objective. All that had been accomplished, politically and militarily, was placed at risk.

Arguably, Somalia does not offer us a fair test of the Bush strategy of humanitarian intervention. It certainly is not a fair test of the evolving concept of "peace enforcement" conducted according to Chapter VII of the UN Charter—a concept that UNOSOM II attempted to carry forward from UNITAF, which had used it so successfully for more limited purposes.

The Somalia "failure" is not a failure of either humanitarian intervention or muscular peacekeeping, but a failure to conduct them steadily and wisely. UNITAF had success during its too brief deployment. Opening up a secure environment for relief while keeping the warlords more or less sweet and somewhat off balance; maintaining and demonstrating military primacy without making a permanent adversary or national hero of any local actor; pushing the military factions towards a locally led political process while opening up that process to civilian elites, without advocating precise formulas; removing heavy weapons from areas of conflict while fostering the restoration of police and government functions—these are undertakings of the highest order of delicacy and complexity in a militarized and fragmented society such as Somalia's. These UNITAF accomplishments in fact went far beyond the one-line goal of creating a "secure environment for humanitarian relief" discussed publicly by U.S. officials during the UNITAF phase. The goals required world-class leadership as well as a well-oiled military-civilian bureaucratic machine capable of acting quickly and coherently.

Does Somalia, then, tell us that the United Nations is just not up to managing "peace enforcement" operations in a dangerous environment where challenges to UN authority are likely? Should we oppose placing the United Nations in charge of ambitious mandates to supervise disarmament arrangements linked to political transitions and humanitarian relief and resettlement? These are two separate questions, and the answers do not fit on a bumper sticker. The United Nations has achieved some dramatic successes in dangerous, complex situations with wide-ranging mandates. Its performances in Cambodia and Namibia were highly effective, professional exercises that unquestionably enabled these fragmented, wartorn lands to get on their feet.

But the United Nations' ability to handle a militarily challenging peace enforcement operation under Chapter VII provisions has not yet been demonstrated. Somalia tells us that change is needed in the modus operandi of the UN system itself: You cannot enforce peace when your own structure is an undisciplined and often chaotic set of rival bureaucratic fiefdoms that characteristically resist unified command and control in the field at both civilian and military levels. Basic change is needed on the issues of delegation to the field, unity of command in the field, professional military backstopping and oversight in New York, and many other matters. We knew these things already, and now we know them better. After Somalia—and with the experience of Bosnia (as well as Cambodia, Namibia, Mozambique, and Angola)—we are better prepared for discussion of how best to upgrade worldwide capabilities for handling the sorts of challenges we have faced in these places and will face again elsewhere.

Equally important, Somalia reminds us of the need for improvement in the way we—the UN's leading member—conduct ourselves when we define missions, review and approve peacekeeping mandates, and approve UN force levels and budgets. This book points clearly to the conclusion that the United States and the United Nations overreached when they expanded the initial mandate—without making it possible to carry it out. The authors confirm that a debate over disarmament of the factions raged out of public view between UN Secretary-General Boutros Boutros-Ghali and both the Bush and Clinton administrations. In the end, of course, the United States won the debate, refusing to take on this time-consuming task before handing off to UN command and UNOSOM II, whose members pleaded for UNITAF to stay on a few months longer. The authors conclude that there is little doubt UNITAF could have done much more to demilitarize and disarm Somalia (more or less voluntarily, without our getting bogged down or incurring significant losses) if the United States had been prepared to keep the necessary forces in place longer and if the UN Security Council had directed the organization to plan and take over responsibility for this longer-term task.

Sensing the more open-ended time frame and resource implications of disarming the Somali factions, and realizing the possible negative fallout on the home front, both U.S. administrations strongly opposed it. Nothing was done to develop a comprehensive and systematic program of removal of heavy weapons, disarmament and demobilization. Clearly, much more could have been done to pave the way for the ambitious nationbuilding mandate contained in UNSC Resolution 814 if UNITAF had stayed on for a few more months in parallel with and under UNOSOM II. This ball, apparently, was simply dropped by the administration in Washington as well as by the secretary-general and the Security Council in New York. As a result, the United Nations received a bolder mandate than the one Bush had given UNITAF (as expanded on the ground by Oakley and Johnston), but it was given woefully inadequate means for carrying it out. These things should never have been permitted to happen. Either the mandate under Resolution 814 should have been drastically revised, or the means to implement it should have been mobilized.

In sum, the contrast between the peacekeeping operations documented here is dramatic. At the levels of strategy, mandate, military resources, tactical and strategic leadership, reporting channels and lines of authority, and of course ultimate responsibility, Somalia has experienced several distinct types of peacekeeping, as Hirsch and Oakley make clear: the minimalist and ineffective UNOSOM I; the skillfully managed, U.S.-led UNITAF; the overstretched, coercive nationbuilding phase of UNOSOM II; and the final scaled-back, more accommodative UNOSOM II. As a result, the Somali case will be a laboratory for years to come, from which vital lessons can be learned about how best to refine the instrument of peacekeeping that we will so obviously need in the years ahead.

I would underscore a handful of the most striking lessons that flow from the Oakley-Hirsch account:

- The need is obvious for the United States and other leading nations (within or outside the United Nations, as appropriate) to swing into action through preventive diplomacy before states fail and societies implode. Once the men with the guns seize the initiative as political actors, it becomes more complex to accommodate the interests of their peculiar hierarchies in addition to those of the broader political system. And it becomes more costly for external peacemakers to apply their will.

- The linkage between UN peacekeeping mandates, whether under Chapter VI or VII provisions, and the resources made available by member states must be better understood by Security Council members when they approve such missions. There can be no excuse for approving grandiose missions that will expose UN peacekeepers to severe risk and the United Nations itself to ridicule and discredit. But at the same time, there is no excuse for underfunding and under-staffing missions that—in our considered judgment—warrant our support. It is simply irresponsible (as well as dishonest) for American commentators to blast the United Nations for problems arising from ill-conceived or poorly drawn mandates. If we are angry at the some-times disappointing fruits of Security Council resolutions, we must forcefully remind ourselves, our media, and our public opinion that the council is a mirror of the actions, inactions, fudges, and fantasies of the leading members, who can veto anything they do not like.

- The clear and continuing shortcomings in the United Nations' capacity to manage peacekeeping, and peace enforcement in particular, argue strongly for a sustained push for UN institutional reform, restraint and selectivity in undertaking enforcement missions, and creativity in sup-porting their management. For some time to come, the UN structure will be capable of success only with the support of big powers (or NATO). Historically, UN operations have prospered when they enjoyed the determined, focused backing of one or more major powers with the demonstrated will and capacity to support them. This was the case with the far-reaching but highly successful Congo operation of the 1960s. It was the case as well with intricate, multipurpose UN oper-ations in Namibia and Cambodia in more recent times. Somalia during the UNITAF phase enjoyed such backing, but the successor UNOSOM II operation was orphaned by both Washington and New York.

- It is essential that both United States and United Nations authorities assign responsibility for the success of such operations to world-class people and then aggressively support them, while forcing operational reviews and fresh decisions if things turn sour. UNOSOM II got off to a poor start and was permitted to slide toward a humiliating crisis in October 1993 before being redefined under duress—the worst of outcomes from the standpoint of United Nations (and United States) credibility worldwide.

- In the conduct of UN operations, it is essential to strive toward greater delegation of authority to a more coherent and streamlined structure of field leadership (unity of command) that avoids multiple reporting channels back to New York. UNOSOM II clearly suffered from the United Nations' byzantine bureaucratic structure, a problem compounded by compartmentalization within the U.S. military command.

- Peacekeeping initiatives should not be launched without some assurances of stability of leadership in the field, some hope for continuity of backstopping in Washington (and New York), and some clear hierarchy of accountability for the whole business in the appropriate capitals and in the UN Security Council. Continuity of leadership and seamless handoffs are the sine qua non of effectiveness in peace operations. Sudden changes in either resources made available (including key combat components) or the leadership relationships and reporting channels between the field and key capitals must be avoided.

At the strategic level, the Somalia story obliges us to consider another set of questions that can only be touched on here. What are the logical limits to United States and United Nations involvement in nationbuilding or restoring failed states? Can and should the United States insist on a carefully worded national interest standard for support of (and participation in) such operations? What obligation is there to respond when no such interest exists or to remain engaged with U.S. forces after headline humanitarian goals have been accomplished? Books will be written on these matters, but a close reading of the Oakley-Hirsch narrative suggests a few basic themes:

- The United Nations and its leading members, by overreaching as dramatically as they did with Resolution 814, created a reaction and a backlash. There is no enthusiasm in most parts of the world for a latter-day, UN-managed colonial era. The sweep of the Resolution 814 mandate and the manner of its implementation changed the Somali political climate from humiliated acceptance of an external helping hand to renewed polarization and the emergence of nationalist martyrs. At home, support for an initially popular undertaking collapsed amid total confusion about U.S. purposes. Was this a humanitarian relief mission, a manhunt for a wily warlord, or a nationbuilding program? There is no enthusiasm in Western societies to become global police. It will not be easy for Western leaders to rally their nations to go to war for the new world order.

- George Bush was right—politically, strategically, and ethically—to launch Operation Restore Hope, and Bill Clinton was right to support that decision. It is not useful, as we near the end of the 20th century, to limit our understanding of the national interest to such things as defense of the homeland, access to oil, security of lines of communication, or control of key industrial assets or natural resources. Categories of national interest that relate to global order (e.g., sanctity of borders) and to global standards (e.g., mass humanitarian catastrophe) must be recognized as we consider the U.S. (and UN) role in post-Cold War security.

- This does not mean a lurch to indiscriminate global interventionism. It suggests, however, that our security policy cannot redline the world's bad neighborhoods as off limits for humanitarian operations. Would we have stood by if losses as large as Somalia's in 1991–92 had been occurring in Greece, Ireland, Israel, or Poland? Operation Restore Hope was an act of human solidarity without regard to race, religion, or national origin. That is why Congress and the American people supported it. And that is why no one is especially proud of our performance in Rwanda, the first victim of the post-Somalia backlash. It is hard to argue that Americans should behave otherwise, and harder still to claim that we can sustain a global leadership role if we have one set of lines in the sand for good neighborhoods and another for the Somalias.

- The criteria for judgment on the use of force for humanitarian ends are not primarily regional or geographic. What, then, are they? It has somehow been claimed that we should not intervene (or encourage the United Nations to do so) in Somalia unless we are also prepared to do so in Sudan, Liberia, or Tajikistan. But this quest for consistency only confuses the picture. It cannot be U.S. policy to do nothing anywhere unless we can be effective everywhere. The real issue is whether humanitarian intervention is likely to be effective and whether it can be effective at an acceptable cost to those who intervene. It will be apparent that a wide range of factors must be examined, including logistics, terrain, the nature of opposing forces on the ground, the likelihood of armed opposition to the intervention, and whether the intervening party can maintain "strategic neutrality" between the local parties, as Oakley did in Somalia.

- But even this analysis provides only part of the answer. We need to know more about exits from humanitarian interventions. The act of intervening (assuming it is done effectively) has a decisive impact on the local balance—the balance between armed factions and innocent civilians as well as the balance between the factions themselves. Operation Restore Hope was no exception. It dramatically strengthened Somalia's vestigial civil society and challenged the warlords' political monopoly. By stopping the factional strife, it also froze in place the military situation, denying the initiative to the stronger factions and protecting, for a time, the weaker. In this way, a new state of affairs developed to replace the hideous one that prompted the intervention.

- Viewed in this light, we need to do better at identifying and analyzing what will replace this new state of affairs so that the previous one does not return. This point has inexorable logical implications. It means that we must answer not only the question of when and how to exit but also the question of how humanitarian operations will bridge into a political settlement strategy so that something can emerge to replace the temporary structure created by intervention. The Bush administration solved this one by pointing to a quick hand-off to the United Nations—begging the question of whether the United Nations would be up to the task, and leaving unaddressed the problem of the UN's exit strategy. It was left to Oakley's team to improvise (under a UN umbrella) the political settlement strategy that began to take shape in early 1993 but was dropped in May. After reading the Oakley-Hirsch account, it is hard to escape the conclusion that humanitarian intervention requires a linkage to political strategies of peacemaking and conflict resolution. The humanitarian purist cannot have it both ways: If there is an appeal for outside force, it must be accompanied by an outside strategy for leashing the dogs—while healing the wounds—of war.

Chester A. Crocker
Georgetown University

Preface

*T*his book emerges from our shared experience in Somalia, first in the mid-1980s as ambassador and deputy chief of mission at the U.S. Embassy in Mogadishu, and later during Operation Restore Hope. It is also the result of our separate but related professional careers in the U.S. Foreign Service, where we have dealt with the complexities of peacekeeping and peacemaking in the Middle East and elsewhere long before the Somalia situation reached crisis proportions. Robert Oakley's experience in Vietnam and Lebanon, John Hirsch's tour in Israel, and our separate assignments at the U.S. mission to the United Nations and in Pakistan in the 1970s and 1980s provided firsthand contact with peoples caught up in ethnic, religious, and territorial conflict, as well as with several UN peacekeeping operations.

It was perhaps fortuitous that Oakley chaired two study groups at the United States Institute of Peace. The first, on the professionalization of peacekeeping, begun in spring 1992, attempted to go beyond the new theoretical arguments for a more assertive UN peacekeeping role to the practicalities of what was needed for success in the field. The second, later that year, involved a cross-section of Somalis resident in the United States in an attempt to define the multiple nature of the crisis and to suggest ways in which the international community could help to resolve it. Thus when President Bush and Joint Chiefs of Staff Chairman Colin Powell asked Oakley to go to Somalia as special envoy, he had a headstart on the issues we would face.

We decided to write this book one evening in January 1993, at the U.S. Liaison Office in the Conoco compound, a mile from United Task Force headquarters on the site of the gutted U.S. embassy in Mogadishu and down the rutted street from the residence of faction leader Mohamed Farah Aideed. It struck us that we were living through a unique experience, which should be made available for public interest generally and especially for those interested in peacekeeping. Officially, Operation Restore Hope was a limited humanitarian intervention intended primarily to get relief supplies through to the famine triangle. However, Oakley and Lieutenant General Robert Johnston, with encouragement from Washington and Central Command (CENTCOM), also saw the international presence as an unofficial umbrella under which Somalis could perhaps begin to sort our their political future after twenty-one years under Siad Barre's rule and two years of devastating civil war, drought, famine, and disease. Clearly UNITAF was a transition to the long-term, broader UN operation that was expected to follow.

Operation Restore Hope and UNITAF were unique on several counts. For the first time in history, the United States had sent a large military force to an area without strategic interest on a strictly humanitarian mission. For the second time, the U.S. military was deeply involved in relief and rehabilitation. Operation Provide Comfort, which helped the Kurds in northern Iraq after Operation Desert Storm, had been the first. It was a new venture in peacekeeping because the Security Council for the first time approved the dispatch of a UN-approved force without the request of the local government, even though on some previous occasions that government had been in exile. Moreover, the United States wanted a more traditional UN peacekeeping force to follow UNITAF and work on broader issues and was prepared to leave noncombatant U.S. troops under UN command in order to make the follow-on succeed. In a humanitarian context, an operation taking place under Chapter VII of the UN Charter also constituted a significant new departure. The UNITAF peacekeepers were allowed to use force if necessary to attain their objective of restoring security so that humanitarian operations could proceed. But Johnston and Oakley were determined to avoid any confrontations with the Somali factions so long as UNITAF's mission was not compromised, and to ensure that if force were used it would not lead to permanent hostilities.

However, as events unfolded in 1993 the original focus had to be revised. Thus we found ourselves writing at length about the second UN Operation in Somalia, UNOSOM II, the successor to UNITAF, even though we had not been present. This part of the narrative—particularly the June 5 killing of the Pakistani peacekeepers and the ensuing war between the Somali National Alliance, UNOSOM II, and the U.S.—draws heavily on interviews with those who were there, as well as on interviews with knowledgeable individuals at UN headquarters, and the Departments of State and Defense, as well as on press and other public accounts. It was originally supposed to occupy only a single chapter. Again our plans for the book changed due to developments on the ground, the significance they subsequently took on, and Oakley's renewed participation.

When Oakley was called back into service as special envoy by President Clinton on October 6, after the confrontation in which eighteen Americans were killed and seventy-eight wounded, the entire international enterprise was on the line. Somalia's future, the role of the U.S. in other peacekeeping operations, and the capability of the UN to support future operations hung in the balance. Clinton's decision to keep U.S. forces in Somalia and reinforce support for UNOSOM II for a further five months gave renewed impetus to diplomacy and allowed the Somalis one last chance to start rebuilding their country with international support. It also slowed the negative trend in attitudes toward peacekeeping generally. So the third part of our narrative became an account of Oakley's renewed mission.

As direct participants, we do not claim the dispassionate impartiality of the scholar or historian. Much of this work is drawn from our own recollection of events; discussions and interviews with others who were present or involved in the same issues in Washington, New York, or foreign capitals; and numerous articles and conferences that sought to analyze these events. We have tried to avoid the polemics that surrounded various phases of the operation, to eschew assigning credit or blame, and certainly not to presume that we have, or have had, all the answers. The reader will not find juicy gossip or accusatory rhetoric, nor are confidential documents revealed, because none was used. We believe it is an honest account of what happened, and that it answers some questions about why.

Peacekeeping in Somalia was complex and difficult. Policy directions taken initially by the departing Bush administration were changed by the Clinton administration. The UN Security Council and the secretary-general, with full U.S. support, drastically expanded the mandate and began to establish what many observers, especially proud Somalis, saw as a de facto trusteeship. The transition in Washington coincided with a new, optimistic perception of the UN role and capabilities. This raised excessive expectations and placed impossible demands on the UN, especially in the peacekeeping area. Subsequent setbacks on the ground inevitably led to a reassessment in Washington and in New York as to what peacekeeping entails, a reconsideration which has had resonance in Bosnia, Haiti, and Rwanda. Although the pendulum has stopped swinging away from peacekeeping, the experience will inevitably affect the international community's approach to other conflicts and crises that lie ahead.

The four successive peacekeeping operations—UNOSOM I, UNITAF, and two distinct phases of UNOSOM II—cannot simply be labeled successes or failures. Their respective strengths and weaknesses are part of the learning process for those at the United Nations who plan and conduct peacekeeping operations and for the member states that support and take part in them. Our concluding reflections are offered in the spirit of a constructive contribution to the continuing debate and assessment about when and how such efforts should be undertaken and how UN peacekeeping capabilities and effectiveness can be enhanced.

We wish to express our deep appreciation to the board and staff of the United States Institute of Peace, under whose auspices this book has been written. Thanks particularly to Richard Solomon and Charles Nelson, the Institute's president and vice president, to Sam Lewis, the Institute's previous president, and Chester Crocker, chairman of the Institute's board of directors. Thanks to David Smock, Ken Jensen, Tim Sisk, Jackie Schwartz, Maryann Heimgartner, and Barbara Cullicott for professional, secretarial, and administrative assistance. Priscilla M. Jensen did an outstanding job in helping with research, editing the text, putting it through multiple revisions, and keeping the two of us reasonably coordinated and of good cheer as the manuscript evolved. Jennifer Mason, an Institute summer intern, provided useful research. The Institute's publications department, with special help from Dan Snodderly, prepared the final stages of the manuscript.

We also wish to thank all those who reviewed the manuscript for its content, accuracy, and conceptual framework. Chester Crocker of Georgetown University; Sir Brian Urquhart of the Ford Foundation; Professor Hussein Adam of the College of the Holy Cross; Ambassador Mohamed Sahnoun, the UN secretary-general's first special representative to Somalia; and Bill Garvelink, director of the Office of Foreign Disaster Assistance at the U.S. Agency for International Development, reviewed the manuscript in draft. Other commenters included Olara Otunnu and Michael Doyle of the International Peace Academy, Enid B. Schoettle of the Council on Foreign Relations; and Bill Durch of the Stimson Center.

Retired general Aboucar Liban provided useful perspective on Somali political developments. All the commenters made many valuable suggestions, corrected errors of fact, and filled in gaps on events preceding the deployment of Operation Restore Hope as well as on Operation Provide Relief and UNOSOM I.

The authors are very grateful to all those who agreed to be interviewed and who shared their recollections, knowledge, and impressions of the events and personalities involved in the various aspects of Operation Restore Hope, the activities and policies of the United Nations, and the Somali political and social scene. At UN headquarters, Under Secretaries-General Kofi Annan, James Jonah, and Jan Eliasson; Elizabeth Lindenmayer; and Johannes Mengesha were more than generous with their time. David Bassiouni of UNICEF provided insights on his tenure as the first humanitarian affairs coordinator.

We received strong support and assistance from the officers and staff of the United States Marine Corps, who occupied key positions in the UNITAF command structure in Somalia. General Joseph P. Hoar, Commander in Chief, CENTCOM, and Lieutenant General Robert B. Johnston, Commander UNITAF, personally reviewed the text, as did Lieutenant General Anthony Zinni and Major General Frank Libutti. John Hirsch spent a most productive day at Camp Pendleton, California—home of the First Marine Expeditionary Force—where he discussed the text with Major General Charles Wilhelm, Colonel Bill Steed, Colonel "Irish" Egan, Colonel Bancroft McKittrick, Lieutenant Colonel G. I. Wilson, Major Michael Heisinger, and Major Bob Rea. John Nelson of the Center for Naval Analysis provided valuable information, explaining marine and naval operations in layman's terms.

Both Major General Tom Montgomery, deputy commander of UNOSOM II military forces and senior U.S. forces commander during UNOSOM II, and Michelle Flournoy, special assistant to the assistant secretary of defense for strategic plans and policy, read chapter 7 carefully and provided us with numerous factual inputs or corrections, as well as extremely valuable insights and criticisms. Major Michael Sheehan, USA, assigned to the U.S. Mission to the United Nations, clarified the text on a number of points. Mari Borstelmann of the Department of the Army provided useful data on public information activities conducted by UNITAF.

In Washington, former Joint Chiefs chairman General Colin L. Powell; Ambassador Herman J. Cohen, previously assistant secretary of state for African affairs; Under Secretary of Defense Frank Wisner; Ambassador

David Shinn, the State Department coordinator for Somalia; Ambassador Brandon Grove, Jr., of the Somalia Task Force; Rear Admiral Frank Bowman and Colonel Perry Baltimore of the Joint Chiefs of Staff; Ambassador James Dobbins of the Somalia Working Group; and Lieutenant Colonel Donald Johnston of the Office of International Security Affairs provided insights on the decision-making process leading to Operation Restore Hope, on the U.S. dialogue with the United Nations, and on developments during UNOSOM II. Bill Garvelink, Kate Farnsworth, and Valerie Newsom in USAID's Office of Foreign Disaster Assistance provided us with their monthly situation reports and other documentation as well as describing their personal experiences in Somalia. Andrew Natsios, former USAID assistant administrator, Philip Johnston, president of CARE USA who was UNOSOM coordinator for humanitarian aid, and Colonel Kevin Kennedy (Ret.), UNOSOM II's deputy coordinator of humanitarian aid and the former head of UNITAF's Civilian-Military Operations Center, were most helpful in analyzing for us the interaction between the humanitarian relief community, the UN system, and the U.S. military and civilian operations.

The Department of State gave John Hirsch leave to begin the manuscript at the Institute of Peace and a fellowship year following, at the Council on Foreign Relations. The Council provided a most cordial setting which is deeply appreciated. Ashok Chaudhari of the Council staff provided valuable assistance.

This book is dedicated to all the men and women of Operation Restore Hope, the UNOSOM operations, and the United States Liaison Office; to the humanitarian relief workers from around the world who worked so hard and gave so much of themselves; and to the Somali people, especially the women and children, who bore the brunt of the disaster.

The authors alone take full responsibility for the text. The views reflected are theirs and do not reflect positions of the Department of State or the United States Institute of Peace.

Abbreviations

CENTCOM	United States Central Command
HRS	Humanitarian Relief Sector
ICRC	International Committee of the Red Cross
NGO	Non-governmental organization
NIF	National Islamic Front
OAU	Organization of African Unity
OFDA	Office of Foreign Disaster Assistance, USAID
OIC	Organization of the Islamic Conference
SACB	Somali Aid Coordinating Body
SDA	Somali Democratic Alliance
SDM	Somali Democratic Movement
SNA	Somali National Alliance
SNDU	Somali National Democratic Union
SNF	Somali National Front
SNM	Somali National Movement
SNU	Somali National Union
SPM	Somali Patriotic Movement
SSDF	Somali Salvation Democratic Front
SSNM	Southern Somali National Movement
UNDP	United Nations Development Program
UNHCR	United Nations High Commissioner for Refugees
UNITAF	United Task Force
UNOSOM I	First United Nations Operation in Somalia
UNOSOM II	Second United Nations Operation in Somalia
USAID	United States Agency for International Development
USC	United Somali Congress
USF	United Somali Front
USLO	United States Liaison Office
USP	United Somali Party
WFP	World Food Program

SOMALIA AND OPERATION RESTORE HOPE

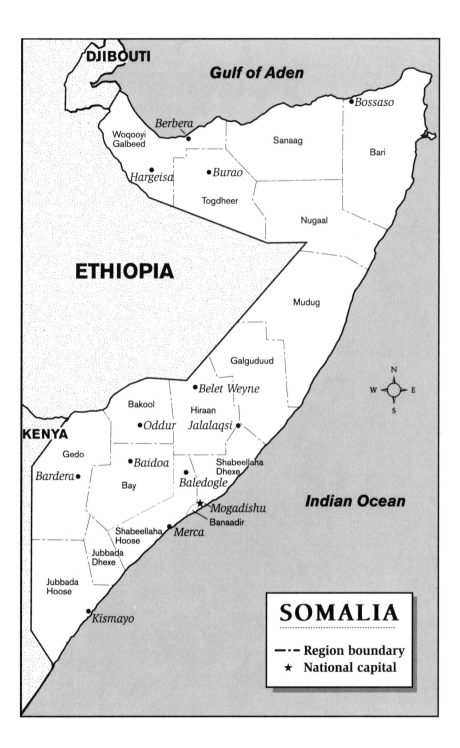

DJIBOUTI

Gulf of Aden

•*Bossaso*

Berbera

Woqooyi
Galbeed

Sanaag

Bari

•*Burao*

Hargeisa

Togdheer

Nugaal

ETHIOPIA

Mudug

Galguduud

•*Belet Weyne*

Bakool

Hiraan

KENYA

•*Oddur*

Jalalaqsi•

Gedo

Shabeellaha
Dhexe

Bardera•

•*Baidoa*

Bay

Baledogle

N
W ◄◆► E
S

Indian Ocean

★*Mogadishu*

Banaadir

Shabeellaha
Hoose

•*Merca*

Jubbada
Dhexe

Jubbada
Hoose

•*Kismayo*

SOMALIA
- - - **Region boundary**
★ **National capital**

Origins of a Crisis

*F*or centuries before the European colonial era, Somalia was a pastoral and nomadic society. Herders of camels, cattle, and sheep lived in a world of "egalitarian anarchy"[1] where the main preoccupation of clan families was the well-being of the herd. With the exception of small Bantu communities along the Juba and Shebelle Rivers, there were no ethnic or religious minorities. It was a singularly homogeneous culture that in theory should have come into the modern era in a cohesive and stable way.

Throughout the precolonial era, the clan structure had functioned cohesively even as the Somalis eked out their nomadic livelihood in a harsh and difficult terrain. From the tenth century on, ethnic Somalis were dispersed throughout the Horn of Africa in a continuous search for forage and water for their herds. In the riverine area between the Juba and Shebelle, a small number practiced maize and millet agriculture, and a small trading class along the coast maintained contact by sea with the Arabian Peninsula.

Somali clans have been compared to Greek or Hebrew tribes, sharing a common ethnic and linguistic identity but distinguished from each other by lineage, history, and custom. Somali society is composed of five principal clan families, the Hawiye, Darod, Isaaq, Dir, and Rahanwein, which according to tradition shared a common ancestor. Each clan is divided into five or more smaller clans which in turn divide into sub-clans. Clan relations are the equivalent of tribalism in other societies, with their own inner codes and culture.

---

[1]Said S. Samatar, "Somalia: A Nation in Turmoil," Minority Rights Group Report, August 1991, p. 6.

Over many centuries clanism has been at times a source of conflict and at others a basis for reconciliation. When parochial interests prevailed, clanism was negative and divisive; it was often a form of elite manipulation through which leaders turned one clan or subclan against another in a competition for power. Historical conflicts between neighboring subclans for water, livestock, and other resources carried over into post-independence politics. On the positive side there is a long history of clan relations promoting mediation by elders, and extensive intermarriage has often brought rival groups together.

The British scholar I. M. Lewis's characterization of Somali pastoralism, though he is specifically referring to the culture of the north, applies as well to the country as a whole and sets the stage for the struggle and violence that have engulfed Somalia in the modern period:

> Like many pastoral nomads who range far and wide with their herds of camels and flocks, the Somali have no indigenous centralized government. And this lack of formal government and of instituted authority is strongly reflected in their extreme independence and individualism. Few writers have failed to notice the formidable pride of the Somali nomad, his extraordinary sense of superiority as an individual, and his firm conviction that he is sole master of his actions and subject to no authority save that of God. If they have perceived it, however, they have for the most part been baffled by the shifting character of the nomad's political allegiance and puzzled by the fact that the political and jural unit with which he acts on one occasion he opposes on another.[2]

By virtue of its remoteness and isolation, Somalia remained untouched until the nineteenth century by the broader currents of international politics. It took the opening of the Suez Canal and competition among Britain, Italy, and France for control of the Horn of Africa to bring Somalia into the modern world. The division and colonization of Somalia in the 1880s into areas under Italian, French, and British control was inherently artificial. Ethnic Somalis lived in French Somaliland (later Djibouti), northern Kenya, and the Ogaden, as well as in what is today Somalia. But none of the European powers was truly interested in the development or unity of Somalia. The big prize was always the kingdom of Ethiopia.

When in 1897 Britain gave the Ogaden—the vast central region through which Somali camel and cattle herders had moved for centuries—to

---

[2]Ibid.

Ethiopia, it set the stage for later conflict in the Horn. After World War II, Italy retained its former colony as a trusteeship in the south, and the British continued to administer Somaliland in the north until an independent and unified Somali Republic was declared on July 1, 1960. The bitter reality, however, was that neither colonial power had prepared the country for self-government. Civil administrations in the north and south had inherited different European languages, cultures, and administrative structures from the colonial period. With no cohesive, trained civil service, and no accepted political norms, individual rivalries for power quickly took their toll. The nine years of democratic civilian government from 1960 to 1969 were notable primarily for the plethora of competing political parties and the dispersal of patronage on the basis of clan and personal relationships. There was a rudimentary private sector based on livestock exports and farming, but public frustration over limited economic development, and dissatisfaction with perceived Western parsimony led Somalia to seek support from the socialist countries of Eastern Europe. Lacking a sizable army, and rebuffed by the West in their requests for military equipment, the civilian governments of the 1960s were unable to respond to popular sentiment for regaining the Ogaden, northern Kenya, and Djibouti, where ethnic Somalis were in the majority. As early as 1964 Somalia had turned to the Soviet Union for arms, and by 1968 the army had fallen under Soviet tutelage. When Somali President Abdi Rashid Ali Shermarke was assassinated by a bodyguard in October 1969, the stage was set for a military takeover. As in many other African countries, the experiment in democracy was unsuccessful.

THE LEGACY OF SIAD BARRE

Major General Mohamed Siad Barre's coup in October 1969 ushered in twenty-one years of military dictatorship. He set up a highly authoritarian regime, centered on his own Marehan clan. In the first year, he enjoyed broad public support based both on his demagogic appeals to Somali nationalism and irredentism and on his call to overcome clan divisions and act as a united people. Among other things, he launched a massive literacy campaign that included a new form of written Somali[3] made compulsory in all schools, rejecting the colonial languages, Italian and English.

---

[3]Previously it had been transliterated into Arabic characters.

From the outset, Siad Barre counted on his alliance with the Soviets for the military equipment he needed to take back the territory he claimed for Somalia. Relations with the West quickly deteriorated. When Somali-flagged merchant ships were discovered delivering arms to North Vietnam, President Nixon cut off residual economic assistance.

Flushed with the exhilarating popular response to his own emotional appeals, and with an exaggerated sense of both Somali military strength and potential Soviet support, Siad Barre miscalculated. When he launched a war against Ethiopia in October 1977 in an effort to regain the Ogaden, the Soviets quickly took the first step in reversing alliances, throwing their military support to the Marxist regime of Mengistu Haile Mariam. In response Siad Barre ejected the Soviets, including military advisors, from Somalia. But while Soviet advisors and equipment and Cuban troops flowed into Ethiopia, by March 1978 the Somali army, without support for its Soviet equipment, was routed. At the same time, the Somali economy collapsed after a decade of Soviet-style collective agriculture, discouragement of the private sector, and establishment of clan-controlled state monopolies. By the end of the decade, Somalia had hit rock bottom, and Siad Barre decided to turn westward once again.

But the conflict between Somalia and Ethiopia had come to be perceived by Washington and Moscow as an extension of the Cold War into the Horn of Africa, and by the late 1970s a new regional situation faced U.S. policymakers. Somalia's defeat by Soviet-supported Ethiopia coincided with dramatic developments in the Middle East, the Persian Gulf, and South Asia. The fall of the shah of Iran in 1979 and the rise of Ayatollah Khomeini, as well as the Soviet invasion of Afghanistan, presented the United States with two challenges—the threats of Soviet expansion and of Islamic extremism—that it feared could lead to Soviet control over the Persian Gulf. The "Carter Doctrine" set forth a strategy to defend the vital oil reserves and sea-lanes of the entire region. Somalia, 3,000 kilometers to the south, suddenly had strategic importance, coinciding with the massive Soviet support for Ethiopia and its large-scale military presence there, and with Siad Barre's decision to turn back to the United States. The "Carter Doctrine" led to the creation of the Rapid Deployment Force, quickly renamed Central Command (CENTCOM), and the establishment of a chain of bases and support facilities in Diego Garcia, Mombasa, the island of Masirah off the coast of Oman, and the strategically located airfield and port facilities built and formerly used by the Soviets at Berbera. The United States declined, however, Siad Barre's additional offer to use Somalia as CENTCOM forward headquarters.

During the 1980s the United States entered on a large-scale program of economic assistance along with a limited military program to rebuild Somalia's basic infrastructure without giving it the capability to renew hostilities against its neighbors. By 1985 the U.S. economic aid program was the second largest in sub-Saharan Africa. For a brief period it was hoped that this would encourage revival of the private sector and liberalization of the government's statist economic policies.

In the mid-1980s Somali government policies still seemed to be moving in the direction of economic liberalization and political reform. Somalia was following International Monetary Fund (IMF) guidelines and had accepted a World Bank structural adjustment program through which foreign currency could be bought at market prices. The U.S. Agency for International Development (USAID) and European donors undertook to help Somalia rebuild its agricultural sector, improve exports, and develop light industry. Exports of livestock, fruit, and fish were increasing, and as late as 1987 a donor consultative group was looking favorably on Siad Barre's proposals for construction of the Bardera Dam (near his hometown) and a massive rural electrification project between Kismayo and Mogadishu. The donors were prepared to continue development assistance, encouraged by assurances that Siad Barre intended, following his uncontested "reelection" in 1987 to a seven-year term, to make his government more responsive and open politically, as well as to continue economic reform.

The United States continued to support Somalia in its confrontation with Ethiopia, the USSR, and other radical states. Armed dissidents operating with direct Ethiopian support in low-intensity cross-border operations were regarded as an extension of the Cold War rather than as part of the age-old rivalries in the Horn. However, the United States was also aware of serious internal Somali problems and tried to use its influence to promote change, actively discouraging armed dissidents whom Siad Barre was supporting against Somalia's neighbors in pursuit of his irredentist ambitions. In coordination with the IMF, the United States urged macroeconomic reform and movement away from state and party controls to private enterprise. By 1985–86 this had begun to significantly improve agricultural production as well as exports and imports.

The United States also kept watch on human rights and corruption problems, intervening in specific cases of abuse and making a special effort to check oppressive regime attitudes toward the Isaaq in the north. During the mid-1980s the United States did not believe that the internal situation warranted an anti-Siad policy or cutbacks in assistance beyond those stemming from Gramm-Rudman-Hollings ceilings, although it did not insulate Somalia from the cuts as it did some higher-priority countries. Military aid fell from $33 million in fiscal 1984 to $14 million in 1985 and $7 million in 1986. Economic aid fell from a peak of $100 million to $70 million in the same years.[4]

By the late 1980s it was clear that indications of long-term reform had turned out to be deceptive. By 1987, Siad's Marehan elites had found their financial interests, dependent on state control, undercut by privatization and the more dynamic private Isaaq businessmen of the north. Their counterpressure brought the process of economic liberalization and loosening of government control to a halt. Somalia also abandoned the structural adjustment and stabilization programs and began to move back to fixed currency rates and state control. Unchecked corruption, false invoicing, faked contracts, and outright theft led to massive inflation and deep trade and payment imbalances. Somalia returned to its prior status as an insolvent debtor.

At the same time Siad's hold on government became ever more authoritarian, focused on power and patronage for his Marehan clan. In the January 1988 government reshuffle, Marehans took over the command of every ministry where money was to be made. Disaffection among the other clans in the north and south was on the increase.[5] Foreign donors' hopes for political liberalization faded as Marehan-Isaaq tensions degenerated into severe repression by the Somali government in response to guerrilla warfare launched by the Isaaqs and their organization, the Somali National Movement (SNM), with Ethiopian support.

DIVIDE AND RULE: CLAN MANIPULATION AND FAVORITISM

In the early years of the revolution, Siad Barre had sought to eradicate clanism by outlawing references to clan identity, stressing national unity,

---

[4]In 1988, when Siad Barre was carrying out brutal reprisals against the Isaaqs in the north, new U.S. military aid was suspended; in 1989 all economic and military aid was blocked. See Hussein Adam, "A Terrible Beauty Being Born?" in I. William Zartman, ed., *Collapsed States* (Boulder: Lynne Rienner, forthcoming, 1995).

[5]Details of Somali policies in the 1980s, on which this account is based, are drawn from "The Somali State and Foreign Aid: Development and Disintegration," an unpublished manuscript by David Rawson, who served as deputy chief of mission in Somalia in 1986–88.

and emphasizing socialist ideology. From 1978 onward, however, after his defeat in the Ogaden war, an unsuccessful coup attempt by Majerteen clan officers, and what he believed to be a growing Ethiopian-USSR threat, Siad Barre turned clan politics into the primary instrument of the regime.[6] As opposition mounted, he withdrew into an ever smaller circle of advisors, mainly from his own Marehan clan and the Ogadeni and Dulbahante clans of his mother and principal son-in-law, who was head of the national security service.

As the 1980s progressed, and especially after 1987, Siad's dictatorial regime relied ever more openly on manipulation of the clan system, which he used ruthlessly to oppress entire clans. Oppression was directed not only at the Isaaq and Majerteen clans whose members led the principal insurgencies against him in the early eighties, but also at the Hawiye and others who later opposed the regime as its repression increased. Indeed, as Somali political scientist Hussein Adam has noted, the worst damage Siad Barre did to Somali culture was to politicize clan relations by encouraging conflict at the level of the five clan families. By openly pitting his Darod clan family against the others, he dropped all pretense of promoting socialist ideology and engaged in a raw power struggle that ultimately led to the collapse not only of his regime but of the state.[7]

The progressive transformation of Siad Barre's army and police into instruments of oppression, the aggrandizement of state institutions in the interest of one clan, and the repression of other clans through murder, exile, or imprisonment had a cumulative impact. By the time international attention focused on Somalia in 1992 through ghastly pictures of starvation and death, the Somali state had ceased to exist and the people had fallen back on the only security they could find, the clan system.

INSURGENCY MOVEMENTS

Clan-based insurgencies broke out after the Ogaden war, inspired by opposition to Siad Barre's autocratic and repressive rule and supported by Ethiopia and at least tolerated by the USSR. The Somali Salvation Front (SSF), made up largely of Majerteen military dissidents who fled into Ethiopia, used urban bombings and cross-border attacks to destabilize

---

[6]See Adam, "A Terrible Beauty Being Born?"
[7]Hussein Adam, telephone interview with John Hirsch, August 11, 1993.

the regime. In October 1981 a merger with another splinter group led to the formation of the Somali Salvation Democratic Front (SSDF), led by Colonel Abdullahi Yusef. At the same time, dissident Isaaqs from the northwest formed the SNM in London. The Isaaqs deeply resented the government's policy of distributing scarce resources in favor of the south, leaving the north an economic backwater. The SSDF and the SNM operated along different parts of the administrative border with Ethiopia, using bases inside that country and receiving political, financial, and some military support from the Mengistu regime. Their cross-border activities were inconclusive except for the capture of two border towns, Balenbale and Galgodob. The SSDF's reliance on Libyan funding, Yusef's dictatorial style, and Siad Barre's success in using clan appeals to entice many SSDF troops to return from Ethiopia, caused its power to fade. The SNM did better in raising funds from Isaaq-based communities near the Gulf and elsewhere. It created a solid base in Ethiopia from which it launched cross-border sorties and it conducted an active propaganda effort from London, charging the regime with extensive violations of human rights and dictatorial practices.[8]

CIVIL WAR BEGINS

Siad Barre's use of terror against his opponents progressively intensified, and as armed opposition grew he targeted Isaaq regions for extraordinary punishment. As he turned more and more against innocent civilians, generating fierce resentment and resistance, the state began to collapse from within. Indeed, as Hussein Adam has observed, by 1990 Somalia was beset by an almost overwhelming set of difficulties—"an anatomy of the Somali crisis reveals multiple problems that often appear as single problems in other countries."[9]

The civil war started in May 1988 as a confrontation in Hargeisa and Burao between the SNM and Siad Barre's army. With considerable popular support, the SNM launched a major offensive in the north, sending in thousands of fighters from Ethiopia. Siad's forces counterattacked with a

---

[8]Ironically, the SNM invasion of northern Somalia came the year after the peace accord between Mengistu and Siad Barre banned cross-border operations against each other.

[9]Hussein Adam, statement before the Subcommittee on Africa, House Committee on Foreign Affairs, U.S. Congress, February 17, 1993.

"widespread, systematic and extremely violent assault" on the unarmed population.[10] The assault included aerial bombardment and brutal massacres of civilians, including women and children. In 1988 and 1989, an estimated 300,000 Isaaqs became refugees in Ethiopia, while thousands more were displaced in the north. Hargeisa and Burao, once bustling towns, lay in ruins. The Majerteen-based SSDF, led by Abdullahi Yusef and Mohamed Abshir, was also active in mobilizing northern resistance to the regime. Over the next two and a half years, Siad lost the support of other clans in the south who also became disaffected with the regime. After his army inflicted atrocities on the clans in south-central Somalia, a broad-based alliance of opposition forces including Hawiye, Rahanwein, Omar Jess's faction of the Ogadeni, and Dir of the Southern Somali National Movement (SSNM), formed what in 1992 became the Somali National Alliance (SNA). Its principal political components became General Mohamed Farah Aideed's branch of the United Somali Congress (USC), the Somali Patriotic Movement (SPM) led by Colonel Jess in Kismayo, and the Somali Democratic Movement (SDM) in Baidoa. These clan-based insurgent organizations became the basis for several of the principal factions that contended for power during the civil war of the early 1990s.

As well as clan-based military challenges to the regime, peaceful political efforts to remove Siad Barre were also tried. In May 1990 a group of 144 moderate business and political leaders issued a manifesto calling for a national conference to find a political resolution to the crisis, seeking the support of the international community for the removal of Siad from office. Most of the members of this "Manifesto Group" were living in Mogadishu, and their courageous action in openly criticizing Siad Barre's abuses and calling for him to liberalize or step down constituted a direct challenge to the regime. One of them, businessman Ali Mahdi Mohamed, soon was to find himself in conflict with supporters of General Aideed. Both were members of the USC.[11]

---

[10]Robert Gersony, "Why Somalis Flee" (unpub.), quoted in Herman J. Cohen, "Intervention in Somalia," *The Diplomatic Record, 1992–93*, edited by Allan Goodman (Boulder: Westview Press, forthcoming).

[11]The Manifesto's urgent appeal to the government and the international community constituted an opportunity for UN or other mediation that, if taken, might have averted horrendous devastation. See Mohamed Sahnoun, *Somalia: The Missed Opportunities* (Washington, D.C.: United States Institute of Peace Press, 1994), pp. 12–13.

THE OVERTHROW OF SIAD BARRE

By the last months of 1990 opposition to Siad's rule had spread throughout the country. There was full-scale civil war, and all vestiges of civil society and government institutions had disappeared. As the insurgency closed in on Mogadishu in December, thousands of people were killed in brutal urban warfare.[12] Personnel at the U.S. embassy and several hundred other foreign diplomats and relief workers were evacuated by military helicopter from the embassy grounds on January 5, 1991. General Aideed's USC forces had captured arms and equipment as they advanced eastward from the Ethiopian border. As they entered the city, they took control of the Ministry of Defense and the presidency, adding to their already large stockpile of heavy weaponry. On January 27 Siad Barre was forced to flee the capital. He plundered the city and headed south, where he established himself with his followers near Bardera, his clan homeland near the Ethiopian and Kenyan borders.

From January 1991 to May 1992, Aideed's forces engaged in combat with Siad Barre's army, and it was this fighting back and forth across south-central Somalia that led to the famine there. Aideed initially had not intended to move south from Mogadishu, leaving the liberation of each region to the local clan leader. However, less than a month after his ouster, Siad Barre attempted to retake Mogadishu. Aideed's forces headed south and blocked his reentry, but Siad did not give up. In his flight south and two attempts to regain military advantage against Aideed's forces and return to Mogadishu, Siad Barre's forces pursued a scorched earth policy, gutting tube wells, destroying canals, and rendering agriculture impossible.

As the conflict raged on, the civilian population was caught in the middle and suffered immensely. In and around Baidoa, where many of the battles were fought, Rahanwein agricultural lands were devastated. In spring 1992, there was also heavy fighting around Kismayo. Throughout the region farmers fled into the bush, precipitating the famine that quickly spread to the "Triangle of Death" between Kismayo, Bardera, and Baidoa. In May 1992 Siad Barre's army made one last major push, reaching as far as Baledogle, where they were once again vanquished by Aideed's forces. Siad Barre finally fled to Kenya and then to Nigeria.

---

[12]Richard Greenfield, "Siad's Sad Legacy," *Africa Report*, March–April 1991, pp. 13–18.

By mid-1992 Aideed had proven himself a formidable military leader. He drove Siad Barre back three times, managing to keep his forces in the field with minimal logistics and communication and building up his own military strength by capturing most of Siad's stockpiles. Aideed's later claim to national leadership, fiercely disputed by the other factions, must be seen in this context. He saw himself as having liberated Somalia from the oppressor and believed that this entitled him to be Somalia's future leader.

THE FACTION LEADERS RULE THE REGIONS

With the fall of Siad Barre, effective control passed to the insurgent leaders in the regions. Rather than coming together, those who had been in opposition to Siad Barre now saw the opportunity to assert their own power. They used the politicized clan system for their own benefit, exacerbating differences between them by demagogic propaganda and forming factions based on personal and clan loyalties. Fighting between factions for local and regional control added to the destruction caused by the continuing battle against Siad Barre's forces. This fighting prolonged and intensified the famine and flight of families in the "Triangle of Death," with more than half a million Somalis becoming refugees in Kenya and a roughly equal number scattered far from their homes. In the south, Omar Jess of the Somali Patriotic Movement, supported by Aideed's forces, fought with Siad Barre's son-in-law, General Said Hersi "Morgan," who controlled the remnant of Siad Barre's army in the area between Kismayo, Bardera, and the Kenyan border. The Bay region around Baidoa, stretching to Bardera, was dominated by the Somali Democratic Movement, the main Rahanwein tribal group, and by the Southern Somali National Movement led by Abdi Warsame—and contested by both Aideed's and Morgan's forces. The central region around Galcaio was the scene of ongoing political and military competition between Yusef and Abshir's SSDF (Majerteen and Darod) and Hashi Ganni's SNF forces (Marehan and Darod) on the one hand and Aideed's SNA on the other.[13]

The situation in the north was very different. On May 17, 1991, the Isaaq-dominated SNM, based in Hargeisa, announced its secession from

---

[13]U.S. Department of State, *1992 Human Rights Practices Report for Somalia.*

the 1960 union and declared its independence as the Somaliland Republic. The move was based on its strongly held view that the north would continue to be victimized by any southern-dominated government. While not gaining international recognition, the de facto secession split the country in two. Somaliland had many problems, but once Siad Barre was ousted it was spared the worst depredations inflicted by the competing factions in the south. In the northeast, from Bossasso and Garoe all the way to Galcaio, there was at least a semblance of stability. The area was administered by the SSDF.[14]

THE BATTLE FOR MOGADISHU

The tragedy of Somalia was further compounded by events following Siad Barre's flight. In Mogadishu, the two principal USC leaders who had been united in opposition to the dictator turned against each other. The forces of Ali Mahdi Mohamed of the Abgal subclan, a businessman and gentleman farmer with little previous interest in politics, confronted those of Mohamed Farah Aideed of the Habr Gidr subclan. Aideed was militarily in the dominant position. He had been a general in Siad Barre's army, then imprisoned for seven years, and after his release was appointed ambassador to India. His forces, emboldened by their successes against Siad Barre and with considerable military experience, were far stronger than Ali Mahdi's ad hoc militia. Moreover, they had more heavy weapons, including missiles and rockets, many of them taken from Siad Barre's warehouses.

From January to October 1991 the two sides prepared for battle but did not actually engage in full-fledged hostilities. Fighters loyal to Aideed established themselves in the southern part of Mogadishu while Ali Mahdi's supporters, largely urban dwellers, found themselves confined to the north. Law and order had broken down completely. No one was capable of establishing conditions of security in the city or the countryside. Sporadic fighting between the factions broke out in May and then stopped. Over the summer, the city was very tense as gangs of armed

---

[14]The Somalis used the label "faction" for the essentially clan-based organizations that emerged from the guerrilla wars against Siad Barre and proliferated during the civil wars of the 1990s. Smaller nonmilitary factions also surfaced to afford political protection to smaller groups such as the Bantu. For a good description of these groups, and a list of the factions, see I. M. Lewis, *Understanding Somalia: Guide to Culture, History and Social Institutions* (London: Haan Associates, 1993).

youths roamed the streets. Neither Aideed nor Ali Mahdi could control them. Throughout the summer, according to Mohamed Sahnoun, Aideed and Ali Mahdi were waiting for an outside mediator to broker a compromise.[15]

After the violent confrontation of May, Hawiye clan elders in June hastily convened a USC congress in Mogadishu. Aideed was elected party chairman, a move intended to resolve the conflict. However, Djibouti's President Hassan Gouled Aptidon, with Egyptian and Italian encouragement, convened a conference the next month at which Ali Mahdi again declared himself interim president and formed a large cabinet. Aideed, whose associates were excluded and who had boycotted the Djibouti meeting, immediately rejected its outcome as aimed at excluding him from Somalia's future. He saw the Italian and Egyptian actors in the context of their earlier support for Siad Barre and as inimical to him. So, though it had been intended to find a solution, the Djibouti conference only exacerbated the situation. The stage was set for open combat. Renewed fighting broke out in Mogadishu in September, more intense and prolonged than before.

From November 1991 to February 1992 the battle of Mogadishu raged, virtually destroying the city center, pulverizing the already fragile municipal infrastructure, and inflicting heavy damage. Three months of continuous shelling night and day created a massive civilian disaster. The *Washington Post*'s East Africa correspondent reported 1,000 people dying per week from random artillery and rocket fire into densely populated neighborhoods.[16]

How could Aideed and Ali Mahdi, both leaders of the USC and opponents of Siad Barre, inflict so much damage on each other and their people? Somali social scientist Said Samatar explains the tragedy as resulting from the conjunction of traditional clan politics and the absence of individual accountability with the availability of modern weapons of mass destruction.[17] Sahnoun contends that each side perceived the situation as a battle for personal and political survival in a grievous situation.[18]

---

[15]Mohamed Sahnoun, interview with John Hirsch, June 18, 1993. Sahnoun has spoken and written on several occasions of the international community's missed opportunities to control the conflict through preventive diplomacy. See in particular his speech to the Secretary of State's Open Forum, January 12, 1994.

[16]Cohen, "Intervention in Somalia."

[17]Samatar, "Somalia," p. 26.

[18]Sahnoun interview.

Certainly, virtually all the political leaders saw control of Mogadishu as the key to national power and control. Shifting relationships based on perceived power, clan feuds, and personal ambitions pushed the Somali political structure in ways hard for an outsider to comprehend. For example, there was a strong negative reaction by the mostly nomadic fighters under Aideed's command, who had come from combat in the Ogaden, against what they saw as the luxury and self-serving attitudes of the city-dwellers in Ali Mahdi's camp. Among other things, this led to massive destruction of property. The complete collapse of any semblance of national structure, making the clan the only basis of authority, order, and survival—plus the hot blood created by earlier clashes—led to an attitude of "every clan for itself." The result was further brutality, including the indiscriminate massacre of civilians and the indirect brutality of mass starvation.

It may seem ironic that when Ali Mahdi and Aideed met in December 1992, for the first time in over a year, they embraced warmly and seemed genuinely dedicated to ending the civil war. However, the personal rivalry and competing interests were still strong.[19] Six months later, as the UN forces sought Aideed's arrest after his forces had killed twenty-five Pakistani soldiers, Ali Mahdi said that Aideed's capture was the key step needed to bring peace to Somalia.

---

[19]John L. Hirsch, unpublished diary kept during Operation Restore Hope.

UNOSOM I 2

The United Nations' reluctance to become operationally involved with the crisis in Somalia must be understood in the context of the aftermath of the Cold War. UN hesitation reflected the disinclination of the Security Council to take on new peacekeeping responsibilities, its absorption with the disintegration of Yugoslavia and the Cambodian elections, and its financial crunch. Still, the situation in Somalia was not by any means ignored; in fact it was the subject of six Security Council resolutions and two major, UN-sponsored international conferences during 1992. Though in retrospect it is starkly evident that the UN response was too slow and finally inadequate, Somalia was not relegated to the ranks of the insoluble.

Throughout 1991, the perspective at UN headquarters was that in responding to Somalia's civil war, the main job of the international community should be limited to delivering humanitarian relief supplies. According to Under Secretary-General James Jonah, the senior UN official charged with Somalia policy when the civil war erupted, there was at the time no thought in New York of international political mediation or of the dispatch of UN peacekeeping forces.[1] The Organization of African Unity (OAU) had rebuffed UN involvement in Sudan and Liberia and did not favor a UN political role in Somalia on grounds that there was no government to request international intervention. This sovereignty argument, and Article 2(7) of the UN Charter, which prohibits intervention in internal matters, plagued the United Nations repeatedly as it wrestled with how much action to take in Somalia.

---

[1]James Jonah, interview with John Hirsch, New York, July 19, 1993.

Toward the end of 1991, the situation began to change. Jonah returned from a summit meeting of the Organization of Islamic Countries in Dakar in October 1991 with anguished appeals from their leaders that something be done to help Somalia. However, Javier Pérez de Cuéllar, then secretary-general, was nearing the end of his term and was reluctant to press for new UN action. The Secretariat prepared a letter for him to send to the Security Council proposing a limited UN role in facilitating relief deliveries, but he did not act on it.

In November and December large parts of Mogadishu were destroyed by massive shelling. Boutros Boutros-Ghali of Egypt, preparing to take over as secretary-general and keenly aware of Somalia's problems, discussed his concerns about the need for UN action with Pérez de Cuéllar and Jonah. With Pérez de Cuéllar's approval, Jonah left New York for Mogadishu on New Year's Eve 1991, leading a small fact-finding delegation. Boutros-Ghali instructed Jonah not to negotiate with the faction leaders but to find out if they were prepared to accept UN mediation—and to get their responses in writing.

As Jonah traveled to Somalia, the signs of impending disaster were clear. UN relief operations had been suspended since October, when the civil war broke out in full force in Mogadishu. The offices of UNICEF, the UN High Commissioner for Refugees (UNHCR), and the World Food Program (WFP) had been moved to Nairobi out of concern that safe and productive relief operation was no longer possible in the chaos. Four non-UN humanitarian relief agencies—the International Committee of the Red Cross (ICRC), Save the Children UK, the International Medical Corps, and Médecins sans Frontières—had continued to operate in Somalia. However, the civil war had made it difficult for these non-governmental organizations (NGOs) to continue to function and their situation was exacerbated by the practical and psychological effects of the departure of the UN agencies. A feeling that the United Nations had abandoned them, whatever its objective merits, was shared by some remaining relief workers and a number of Somalis, and the gulf that had opened would take some time to close.

By the end of 1991 there were already an estimated 20,000 casualties of the civil war, more than 600,000 refugees, and several hundred thousand internally displaced persons.[2] As the situation on the ground deteriorated,

---

[2]See Situation Reports 5 (December 10, 1991) and 6 (January 21, 1992), Office of Foreign Disaster Assistance, USAID.

the remaining NGOs stayed active—at considerable risk—in seeking to deal with mounting starvation, disease and death. The ICRC assumed the lead in food distribution and, at the request of USAID's Office of Foreign Disaster Assistance (OFDA), expanded its activities to include operating feeding centers and kitchens as well as providing emergency medical assistance and distributing farm supplies. During 1991 the United States donated 12,000 metric tons of food through the ICRC, an amount that was to increase significantly during the year ahead. By far the greatest part of the subsequent terrible starvation and malnutrition in Somalia during that period resulted from the interruption of relief activity by looting, stealing, and extortion, not from the lack of food and medicine.

THE STATE OF AFFAIRS IN MOGADISHU

Jonah's discussions in Mogadishu in the first days of January 1992 made clear that any political progress toward an internal settlement or broader political reconciliation would be difficult indeed. Jonah focused on the struggle for power between Aideed and Ali Mahdi in Mogadishu; because of the briefness of his stay he did not meet the other faction leaders in the interior. Aideed, still basking in Siad Barre's defeat, was absolutely convinced of the rightness of his claim to lead Somalia, and believed he could handily defeat Ali Mahdi within weeks. Initially Aideed was opposed both to UN political involvement and to a cease-fire, though Jonah, who compared him to Liberian rebel Charles Taylor, warned him that he could not achieve his ambitions at the point of a gun.[3] Ali Mahdi, in the weaker position militarily, welcomed a UN role.

Aideed was very suspicious and vociferous in his criticism of the United Nations, in part because of genuinely strong nationalist feelings, in part because he feared it would hinder his plans to obtain power by whatever means necessary, and in part because he had a strong personal animosity toward Boutros-Ghali, whom he considered responsible for Egypt's strong support of Siad Barre while he was minister of state for foreign affairs. These negative feelings were reciprocated by the secretary-general as well as by Jonah after his initial meeting with Aideed. Their powerful animosities played an important role in the difficulties of the United Nations in Somalia over the next two years.

---

[3]Jonah interview.

Following Jonah's return to New York, Boutros-Ghali, with Security Council support,[4] invited the two faction leaders to send delegations to New York to discuss a cease-fire. Aideed and Ali Mahdi accepted, the former perhaps playing for time while continuing his blitzkrieg. An enormous number of shells were lobbed into north Mogadishu from Aideed's south side while these discussions dragged on. Still, on February 14 representatives of the two sides agreed in principle to a cease-fire.

In late February Jonah undertook a second trip to Mogadishu to nail down the specifics, and after four days of intense negotiations Ali Mahdi and Aideed signed a cease-fire agreement that held—albeit sporadically—until the United Task Force (UNITAF) arrived. Unfortunately, though maintaining the cease-fire was important, it ultimately had little impact on the near-anarchic situation at the port and airport, nor did it prevent large-scale looting of relief supplies and extortion from humanitarian agencies in and around the capital city.

By focusing almost exclusively on Mogadishu the United Nations inadvertently intensified the rivalry between Aideed and Ali Mahdi, each of whom tried valiantly to claim political legitimacy from his international contacts. This focus also contributed to the belief held by other faction leaders, clans, and regions that they were being ignored. Media attention also centered almost exclusively on the Mogadishu leaders. This became a complicating factor for later efforts to build a countrywide consensus on political reconciliation.

The Security Council, in its Resolution 733 of January 23, had called for an increase in humanitarian aid and authorized the appointment of a special coordinator to oversee its delivery. David Bassiouni, who had been UNICEF's Mogadishu representative, took on this task, working from Nairobi until he was allowed to return to Mogadishu in March. In the five months of his tenure, Bassiouni found that the long absence of UN agencies from Somalia had created both practical and psychological difficulties. His task was complicated by the thorny problems of restoring good relations with the NGOs and regaining the confidence of the Somalis. Bassiouni initiated weekly meetings between the NGOs and the United Nations, and for the next months struggled with continuing issues of air and port access for the relief agencies, seeking to prevent looting and extortion and trying to facilitate food distribution throughout the divided

---

[4]See UN Security Council Resolution 733, January 23, 1992.

city. Agreements with Ali Mahdi and Aideed on access and other issues were often broken within hours—if not at their orders, at least with their acquiescence. The mission was also hampered by lack of facilities and personnel and ultimately succumbed to its improvisational nature, weak support from outside, and internal Somali rivalries. As the death toll mounted steadily, it became clear that the ad hoc approach to delivery of relief supplies could not work.[5]

APPOINTMENT OF MOHAMED SAHNOUN AND
ESTABLISHMENT OF UNOSOM I

Reports of impending disaster pushed Boutros-Ghali to conclude that the UN's political role in Somalia could no longer be handled exclusively from New York or even with the help of a relief coordinator, and he decided that a new, full-time political representative was needed. Bassiouni lacked the requisite political stature and seniority, while Jonah's portfolio required that he turn his attention mostly to Angola, Mozambique, South Africa, and other African issues.

In Resolution 751, passed April 24, the Security Council established the United Nations Operation in Somalia (UNOSOM I), providing for the immediate dispatch of fifty unarmed UN observers to monitor the tenuous cease-fire. The resolution also allowed for the possible future deployment of a peacekeeping force of 500—Boutros-Ghali's original proposal to the Security Council—and for the secretary-general to appoint a special representative in Somalia.

To pull the endeavor together, Boutros-Ghali asked an old friend, the experienced Algerian diplomat Mohamed Sahnoun, to undertake an unofficial fact-finding mission in Somalia. Sahnoun, who had represented Algeria at the United Nations and served as an assistant secretary-general of the OAU, was knowledgeable about Somalia's history and had a feel for the Somali character.

In mid-March, Sahnoun arrived in Somalia, meeting with Ali Mahdi and Aideed in Mogadishu and again with Aideed at a location close to the Kenyan border where his forces were engaging the remnant of Siad Barre's army. In the seven months of his tenure Sahnoun held meetings with almost all the faction leaders; he believed he would be able to win

---

[5]This account is based in large part on the Jonah interview (see note 1) and John Hirsch's interview with David Bassiouni, New York, August 2, 1993.

their confidence by responding seriously to their concerns and offering the perspective of a sympathetic outsider. Sahnoun's style of establishing personal contact with all the factions and consulting periodically with regional governments, largely on his own initiative, won the appreciation of many Somalis but eventually precipitated resentment at UN headquarters, where it was felt he was too much an independent player. However, in late March, Sahnoun reported back to the secretary-general. Boutros-Ghali was impressed by his report, agreed that urgent action was required, and asked Sahnoun to become his special representative to Somalia.

Sahnoun returned to Mogadishu on May 4, authorized to work out means for monitoring the cease-fire, to improve the delivery of humanitarian assistance, and to explore possibilities for national reconciliation. He was very active, urging more effort by UN agencies and extending his outreach throughout the country. Wherever Sahnoun went he made a point of meeting with clan elders, women's groups, and others to encourage civic involvement in reconciliation efforts. Sahnoun also met with representatives of Somaliland, the northwestern secessionist area, and opened a dialogue with President Meles Zenawi of Ethiopia, President Gouled of Djibouti, the OAU, the Horn of Africa Committee, and representatives of other governments.

Sahnoun's main concerns, however, were in Mogadishu. Aideed, though he had reluctantly agreed to the cease-fire, was initially opposed to the UN monitors being armed and in uniform—points which were acceptable to Ali Mahdi, who wanted UN support, but which Aideed considered excessive interference in Somalia's affairs. A more serious problem arose when, in mid-June, a Russian plane bearing UN markings delivered military equipment and newly printed Somali currency to Ali Mahdi in north Mogadishu. The perceived UN involvement in secret arms delivery was only that—a Russian transportation contract with the United Nations had expired, but someone had failed to repaint the plane before it was used for other business transactions. Still, Aideed seized on the event to withdraw his consent to the deployment of the fifty cease-fire monitors and to oppose the deployment of 500 armed peacekeepers.[6] Sahnoun called Aideed's suspicions understandable and criticized the UN's

---

[6]See Jonathan Stevenson, "Hope Restored in Somalia?" *Foreign Policy,* Summer 1993, No. 91, p. 145. Also see Secretary-General's Reports to the Security Council, S/23829 (April 21, 1992) and S/24343 (July 22, 1992).

lack of vigilance. His statements irritated UN headquarters but mollified Aideed, who, having made his point, agreed again to the cease-fire monitors, in uniform but unarmed. Pakistani Brigadier General Imtiaz Shaheen arrived on July 5 to be the chief military observer, and the fifty monitors followed on July 20.

THE CRISIS DEEPENS

Over the summer the humanitarian crisis deepened. The secretary-general's July 22 report was extremely pessimistic, describing a critical food situation, with widespread famine in the rural areas. Civil war for more than a year had prevented normal agricultural activity throughout the country—projected food production for 1992 would fall to nearly half normal totals, far short of what was necessary in a country that does not come close to subsistence production even in a good year. Food prices were beginning to skyrocket, and in some up-country locations there was almost no food at any price.

The secretary-general's report estimated that a million Somali children were at immediate risk from malnutrition, with four and a half million people "in urgent need of food assistance." The pastoral economy central to Somalia's well-being and its culture was in ruin, with drought and disease killing off as much as 40 percent of the cattle and other stock. Farmers were unable to work their fields because of clan warfare in the most productive rain-fed and irrigated agricultural areas. There were 350,000 refugees already registered in Kenya, and thousands in Ethiopia as well, with an estimated 300,000 internally displaced. With 1,000 refugees a day crossing the border, the UN projected 500,000 refugees by the beginning of 1993.[7]

Potential public health crises loomed, with the threat of epidemic exacerbated by malnutrition and a disastrous sanitary situation that seemed only waiting for the rainy season to spread disease. Potable water was no longer available. Most clinics in the interior had closed, and treatment programs for such chronic diseases as tuberculosis and malaria had disappeared. Vaccines were unavailable and immunization programs had dwindled as the health care sector collapsed. Of the seventy Somali hospitals working in 1988, only fifteen were still functioning even partially;

---

[7]Secretary-General's Report S/24343.

most lacked running water, electricity, and even the most rudimentary medical equipment.

In spite of laudable efforts by the relief community, supplies of food and medicine could not keep up with Somali needs. Only 79,000 of the estimated 200,000 metric tons of food aid necessary had arrived in the country by July, and little of this had reached those most in need. While the ICRC and the WFP provided food assistance, emergency health care, livestock vaccinations, and other services as best they could, the worsening violence and looting severely limited their effectiveness. Boutros-Ghali ended his report by noting bleakly, "Under these circumstances, it is inevitable that people in Somalia have begun to lose any sense of hope for the future."[8]

OPERATION PROVIDE RELIEF

Against this background, the Security Council, in Resolution 767 of July 26, endorsed Boutros-Ghali's proposal for an emergency airlift to provide food and medical supplies to the "Triangle of Death" in southern Somalia. President Bush responded by authorizing a U.S. airlift—Operation Provide Relief—to deliver humanitarian relief supplies and to bring the first 500 UN peacekeepers to Somalia. The launch of the airlift from Mombasa in late August was marked by a number of operational problems, due primarily to the absence of time for advance planning. For example, changes in the project as it was originally envisioned meant that when Brigadier General Frank Libutti of CENTCOM met OFDA's Bill Garvelink for the first time in Mombasa, they had to create an infrastructure from scratch to support the fourteen planes authorized by President Bush—a jump up from the four that OFDA had been expecting. ICRC and WFP relief supplies initially intended to be delivered by ship were diverted to supply the airlift.

Since the airfields in interior cities like Baidoa and Bardera were unprotected, the local militia quickly adopted the practice of extorting landing fees and looting. Sahnoun worked with clan elders to stop the looters, but it proved more practical in some instances to arrange airdrops at locations other than the airstrips. However, the only reliable way to manage the airlift safely was to rely on the NGO community,

---

[8]Ibid.

which had a presence in many interior locations where the UN agencies did not. Radio communications between the NGOs and Operation Provide Relief aircraft provided essential information on ground security, while the NGOs assumed responsibility for distribution. Coordinating the needs of different entities sometimes proved a surprisingly delicate task. For example, the ICRC has an immutable rule, of great longstanding, that any vehicle bearing its emblem may carry no arms or weapons whatsoever. Practically, that meant the Red Cross emblem had to be detachable from the U.S. Air Force C-130s that performed the airlift so that NGO and UNHCR flights, which carried armed guards, could alternate with the ICRC flights. It also meant the ICRC was obliged to hire Somali guards for their personnel and facilities and to reject UNITAF military protection.[9]

From the end of August to late February 1993, Operation Provide Relief aircraft flew almost 2,500 flights to Baidoa, Bardera, Belet Weyn, and Oddur, delivering more than 28,000 metric tons of relief supplies to airfields in the famine belt.[10] Operation Provide Relief made an important contribution to limiting the extent of the crisis, but it quickly became apparent that even a sustained airlift would have too low a rate of effectiveness to reverse the situation. The cost quickly became prohibitive, and the sheer need for food and medicine could not be met through the airdrops alone. The situation in southern Somalia continued to deteriorate. Looting increased steadily and most food never reached the intended NGO or UN beneficiaries. In fact, even though the volume of food arriving in Somalia increased significantly—in September alone from 20,000 to 37,000 metric tons—the percentage actually reaching people in dire need fell by 40 percent.[11]

There were several reasons for this, above all the lack of protection for relief supplies. In a number of instances, food deliveries were regarded simply as free for the taking, and people took what they could haul. In others, there was organized, intentional diversion and hoarding. OFDA's answer was to flood Somalia with so much food that its market value would decline to the point where looting no longer would be profitable. Unfortunately, this strategy did not work—the looters merely increased

---

[9]In some instances in which they accepted protection, they removed the emblem from their vehicles.

[10]Statistics communicated to author by Brigadier General Frank Libutti, CENTCOM.

[11]For an overview of the evolving situation, see monthly OFDA Situation Reports, especially nos. 13 (September 16, 1992), 14 (October 1), 15 (November 6), and 18 (January 18, 1993).

their depredations to enhance their political power and keep their incomes up even as the cost of food fell.[12]

UNOSOM I DEPLOYMENT: THE PLAN THAT NEVER MATERIALIZED

The Security Council, meanwhile, invoking its traditional concept of small-scale peacekeeping under Chapter VI of the UN Charter, continued to operate in Somalia on the premise that a limited traditional operation requiring the consent of local authorities could be effective. In August the council voted to approve Boutros-Ghali's request to increase UNOSOM I from 500 to 3,500 men.[13] Somewhat oddly, the deployment plan foresaw the dispatch of more troops to Kismayo in the south and Bossasso and Berbera in the north than to Mogadishu, where most of the relief supplies were arriving at the departure point for the main inland supply routes and where there was the most looting.

Problems of logistics, recruitment, and finance crippled UNOSOM I before it ever got going. The first of the 500 peacekeepers authorized in April, a group of Pakistani soldiers, did not begin to arrive in Mogadishu until September, four months later. The remaining 3,000 were never dispatched, though Canadian and Belgian troops had been mobilized and were awaiting deployment by the UN Secretariat by the time President Bush decided to begin Operation Restore Hope.

The problems involved in obtaining permission for the Pakistanis to land illuminate the differences between Sahnoun and UN headquarters. After days of intense discussions with Aideed, Sahnoun finally obtained his formal approval on August 10 for the landing of 500 troops. When, later that month, Aideed and Sahnoun both heard over the BBC that the approved force had grown by 3,000, Aideed was enraged, certain he had been deliberately deceived. Sahnoun, who had received no notice of the change, was equally astonished. He found his credibility severely damaged and was at a disadvantage in trying to convince Aideed to honor his initial commitment and allow the Pakistanis to land peacefully. Eventually he was able to do so, but with severe constraints imposed by the UN principle of getting permission from local authorities.

---

[12]Andrew Natsios, former assistant administrator of USAID, interview with John Hirsch, Washington, D.C., July 13, 1993.
[13]UN Security Council Resolution 775, August 28, 1992.

The mission of the Pakistani battalion was supposed to be to secure the port, safeguard food shipments to and from the airport, and escort food convoys to feeding stations in Mogadishu. However, in the two and a half months before the arrival of U.S.-led forces, the Pakistani battalion remained encamped at the airport, hobbled by stringent rules of engagement that allowed them to shoot only in rigidly defined cases of self-defense and to move only when granted permission. The Pakistanis found themselves in an impossible situation, ridiculed and humiliated by the armed looters and gangs and unable to carry out their mission.[14]

HUMANITARIAN INTERVENTION: THE HUNDRED-DAY PLAN

While UNOSOM was struggling to put a peacekeeping force on the ground, Sahnoun tried to close the communications gaps among the UN relief agencies, the Somalis, and the NGOs. In September he convened twenty Somali community leaders and intellectuals in the Seychelles for a preliminary discussion of such practical matters as more effective coordination of relief deliveries as well as longer-term issues such as national reconciliation. However, little could be accomplished. The UN agencies were seriously understaffed and the United Nations' decentralized personnel system made it virtually impossible to mobilize additional staff quickly.

In September a high-level delegation led by Jan Eliasson, the new under secretary-general for humanitarian affairs, and including the heads of UNICEF, the UN Development Program (UNDP), and the WFP, visited Mogadishu.[15] The reality of the situation hit home. Eliasson later recalled his shock at seeing Mogadishu port with no ships in the harbor, mountains of flour piled up in warehouses, and people starving and dying inland. It was, he said, an "unbearable contrast" that made clear the urgent need to deal effectively with the security and protection of relief supplies if the crisis was to be resolved. Eliasson considered that deals with the faction leaders would never be sufficient to achieve lasting

---

[14]The foregoing account is based in large part on John Hirsch's interviews with Mohamed Sahnoun (June 15, 1993), James Jonah (July 19, 1993), and David Bassiouni (August 2, 1993).

[15]Eliasson's first major assignment after being named to the newly created position in January 1992 was to represent the UN at an April 10 humanitarian conference in Addis Ababa. Eliasson continued his interest in the Horn throughout his tenure, playing an important role in shaping overall policy as well as in providing and coordinating humanitarian assistance.

change; indeed, though such arrangements might have been necessary in the short term, the pitfalls of becoming embroiled in local politics had put the United Nations, the ICRC, and the NGOs in a precarious position.[16] James Grant of UNICEF and Eliasson ordered the development of an urgent action plan, drawing heavily on information provided by UNICEF's excellent Somali field staff.

At a donors conference called in Geneva in October to discuss ideas about helping in Somalia and the bottom line of doing so, Sahnoun suggested a possible path. In a "Hundred-Day Plan for Accelerated Humanitarian Assistance" he presented on behalf of the United Nations a detailed approach for increased food aid; aggressive expansion of supplementary feeding stations; the provision of basic health services, clean water, and shelter materials; and delivery of seeds, tools, and animal vaccines.

The plan was based on two broad objectives which were to remain key targets for the indefinite future. First, it intended to prevent further refugee outflows and encourage repatriation by providing for the immediate needs of the populace. Second, in the longer view, it sought to revive and strengthen Somali civil society at the national, regional, and local levels. While the goals were on the mark, the plan had two immediate drawbacks. At that point there was very little Somali involvement, though it was envisaged, and it could be achieved only in a much improved security environment, at some time in the future—a dubious prospect given that the intended UNOSOM force was not fully deployed, and that the troops that were in Somalia were severely hampered by their immobility and rigid rules of engagement.

The adoption of the Hundred-Day Plan had one immediate result. Eliasson and Sahnoun engaged Philip Johnston, president of CARE, to come to Somalia for three months to take charge of its implementation. Johnston, an enormously creative, dedicated, and experienced professional in humanitarian relief, brought tremendous energy and dynamism to the task as the new coordinator for humanitarian aid. In the next five months Johnston, despite illness and bureaucratic obstacles, became the spearhead not only for emergency relief, but also for conceiving the United Nations' broader development and reconstruction program. Johnston also was keenly alert to the need "to have a process of legitimizing

---

[16]Jan Eliasson, interview with John Hirsch, New York, August 2, 1993.

Somali involvement," shifting away from the previous paternalistic approach by the relief community—including the United Nations, the ICRC, and most NGOs—which had unwittingly fed Somali resentments and xenophobia. The key to long-term reconstruction, he recognized, was to involve Somalis more actively in determining priorities and taking responsibility for their future.

Johnston arrived in Mogadishu on October 25. He immediately set the goal of improving UNOSOM's relations with the NGO community by establishing the base for what later became the U.S.-led Civilian-Military Operations Center (CMOC). More than twenty-five nongovernmental agencies were based in Mogadishu, many with fieldworkers in the interior, and they welcomed his initiative. Without improved security, however, implementing real reforms was a different matter. The most pressing problems were at Mogadishu port, where no more than 3,000 to 4,000 tons of food relief were moving through every few days—barely a third of what was needed for Mogadishu alone. Only one transit shed was functional, the work crews (all from Aideed's clan) worked only one shift, and generator-driven lights would have to be installed in order to put a night shift into operation. In addition, Johnston found the UN agencies "hugely understaffed" for the tasks they were supposed to address and unfamiliar with local conditions because of their long absence in Nairobi. UNICEF did not have the staff to handle the many programs assigned to it; the WFP was getting organized; and UNDP, WHO, and other agencies were even less able to cope.

SAHNOUN AND UN HEADQUARTERS

During September, with the U.S. airlift under way and the first peacekeepers en route, Sahnoun had concentrated his efforts on trying to create a regional approach by dividing Somalia into four zones, in each of which he tried to develop a local leadership of clan elders and community leaders. He also pressed for cooperation from the faction leaders throughout the country. In a controversial move, Sahnoun tried to create a consensus among the faction leaders that would simplify the implementation of UN deployments at selected points in Mogadishu and the other ports— Kismayo, Berbera, and Bossasso—and attempted to allay their concerns that the United Nations would establish a military occupation. He was widely criticized at the time by some who felt he went too far toward giving Aideed an implicit veto over further troop deployments in

Mogadishu.[17] Sahnoun did succeed, however, in winning Aideed's and Ali Mahdi's consent to easing their gunmen out of Mogadishu port by giving them food allotments.

As he was gradually gaining the respect and attention of the local Somalis, however, Sahnoun's relations with UN headquarters began to sour, particularly around his request for greater flexibility. Frustrated by the inertia of the UN humanitarian agencies, Sahnoun proposed to Boutros-Ghali that Sahnoun devote all his time to negotiations on political reconciliation and that someone else assume oversight of the UN agencies. In New York, Sahnoun's travel outside Somalia and his efforts to unify and streamline activities in the field were perceived as disregard of UN protocol and the command relationships of different UN operations, which rankled senior members of the Secretariat and the UN agencies. Sahnoun found himself having to answer to three under secretaries—for peacekeeping, political affairs, and humanitarian affairs—with only minimal unifying direction from the secretary-general. Since the UN agencies in the field were not operationally responsible to Sahnoun, they were inclined to resent his attempts to supervise their activities.

Sahnoun also tended to overlook much of Aideed's anti-UN posturing in the interest of obtaining his cooperation on the ground. This approach created friction with UN headquarters, where Boutros-Ghali and Jonah were disposed to take Aideed's criticisms personally and as an affront to the institution. They felt Sahnoun should defend the United Nations more vigorously, even if it complicated dealing with Aideed.

Finally, in his speech to the donors at the Geneva conference, Sahnoun had expressed dismay that the UN agencies had abandoned Somalia in late 1991 and been so slow to return. He argued that it was essential that UN agency staffing be accelerated and more resources devoted to Somalia. In New York several days later he met Boutros-Ghali, who promised to address his concerns. Upon his return to Mogadishu, however, he received a letter from Boutros-Ghali instructing him to desist from further public criticism of UN headquarters. Sahnoun felt that he had suffered a serious rebuff to his authority. He wrote to the secretary-general requesting clarification (and implicitly a reaffirmation of support), and resigned when he did not get a reply.[18]

---

[17]Sahnoun strongly denies that this was the case. Interview with John Hirsch, Washington, D.C., June 15, 1993.

[18]For a detailed explanation of what occurred during this period, and Sahnoun's reasons for resigning, see Sahnoun's January 12, 1994, speech to the Secretary of State's Open Forum.

Sahnoun's resignation, effective immediately, compounded UNOSOM's logistical and personnel problems and in the short term probably increased Somali suspicion of and antipathy toward the United Nations. In his months in Somalia, Sahnoun had succeeded in obtaining agreement from faction and community leaders for a preparatory UN conference, planned for Addis Ababa in January 1993. Though it is an exaggeration to suggest that Sahnoun was on the threshold of a negotiated settlement that would have obviated the need for U.S. military intervention, his resignation undoubtedly represented a major setback to prospects for a political resolution to the crisis.[19]

SITUATION ON THE GROUND

Sahnoun's departure, problems in sustaining dialogue with Aideed and Ali Mahdi, and the embarrassing paralysis of the Pakistani battalion at Mogadishu airport while the humanitarian crisis continued brought into stark relief UNOSOM I's inability to carry out the mission assigned it by the Security Council. Though thousands of tons of food and relief supplies had been airlifted since the summer, continued banditry and looting prevented the distribution of most food and medicine to those in need. Land corridors for distribution remained blocked, and the famine crisis intensified as civil war continued around Bardera and Kismayo.[20]

The scale of human suffering in Somalia in autumn 1992 is difficult to convey from statistics alone, grim though they are. By early November up to half a million Somalis had perished during the two years of civil war, famine, and disease. According to OFDA, 25 percent of southern Somali children under the age of five had already died. At Annalena Tonelli's clinic in the coastal town of Merca, more than 1,000 Somalis died that month—an average of more than thirty a day. Tonelli, an Italian who had been treating tuberculosis patients in Somalia for more than twenty years, called it the nadir of her time there.[21]

And it was a picture repeated over and over throughout the southern famine belt as starvation and disease took their toll. In the southern city of Baidoa, according to estimates from the U.S. Centers for Disease Control and Prevention, 40 percent of the population, and 70 percent of its children

---

[19]Stevenson, "Hope Restored," p. 151.

[20]Sahnoun and Stevenson both provide descriptions of the problems encountered—and sometimes caused—by UN agencies in delivering assistance.

[21]Annalena Tonelli, interview with John Hirsch, Somalia, January 18, 1993.

under five, had died of hunger or disease. Though death rates amelio-rated somewhat in Baidoa, at first it was because, as one weary relief worker put it, people can only die once. In Bardera the same month, a major battle between forces under General Morgan and Aideed's ally General Warsame caused death rates in that area to skyrocket to levels matching the earlier Baidoa rates of more than 300 per day.

Political developments were also unsatisfactory. In mid-November Aideed had demanded that the Pakistani battalion give up control of Mogadishu airport—a move intended to regain both political and financial control of internal food distribution and to weaken his rival Ali Mahdi. His demand was rejected, but its very boldness underscored the breakdown of communication and diminished respect for the United Nations. Two weeks later, a WFP relief ship was shelled offshore from Mogadishu and forced to depart without unloading its cargo. Only one relief ship had reached port for six months, and the food it off-loaded could not be deliv-ered. A twenty-five truck convoy left Mogadishu for Baidoa in November, but twenty-one were hijacked, and no food reached the people.

These events coincided with the arrival of Sahnoun's successor, Ismat Kittani, on November 8. Kittani, a seasoned Iraqi diplomat who had been a senior member of the UN Secretariat, encountered the same problems faced by Sahnoun. But his personality and style were different. Accus-tomed to the formal relationships at the United Nations, he expected the Somalis to give him the deference due his position as the secretary-general's representative. For example, he asked the faction leaders to come to him rather than moving around Mogadishu himself. At times he asked them to deal through his staff rather than directly with him—a posture perceived as insulting to the prickly amour propre of the faction leaders, particularly the aggressive Aideed.

Kittani was particularly concerned not to leave Aideed with the impression that the United Nations accepted his claim to future political power, or to imply to self-designated acting president Ali Mahdi that he would be recognized as the future president. While Kittani's concern was understandable, the dismissive way these relationships were handled, and the contrast with Sahnoun's more personal, conciliatory style, together with the obvious impotence of UNOSOM I's Pakistani battalion, further damaged relations between UNOSOM I and the faction leaders. By the end of November, Aideed and Ali Mahdi had virtually ceased their discussions with the United Nations—often dealing at a remove by communicating through lower-level representatives.

Even as the situation in Somalia reached a low, the United Nations was proceeding to formulate its plans for longer-term reconstruction and rehabilitation. When Eliasson convened a second humanitarian conference in Addis Ababa the first week in December, the United Nations began its first serious effort to involve Somalis in planning the future. In contrast to the Geneva meeting, Somali NGOs, community leaders, women's groups, and political leaders were present. Eliasson and Philip Johnston insisted they be given a voice in discussing the Hundred-Day Plan and its revision, as there had been no direct Somali input to the original plan. They organized two working groups with Somali participation to discuss immediate security needs and long-term rehabilitation. Oakley, en route to his assignment in Mogadishu, took part with a small American delegation and began to explain the coming U.S. military involvement to groups of Somalis from all factions as well as to women, tribal elders, and religious leaders. It was the beginning of a process of involving Somalis in decisions affecting their future, which was to continue and deepen in coming months.

In the security committee, the Somalis vigorously urged disarmament, acknowledging that the lead must be taken by Somalis, because any externally led disarmament effort would generate armed confrontation with the Somali factions. In the rehabilitation committee, they surprised the foreign community by the detailed information provided on various areas of interest such as health, agriculture, and livestock. Outside the conference, the Somali faction representatives adopted a resolution calling for political reconciliation, a cease-fire, and outside assistance. President Zenawi was active and effective behind the scenes, working to promote reconciliation.

President Bush's Decision to Protect Humanitarian Operations

3

*A*s public distress about the situation in Somalia mounted, pressure on the Bush administration to act came from three main sources—the media, Congress, and the humanitarian relief agencies operating in Somalia. Television news beamed graphic images of looting and banditry, and even more heart-wrenching depictions of women, children, and the elderly in the throes of war-induced starvation and death. The *New York Times* and the *Washington Post,* as well as other nationally distributed newspapers, kept their East African correspondents on top of the situation and reported the crisis of starvation and clan warfare in depth. A parade of editorial commentators challenged the administration and Congress to act before total catastrophe ensued.

The state of Somalia also became an issue in the presidential campaign as supporters of Democratic candidate Bill Clinton criticized President George Bush for inaction in dealing with problems such as Bosnia and Somalia and for weak support of the United Nations. Although Clinton made it plain that his primary concern was with domestic matters, those associated with the Democratic Party and his campaign emphasized the need for more vigorous U.S. leadership in dealing with humanitarian crises and promoting a more active and effective role for the United Nations. This emphasis continued during the initial months of Clinton's administration, focusing primarily on Bosnia, Cambodia, and Somalia.

Rising congressional interest resulted in some action. Early in the year Senator Paul Simon (D-IL), chairman of the Africa Subcommittee of the Senate Foreign Relations Committee, and his committee colleague Senator Nancy Kassebaum (R-KS) called for urgent international action to save the Somali people from starvation.[1] They were to devote much of their energies in the next months to urging U.S. support for United Nations peacekeeping efforts, eventually calling for the dispatch of U.S. forces to undertake humanitarian intervention. In Africa Subcommittee hearings in March, the two senators argued that the Security Council's reluctance to send peacekeeping forces to Somalia would only condemn thousands more to death.[2]

In early July, Senator Kassebaum traveled to Somalia to observe the situation firsthand. Reinforced in the determination that action must be taken, she and Senator Simon introduced a resolution calling for the deployment of UN forces—without the approval of the Somali factions if necessary. The resolution was adopted by both houses of Congress within a week.[3] After further visits to Somalia in the fall, a Senate delegation headed by Senator Simon and a House delegation led by Representative John Lewis (D-GA) called for more security for relief workers and supplies.

Pressure also came from the humanitarian relief community operating in Somalia. Representatives of U.S. humanitarian agencies, including CARE, the International Medical Corps, and Save the Children, met regularly with officials from the State Department and OFDA to report on conditions and make concrete suggestions about what needed to be done. They met as well as with members of Congress to press for greater protection for their personnel and operations. The major non-U.S. NGOs, especially the ICRC, also urged the United Nations to do more to end the crisis.

ADMINISTRATION POLICY EVOLVES

U.S. policy evolved significantly during the year, reflecting a growing tide of international humanitarian concern and ultimately concluding that

---

[1]Paul Simon and Nancy Kassebaum, "Save Somalia From Itself," *New York Times*, Jan. 2, 1992.

[2]U.S. Senate, Committee on Foreign Relations, Africa Subcommittee, Hearings on the Horn of Africa, March 19, 1992.

[3]S. Con. Res. 132, adopted August 10, 1992.

the failure of the traditional UN peacekeeping approach required decisive U.S. leadership and the use of military force. Though the United States had originally been interested in Boutros-Ghali's efforts to make the United Nations the focus for ending the civil war as well as for future reconciliation and reconstruction, there was considerable reluctance to give the United Nations the resources and staffing the secretary-general sought.

Additionally, even after Jonah's fact-finding trip, the Security Council's approach to Somalia for the first months of 1992 had remained minimalist, and—in the eyes of the OAU, the Organization of Islamic Countries, the League of Arab States, and the new secretary-general—insufficient. Indeed, when Boutros-Ghali assumed office, he had challenged the members of the Security Council, accusing them in widely reported remarks of "fighting a rich man's war in Yugoslavia while not lifting a finger to save Somalia from disintegration."[4]

Despite the growing pressure for action and the stalemate at the United Nations, the U.S. administration was still wary of entering what seemed likely to be an open-ended, politically dangerous situation. Though it supported increased humanitarian aid and a mandatory arms embargo on Somalia, it shied away from more direct action. At the State Department both the African and the Human Rights Bureaus argued for greater U.S. involvement, but there was no top-level push to change the cautious approach. The National Security Council (NSC) staff also argued for more action. On the other hand, the Defense Department and the Joint Chiefs of Staff, while concerned, regarded the State and NSC positions as too nebulous, as vaguely asking the military to "fix the civil war." From Defense's perspective, there was no definable mission and no realistic plan.

U.S. reluctance to become more deeply involved reflected a number of other considerations, including Somalia's perceived insignificance in the aftermath of the Cold War. Some critics, such as Representative Howard Wolpe (D-MI), blamed the crisis on U.S. policymakers who in the 1980s had extended economic and military support to the Siad Barre regime. However, officials in the Bush administration countered that responsibility for Somalia's current crisis lay with Siad Barre himself and the former colonial powers, Britain and Italy. Some thought that Italy, which had

---

[4]Remarks in the UN Security Council, July 23, 1992, *Facts on File*, Vol. 52, No. 2700, p. 623.

extended massive support to the Siad regime, should take the lead in helping Somalia deal with the consequences.[5]

The United Nations' own negative assessment of prospects for a successful resolution of the crisis, its view that the Somalis would first have to resolve their own underlying problems, and its involvement elsewhere reinforced its caution. The United States was concerned about the issues of sovereignty that might arise if it intervened without an invitation, even in a situation of virtual anarchy. The cost attached to UN peacekeeping operations was a consideration as well—the United States already was $140 million in arrears on its peacekeeping account, and Secretary of State James Baker had received a cool reception when he asked Congress for another $810 million for 1992–93 peacekeeping operations, not including whatever more might be needed for Somalia.[6] In April the United States had been among the members of the Security Council that watered down the secretary-general's recommendation for a 500-man armed peacekeeping force, arguing legal and financial problems, so that final approval was for the fifty-man unarmed observer mission.

Still, Bush had for some time been considering the need for stronger action. In July, Acting Secretary of State Lawrence Eagleburger informed his staff that the president wanted the department to be "forward leaning" on Somalia.[7] On July 27 the State Department issued a public statement in support of sending armed UN security personnel to Somalia, the first U.S. "pro-security" statement since the crisis began.[8]

While interagency policy deliberations were addressing what more the United States could do, OFDA continued to take the lead in international relief efforts. By August 1992, the United States had already provided $150 million worth of food and other emergency aid.[9] On August 3, OFDA announced that the United States was prepared to send an additional 80,000 metric tons of food to Somalia—28,000 immediately. Problems of looting and banditry were rampant—at the time of the announcement, 7,000 tons of food were blocked in Mogadishu harbor by gunfire in the neighboring area.

---

[5]Peter J. Schrader, "The Horn of Africa: U.S. Foreign Policy in an Altered Cold War Environment," *Middle East Journal*, Vol. 46, No. 4 (Autumn 1992), p. 585.

[6]Paul Lewis, "Security Council Weighs Role in Somali Civil War," *New York Times*, March 18, 1992.

[7]Cohen, "Intervention in Somalia."

[8]Ibid.

[9]OFDA Situation Report, September 16, 1992.

Over the summer, the interagency debate on Somalia policy continued without reaching a consensus. Various ideas were floated in the NSC Deputies Committee, from backing an "all necessary measures" resolution in the Security Council that would allow the use of force against those who blocked relief efforts, to mounting a military rescue operation like Operation Provide Comfort, undertaken to assist the Kurds in northern Iraq after the Gulf War.[10] President Bush's August 14 decision to start Operation Provide Relief broke the logjam. The White House announced that the United States was ready to transport UN peacekeeping forces to Somalia for humanitarian purposes. The Department of Defense was instructed to begin an emergency food airlift to northern Kenya and Somalia—the United States planned to send an additional 145,000 tons of food. U.S. ambassador to the UN Edward Perkins was authorized to hold consultations with Security Council members on additional measures to assure that humanitarian food relief could be delivered. USAID's Assistant Administrator Andrew Natsios was appointed the president's special coordinator for Somali relief, and a UN humanitarian donors conference was to be convened.

DIALOGUE WITH THE HUMANITARIAN RELIEF AGENCIES

Both Natsios and OFDA director James Kunder used public diplomacy to highlight the crisis and solidify popular support for the proposed U.S. assistance. Kunder's press conference after returning from Somalia in early August had stressed grim reports of mass starvation and chaos. In a reflection of growing interest, it was attended by thirty journalists—up from the four who had attended earlier OFDA press conferences. Also that month, OFDA started meeting regularly with representatives of the American NGOs operating in Somalia (World Concern, CARE, the International Medical Corps, and World Vision) to pool information and discuss issues of food distribution, public health, and security.

Meanwhile the U.S. NGOs were intensifying their campaign for further government action. Most were circumspect, recognizing the potential problems raised by a call for forces during a presidential campaign. By November a disaster response committee from Interaction, the NGO

---

[10]Security Council Resolution 688, adopted in the flush of UN activism related to Iraq's invasion of Kuwait and new U.S.-USSR solidarity, was the first express authorization of the use of force in support of a humanitarian mission without the consent of the local government.

coordinating agency, was meeting weekly with State, Defense, and OFDA representatives. In late November the NGOs sent a letter to President Bush, asking the United States to enhance the capacity of the United Nations to provide security for relief operations. It was an indirect way of calling for direct U.S. military involvement.

Though some field representatives argued that the dispatch of U.S. ground forces was unnecessary or even counterproductive, this was not the view of the senior executives of the relief agencies. By early fall, virtually every field representative suggested a multilateral armed intervention, although some did not want a unilateral U.S. intervention.[11] Shortly after the president's announcement of Operation Restore Hope, Natsios accompanied a delegation of U.S. NGO representatives to CENTCOM Headquarters in Tampa, where General Freeman, the deputy commander, briefed them on outlines of an operational plan. They welcomed the president's decision, agreed with the focus on providing security for humanitarian relief operations, and described where their operations were taking place and where protection was most needed. The contributions of the knowledgeable NGO personnel were invaluable for correctly assessing the state of affairs in Somalia, helping with a sort of triage to identify the most urgent humanitarian tasks, and planning the logistical approaches to them.

DECISION ON INTERVENTION WITH U.S. FORCES

President Bush's August decision to mount an airlift had shifted discussion within the administration and created an "activist consensus" that had not existed previously.[12] Though he did not relate it to Somalia directly, in his October address to the UN General Assembly, Bush announced that the U.S. military would have a new and more active role in peacekeeping efforts in the "new world order" and that the Pentagon needed to prepare for it. However, he stressed logistics, communications, training, and other roles, stopping short of actual participation in peacekeeping operations under UN command.

By mid-October, interagency deliberations had brought the Pentagon to the conclusion that an ad hoc approach to the Somali crisis was going to be seriously counterproductive and that broader long-term planning

---

[11]William Garvelink, OFDA, interview with John Hirsch, Washington, D.C., July 15, 1993.
[12]Cohen, "Intervention in Somalia."

and better coordination of international efforts were needed. The airlift operation from Mombasa was barely scratching the surface of the humanitarian crisis. The piecemeal approach of establishing "points of security" where airdrops could be made, and waiting for the deployment of still-absent UN peacekeepers to prevent looting, was neither appropriate to the magnitude of the problem nor cost-effective, and the Joint Chiefs were not prepared to commit to an open-ended funding of the marginally useful military airlift.

A Defense Department paper outlining a strategy that would simultaneously address diplomatic, political, security, and humanitarian requirements became the basis for discussions in the Deputies Committee. CENTCOM and the Joint Chiefs had begun to define a mission to ensure the safe delivery of relief supplies to the famine belt, in contrast to the nebulous concept of finding a way to end the civil war. They recognized that even 4,400 peacekeepers, as requested by the secretary-general, would be insufficient for that purpose. Effective security would require a force of 12,000 to 15,000, though the use of U.S. troops was still not envisaged.

During this time, the State Department and the NSC had become more active in exploring alternatives. Frank Wisner, who had considerable familiarity with African affairs, was appointed undersecretary of state for international security affairs and given responsibility for Somalia.[13] Wisner and Boutros-Ghali, whom he knew from having been ambassador to Egypt, began informally to discuss avenues of action. The secretary-general, recognizing that UNOSOM I was bogged down, explored with Wisner the possibility of an enlarged peacekeeping operation in which the United States would supply logistical support while the Canadians, Belgians, and others would supply troops. Boutros-Ghali also indicated that he did not want U.S. forces, which he thought were unavailable in any case.

Only in mid-November did the need to intervene with U.S. forces come into clear focus. By then the situation in Somalia had become completely untenable. The beleaguered relief workers and the frustrations of humanitarian agencies that could not get food to the intended recipients,

---

[13]At the NSC, Dick Clark, formerly director of the Political-Military Bureau of the State Department, worked closely with Admiral Jonathan Howe, Scowcroft's senior deputy. They had responsibility for coordinating U.S. activities in Somalia, and Howe later became the secretary-general's special representative there. Jim Woods, deputy assistant secretary for Africa and international security affairs, who had more than a decade of experience with African issues, was the key official at Defense.

combined with the horrifying evidence of thousands of dying Somalis, put intense pressure on the president and the administration to act.

It was apparently at this point that Joint Chiefs Chairman Colin Powell took the lead in the Defense Department's decision to propose a large-scale U.S. military intervention, going considerably further than the JCS staff had originally been prepared to go. The idea appears initially to have involved only Powell, Secretary of Defense Dick Cheney, National Security Advisor Brent Scowcroft, and General Joseph Hoar, commander in chief of CENTCOM, who was tasked with preparing a basic approach. By mid-November, CENTCOM had developed a mission statement and concept of operations, even though no formal decision had yet been made. Consideration of direct U.S. military intervention, a response to growing pressure for action, represented a complete turnaround in Defense Department thinking from the middle of the year.[14]

The NSC Deputies Committee, a group of senior staff just below cabinet level, convened four times between November 20 and 26. Though the subject had been under lively discussion for some time, the atmosphere at the Deputies Committee meetings changed rapidly. Somalia had emerged as such an overwhelming humanitarian crisis that there was no longer a question of inaction. Moreover, a definable mission had emerged, one which no other nation was likely to undertake. And the goodwill to be gained from helping out in Somalia might help offset the widespread criticism that the United States was dilatory in responding to aggression in Bosnia. Such action would also help mute criticism of the United States in the Arab world for not helping their Muslim coreligionists in Bosnia.

The Deputies Committee was considering three options: increased U.S. support for UN peacekeeping efforts; a U.S.-organized coalition effort without the participation of U.S. ground troops; or a major U.S. effort to assemble a multinational force in which U.S. ground troops would take the leading role, as in Operation Desert Storm. Though the secretary-general had appealed to Wisner for more help earlier that week, he had not raised the issue of U.S. ground forces, and the changed think-

---

[14]CENTCOM had begun to prepare for a mission of this sort following the lengthy search in Ethiopia for the crashed plane carrying Rep. Mickey Leland (D-TX) in 1989. It developed new plans for humanitarian assistance in cooperation with OFDA, and had conducted an exercise to test them in early 1992, with the First Marine Expeditionary Force designated as the action element. This made it much easier for CENTCOM to organize Operation Provide Relief and to quickly develop plans for Operation Restore Hope.

ing at Defense had not yet been mentioned. Most participants at the November 20 meeting, therefore, still did not think the use of ground forces was a serious option. On November 21, committee vice chairman Admiral David Jeremiah, Powell's representative, startled the group by saying, "If you think U.S. forces are needed, we can do the job." He presented an initial concept, developed at CENTCOM, to deploy two divisions, parts of which might be coalition units from other countries. At the end of the committee's deliberations, a detailed description of the paper, with three options, was sent to the president without a recommendation. It would be up to him to decide.

Bush met with his senior advisors on the day before Thanksgiving, November 25. Powell wanted to be sure the pitfalls were reviewed before a decision was made. He questioned, too, whether conditions in Somalia would permit a smooth handoff to a UN peacekeeping force after a relatively brief U.S. deployment, which all present believed to be an essential limit on the U.S. involvement. After broad discussion, the president decided that if the Security Council concurred and other nations agreed to join the effort, U.S. ground forces would lead an international force to try to stop the death and famine in Somalia. He had chosen the strongest option available and embarked on a major humanitarian intervention.[15]

MILITARY PREPARATIONS AND PLANNING

For nearly a month before the announcement of Operation Restore Hope, CENTCOM, working with the Joint Chiefs, had been developing a mission statement and concept of operations, including defining an appropriate force structure and rules of engagement. Recognizing that operations would take place in a situation of near anarchy, General Hoar proposed using unprecedented Chapter VII authority for peace enforcement "by all necessary means." This would "allow the on-scene commander maximum flexibility to determine what constituted a threat and what response was appropriate, including first use of deadly force."[16]

---

[15]The foregoing account is based on interviews with several senior participants in the interagency process. The best public account is by Don Oberdorfer, "The Path to Intervention," *Washington Post*, December 6, 1992.

[16]Joseph P. Hoar, "Humanitarian Assistance Operations Challenges: The CENTCOM Perspective on Somalia," *Joint Forces Quarterly*, Vol. I, No. 2 (November 1993). This article contains a useful account of the development of the deployment plan for UNITAF and reflections on what was learned for future humanitarian undertakings.

The force structure drew on U.S. naval forces already in the Indian Ocean area. The amphibious ready group (ARG) with its embarked Marine expeditionary unit (MEU) became the core of the Joint Task Force. Hoar turned to his Marine component at Camp Pendleton, California, under the command of Lieutenant General Robert Johnston and built around the First Marine Division commanded by Major General Charles Wilhelm, to head the task force and added the Army's Tenth Mountain Division commanded by Major General Steve Arnold, as well as Air Force and Navy units. Building on CENTCOM's strategic concept, Johnston, in daily contact with Hoar, quickly prepared for deployment and undertook planning for its execution.

The operation would have four phases. Phase I would involve a Marine landing in Mogadishu, establishing control of the port, harbor facilities, and airfields. In Phase II, U.S. Army and allied forces would join the Marines in securing areas inland. Phase III would extend operations south to Kismayo, and Phase IV would see the handoff from UNITAF to UNOSOM II, the subsequent UN peacekeeping operation.

POLITICAL CONSULTATIONS ON U.S. INTERVENTION

On the day before Thanksgiving, President Bush sent Acting Secretary of State Eagleburger to New York to advise the secretary-general of his decision. By that point, Boutros-Ghali had arrived at a similar conclusion: the horrors of Somalia warranted more forceful action by the international community. These views were expressed very clearly in his November 29 report to the Security Council. Boutros-Ghali was generally receptive to the proposal presented by Eagleburger, since decisive action seemed essential in light of the horrors on the ground and pressures from the international community, and there was not enough support for further efforts to strengthen UNOSOM I. Still, a great deal of work would be required to fit the plan into a suitable UN framework.

During the next week Ambassador Perkins and his staff held intensive consultations with the secretary-general, members of the Security Council, and selected others, including some from Africa as well as from NATO countries, which confirmed that there was strong support for the U.S. proposal. En route to Somalia, Oakley and Perkins met privately for an hour on December 1 with Boutros-Ghali, Under Secretary for Peace-keeping Marrack Goulding, and Under Secretary Jonah to discuss how the U.S.-led effort could be coordinated with the United Nations. In all these consultations, the top UN officials rejected the idea that the U.S. initiative should eventually become a UN peacekeeping operation. It was seen as a corruption of traditional peacekeeping involving too much emphasis on use of force and too great a role for the United States. Oakley's suggestions that there might be an analogy to UN peacekeeping operations in the Congo in the early 1960s and that in this case a strong show of force might be the key to success were rejected out of hand.

President Bush made personal telephone calls to a number of heads of state asking for participation in or support for the proposed operation. All but British prime minister John Major pledged to send troops or provide other assistance.[17] On December 3, the Security Council unanimously adopted Resolution 794, endorsing the offer "by a member state" to constitute and lead an international force to protect humanitarian relief operations in Somalia. It would be not a UN force, but one endorsed by the Security Council, much as the 1950 U.S.-led force for Korea and the 1991 U.S.-led force for Kuwait had been. Although Eagleburger and Oakley had informed the secretary-general and key members of the Security Council that the administration was prepared to make the U.S.-led mission into an official UN peacekeeping operation, the response was that a U.S.-led, UN-approved operation would be more acceptable. The forceful approach envisaged by the United States did not fit UN peacekeeping practice or theory at that time.[18] The Security Council was silent on the implied relationship between UNOSOM I and the proposed operation and did not address the implications for long-term solutions to Somalia's problems.

---

[17]The United Kingdom eventually sent two RAF aircraft to Mombasa to join Operation Provide Relief.

[18]In his "Agenda for Peace" of 1992, Boutros-Ghali had called on the Security Council to consider establishing "peace enforcement" units that would be on call to operate under Chapter VII for such low-level conflicts. The Security Council had not endorsed the idea. In Operation Provide Comfort, the Security Council had established a precedent for forceful international intervention in a humanitarian situation without consent of local authority (Security Council Resolution 688, April 5, 1991). Yet in deciding to send peacekeeping forces to Somalia, the Security Council pulled back to a more traditional approach with Resolution 751 of April 24, 1992, referring to agreements signed by Somali leaders and the mechanism for monitoring the cease-fire and to "consultations with the parties in Mogadishu" as the basis for sending fifty UN observers and establishing a "UN Security Force." Security Council Resolution 775 (August 28, 1992) increased the number of peacekeepers to be deployed but did not explicitly approve the principle of nonconsent, leading to the immobilization of the Pakistani contingent. The movement by the UN during 1991–92 on the issue of "forcible humanitarian intervention in a state" is discussed in "Three Views on the Issue of Humanitarian Intervention," a report published by the United States Institute of Peace (Washington, D.C., June 1992).

On December 4, President Bush announced that U.S. and other forces would soon land in Somalia. This announcement was followed by a press briefing on details and logistics from Cheney and Powell. Cheney described the mission objectives as the establishment by U.S. forces of a secure environment for the delivery of relief supplies and the consolidation of the security framework so that it could be handed over to regular UN forces. U.S. forces were committed to be in the lead in large numbers for only a few months. Both Cheney and Powell, however, explicitly rejected reports from anonymous White House sources that U.S. troops would leave by January 20.

Powell explained the president's decision as arising from the need for a totally new strategy because "the level of violence was increasing faster than the humanitarian effort to try to deal with the situation." A large force, capable of controlling the violence, not just in Mogadishu, would make clear to the faction leaders that order would be restored with or without their cooperation. More than a dozen other countries, he noted, already had volunteered to participate.

Powell also indicated that the United States had given considerable advance thought to the transition and an eventual U.S. role in the succeeding UN peacekeeping operation. First, he envisaged that as early as January forces slated for UNOSOM II would begin to arrive to replace U.S. forces. The handoff would be "in such a security environment, such a level of stability, that it will be fully within the capability of [the] peacekeeping operation to maintain that humanitarian effort." Powell indicated that some limited U.S. forces with unique capabilities, such as logistics and support units and a quick reaction force, would remain as part of the UN peacekeeping operations while the amphibious ready group with its marine expeditionary unit could remain off the Somali coast for a brief time to assist if problems developed.

Although it went largely unnoticed at the time, the briefing made explicit a major change in U.S. policy toward UN peacekeeping. Previously, the Pentagon had been unwilling for U.S. forces to serve as members of UN peacekeeping forces, although they had participated as observers, provided logistics support for peacekeeping operations, and participated in U.S.-led, non-UN multilateral forces (e.g., as observers in the Sinai). However, Cheney and Powell clearly stated their readiness for U.S. forces to serve as full members of the UN peacekeeping force that they expected would follow the U.S.-led coalition.

Moreover, an essential part of this new policy was the clear implication that peacekeeping should be conducted along the lines of the so-called Weinberger-Powell Doctrine of a clear, finite, "doable" mission, involving the deployment of overwhelming, efficient force, with rules of engagement that allowed the expeditious use of force when necessary. This view was diametrically opposite to the traditional peacekeeping doctrine under Chapter VI of the UN Charter, which calls for deploying as few forces as possible, with strict limits on the degree and circumstances of the use of force and with the requirement for approval from local authorities.

The secretary-general and his principal advisors were prepared to go along with the planned Operation Restore Hope, even though they were somewhat uneasy about an operation not directly under UN authority. However, they, like the Security Council, did not agree with the U.S. idea that the United Nations should take responsibility for Somalia in the near future, replacing the proposed UNITAF with a UN peacekeeping force very soon.

Indeed, in subsequent public statements and a letter to President Bush on December 11, Boutros-Ghali made it quite clear that he also did not accept the limited scope of security and disarmament to be provided by UNITAF. He called instead for the U.S.-led forces to conduct a full-scale, total disarmament program over the entire country, using whatever force might be required. This failure to clarify the UN-UNITAF relationship at the outset was to plague both parties and create a myriad of problems, small and large, on the ground.

Operation Restore Hope

Operation Restore Hope was a new direction in international engagement for the United States. Neither a traditional peacekeeping mission nor a textbook military undertaking, it sought to combine elements of each for a rapid and productive venture. Such departures from the beaten path often hold out great promise; at the same time, their pitfalls can be unexpected and costly. But for the situation in Somalia, there seemed no alternative to a new approach.

Organizationally, the operation took shape along established military pathways. UNITAF was made up of U.S. and allied troops under the command of Lieutenant General Robert Johnston,[1] who in turn reported to General Joseph P. Hoar, commander in chief of CENTCOM, and reporting responsibilities went directly up the military hierarchy through the Department of Defense and the Joint Chiefs of Staff to the president. Thus, though Operation Restore Hope had been endorsed and supported by Security Council Resolution 794, command and control were firmly retained within the American military. The secretary-general and the Security Council were kept informed of developments.

During planning for Operation Restore Hope, the need for an active political presence had been quite clear, and President Bush was urged to appoint a political representative with enough seniority and experience to provide balance to the military aspect. Robert Oakley, who had served as ambassador to Somalia between 1982 and 1984, was well known to the

---

[1]Johnston had served during Operation Desert Storm as chief of staff to General Norman Schwarzkopf, the overall commander, gaining excellent experience in coalition operations. Previously he had served as senior officer during the early phase of U.S. peacekeeping activities in Beirut, dealing with a number of political factions, including the PLO.

political and military officials with whom he would need to work. As Bush's special envoy Oakley had easy access to the Department of Defense and the NSC as well as the State Department, which set up a special Somalia Interagency Task Force to coordinate civilian planning and operations with those of the military.[2]

No formal guidelines were established for the Johnston-Oakley relationship. Oakley's brief was to act as overseer and coordinator of all U.S. civilian activities in Somalia, to provide political advice to UNITAF, to act as liaison with UN special representative Kittani, and to work closely with the NGO community to get humanitarian operations moving. Johnston was charged with providing the security necessary to achieve this goal. By good fortune in this particular case there were no problems in establishing a close, comfortable working relationship based on mutual respect. This was a dividend, however, not only of a fortunate compatibility between the two personalities, but of the flexibility afforded them by their superiors to avoid bureaucratic stiffness and emphasize getting the job done. Much of what had to be done in Somalia was without established doctrine or precedent, and priority was given to adaptability, initiative, and good judgment.

Oakley's assignment was complex and delicate. UNITAF's mission was explicitly focused on protecting the delivery of relief supplies and other humanitarian operations in southern Somalia. It was not he but Kittani who was officially charged with conducting negotiations with the Somali faction leaders and others on such political issues as eventual national-level reconciliation, coordination of humanitarian operations, and economic reconstruction.

But local attitudes toward the United States and the United Nations had begun to diverge, sometimes rather awkwardly. Not only did the U.S. military presence overshadow the United Nations' by early 1993, but the perception of the United States as the remaining international superpower affected the response of Somali leaders. It was perhaps inevitable that Aideed and Ali Mahdi, jockeying for future political position, looked to Oakley as their principal interlocutor on the broader issues facing Somalia. Even though Oakley repeatedly made clear the limits of the U.S.

---

[2]The task force, under the direction of Under Secretary Wisner, was chaired by Ambassador Brandon Grove, Jr., assisted by Ambassador David Shinn. It worked around the clock to coordinate domestic civilian activities in support of Operation Restore Hope and to provide instant responses to the needs of the U.S. Liaison Office (USLO). Grove worked closely on the military side with Rear Admiral Frank Bowman of the Joint Chiefs.

mandate and stressed the need for Somali cooperation with the United Nations, the Somalis believed that the United States was more likely to make things happen. (An element of flattery, not unrecognized by its American objects, was also at work.) The media inadvertently contributed to enhancing the role of UNITAF, which offered a new and exciting approach after the uninspiring record of UNOSOM I. And the widely held perception, fostered energetically by Aideed, that Boutros-Ghali had been a supporter of Siad Barre further complicated the ticklish relationship.

Both UNITAF and the U.S. Liaison Office (USLO), the U.S. diplomatic presence in Somalia, were intent on moving as rapidly as possible to carry out their humanitarian mission. They were equally intent on not taking sides among the several Somali factions and on avoiding confrontation and long-term animosity, which would have interfered with the achievement of their goals and increased the possibility of casualties. However, they wanted also to contribute to longer-term stability and to the prospects for political reconciliation. They had the resources to implement major activities, did not hesitate to improvise where there was no proven plan, and had good cooperation in the early months from the Somalis as well as the NGO community. Aware of the desirability of keeping the United Nations informed, both Oakley and Johnston met regularly with and briefed Kittani on developments. Their staffs also cooperated with Kittani's staff and that of Brigadier General Shaheen, military commander of UNOSOM I.

Inevitably, there were occasions when UNITAF acted without first informing the United Nations, at least partly because of the vagueness of their relationship. There was also a tendency on the part of Kittani and Shaheen, stemming from the mandate of the Security Council and the secretary-general's preferences, to take no action without approval from UN headquarters, which was slow in providing such guidance—too slow for the operational requirements of UNITAF and USLO. Moreover, both UN headquarters and its representatives in the field preferred to deliberate carefully over the development of long-term programs such as the creation of Somali governmental institutions. Since there were no completed plans, no immediate prospect of implementing such fundamental political change, and only a small UN field staff, UNOSOM generated little action on the ground.

All of this inevitably created some UN-U.S. friction, played on variously by Somalis, NGOs, and the media. The weakness and small numbers of UNOSOM I's civilian staff added to Kittani's frustrations, and

A "technical" patrols a road outside Mogadishu in December 1992, before the U.S. Marine landing.

Robert Oakley is sworn in as U.S. special envoy to Somalia in December 1992 as General Robert Johnston and John Hirsch look on.

UNITAF forces stand guard outside the the former Central Bank in Mogadishu in January 1993.

Oakley speaks at the January 1993 dedication of a bridge built near Kismayo by U.S. troops.

Somali workers distribute relief supplies at a village near Jalalaqsi in January 1993.

reinforced the common tendency to turn to UNITAF for help. It also exacerbated problems caused by the divergent views of the Bush administration and the secretary-general on issues such as disarmament and the scope of UNITAF's mission, and by the failure to spell out the relationships between U.S. and UN operations in the field. Nevertheless, despite the difficulties, UNITAF, USLO, and Kittani kept in mind that Operation Restore Hope was a short-term, limited-scope operation and that the United Nations had to be bolstered so that it would be in a position to take over when UNITAF departed.

PHASE I: SECURING MOGADISHU

Oakley and Johnston, who had never met, arrived in Mogadishu within days of the Marine landing. Oakley, who arrived two days before, prepared the groundwork for the landing and established a pattern for the combined political-military effort that ensued. On December 7–8, he met separately with Aideed and Ali Mahdi to enlist their cooperation in ensuring the unchallenged arrival of U.S. forces on Somali shores. Each promised to use his radio station and political-clan organization to urge everyone to stay away from the port and the airport landing sites after midnight December 8. Aideed also intervened with the Murasade, an allied Hawiye subclan, to move several hundred armed fighters away from barracks adjacent to the airport. It was perceptible, beneath the apparently warm welcome, that he still harbored deep reservations about the effect of foreign forces on his interests, but it was even clearer that he was not in a mood to challenge them at the outset—he had even made a public statement welcoming the U.S. forces, and his militia was on its best behavior. Ali Mahdi's welcome was more obviously sincere, though he inquired about the arrival of the Italians, and asked when and where they would land.

In the event, apart from unexpected encounters with the massed floodlights of international television crews, the landing went forward without a hitch.[3] The immediate military objective of securing the airport and the port was quickly attained by the first 1,300 Marines who

---

[3]Back in Washington, Defense Department public relations had informed the media of landing timetables but had neglected to tell those conducting the landings that they had done so. Without the extraordinary restraint of Marine Corps personnel, a number of media casualties might have resulted.

landed by helicopter and came ashore in amphibious craft from the USS *Tripoli* and other ships of the amphibious ready group.

A DELICATE BEGINNING

For more than a year Mogadishu had been a divided city, with an east-west "green line" of barricades running through a rabbit warren of alleys and destroyed buildings in the city center. Both Ali Mahdi's and Aideed's factions had amassed a sizable amount of weaponry in the city, including the famous "technicals"—jeeps and landcruisers mounted with heavy weapons. It was extremely hazardous for relief workers and food convoys to move in either direction, and most Somalis dared not cross from one territory to another. Thus, given UNITAF's tough rules of engagement, possibilities for confrontation and conflict with U.S. forces were high. The Somali leaders recognized the dangers of such a situation and preferred at least to start out on the good side of U.S. military and civilian leaders.

Oakley invited the two leaders to join him, along with Johnston and Kittani, for lunch at the USLO offices on December 11 to discuss how to avoid potentially disastrous problems for the Somalis should they "unintentionally" clash with U.S. forces. (Oakley recalled for them the massive firepower used so effectively by the United States during Operation Desert Storm.) The site—at what had been the Conoco compound—offered a neutral and secure venue, and the meeting was intended to clarify what the parties could expect of one another.

The desire to avoid what could be major problems and to get on good terms with the United States was an important factor in the decision of the two rivals to meet for the first time since the civil war began in earnest. However, there was also an evident feeling on both sides that it was time to test the waters for possible reconciliation. Several other attempts to arrange a meeting between the two had almost but not quite succeeded. The U.S. command invitation provided the needed deus ex machina, allowing both to attend without losing face.

Though Aideed initially protested Kittani's presence, Oakley insisted that the objectives of the meeting required that he be present. Given the obvious implication of the meeting for long-term political reconciliation, it would have been a serious mistake to exclude him, sending a signal that the United States was not supportive of the United Nations and that Aideed could get his way in opposing it.

Ali Mahdi, for his part, protested the meeting site as being too dangerous because of proximity to Aideed's headquarters. It took more than thirty minutes and a threat to cancel the meeting to convince Ali Mahdi's retainers that it would be safe for him to come to USLO even with a U.S. armored escort. Eventually agreement was reached, and the meeting was held as proposed.

In typical Somali fashion, each faction leader was accompanied by an entourage of six or seven aides, probably both to establish status and to ensure against later misrepresentation. When they met, Ali Mahdi, Aideed, and their followers all embraced. That the action was genuine seems in little doubt. It was not for outside observers; there were no foreign media present. There seemed to be at that moment genuine relief that the United States had done for them and the Somali people what they could not do for themselves—stop the cycle of death and destruction.

And though each clearly remained very cautious of the other, it was Aideed and Ali Mahdi who put together the "Seven Point Agreement" after listening to points raised by Johnston, Oakley, and Kittani at a small working lunch. They surprised their U.S. hosts—who had expected them to work out an agreement more easily with outsiders present to push the process if it got stuck—by asking to rejoin their delegations for a combined discussion with no foreigners present. (This was not the last time foreigners failed to understand how Somalis negotiate and agree.) At the end of two hours they called for the United States and UN representatives to witness the signing of their agreement, and then held a joint session outside with the international and Somali media to read the agreement and shake hands for the television cameras. Both sides were pleased with the favorable attention from so many top U.S. and European television and print media.

This event was the starting point of the U.S. strategy for creating a benign security environment. As far as possible, the goal would be achieved by dialogue and cooption, using the implicit threat of coercion to encourage the faction leaders to gain prestige by showing leadership at home and to the international community. Over a period of time, Oakley urged the Somali faction leaders to take a series of specific steps, first to allow for humanitarian activities and stop fighting and then to end the civil war and begin the process of national reconciliation.

These steps were also explained to them as the best means of obtaining much-needed international material help for relief, rehabilitation, and eventual reconstruction. The keen Somali interest in international material assistance was a significant incentive for at least a degree of cooperation.

Once an internal Somali agreement was concluded, the U.S. approach was to insist on its implementation, since experience soon showed that signing an agreement did not mean that either party necessarily intended to do anything about it, at least not of his own volition, or soon. It might mean a desire to appear cooperative, or that the elements in the agreement were not utterly unacceptable and might be implemented under certain circumstances. It rarely meant what the United States understood formal top-level agreements to mean. In response, UNITAF and USLO devised an approach that focused on selecting the most positive feasible elements of agreements between the two factions and concentrating on getting them implemented. Their means of doing so included providing material assistance as well as persuasion, pressure, and the threat of force.

At that time, Aideed and Ali Mahdi were rivals in projecting themselves as responsible national leaders worthy of U.S. support. Each also wanted to avoid conflict with UNITAF and save face at home. Therefore, they could usually be persuaded, pressured, or cajoled into reaching agreement and cooperating at least minimally with UNITAF.

These initial meetings with Aideed and Ali Mahdi revealed an interesting pattern that prevailed for almost all the many subsequent meetings, and offered insight into their respective strengths and political situations. Aideed attended alone except for a note taker, did all the talking, and presented a number of points in the form of letters as well as orally. Aideed's was very much the approach of a general who wished to show himself in full command of a disciplined organization. Ali Mahdi, on the other hand, was openly collegial, offering few specifics and inviting a great deal of discussion—he frequently consulted with his seven or eight advisors before responding to a question or taking a position.

BUILDING A MORE SECURE ENVIRONMENT

In the case of the December 11 communiqué it was critical that the two leaders be held to the agreed-on cease-fire and the explicit undertaking to remove heavy weapons from the streets of Mogadishu to designated compounds. Other elements of the agreement—for example, removing barricades from the green line—could be implemented later, when conditions were right. The cease-fire in Mogadishu, which was already tentatively in effect, took firm hold at once, but it took until December 26 for both sides to begin cantoning heavy weapons.

During the two weeks of discussion between the Aideed and Ali Mahdi factions, and between them and UNITAF and USLO, about removing heavy weapons, the two Somali factions established what they called a joint security committee. Composed of senior military leaders, it met almost daily between January and April at the Conoco compound, relying on the United States to provide safe transportation for the Ali Mahdi representatives as well as a safe and neutral meeting place. Senior UNITAF and USLO officers found this body invaluable for encouraging dialogue and understanding between Somalis and Americans, not only on the specific issue of removing heavy weapons, but on other issues where there were or could be problems or misunderstanding. Many of the Somalis genuinely welcomed the opportunity to reduce tension and increase mutual understanding, establishing firm personal relationships.

Thus there were almost daily meetings of the security committee, often with U.S. officers and civilian officials, sometimes with only Somalis. The Somalis thus became more accustomed to dialogue and problem-solving and conflict prevention and resolution. Continued efforts toward such goals as removing roadblocks and resolving violent property disputes helped bolster a sense of sharing a common goal. The meetings continued regularly until the United Nations formally assumed responsibility on May 4, even when Aideed or others were in a period of tense relations with UNITAF. Oakley and Zinni occasionally joined meetings to press for action on such key issues as resolving property conflicts. After May 4, however, UNOSOM II did not continue the pattern of frequent meetings, the joint security committee withered away, and tension mounted.

In mid-February 1993, Ali Mahdi turned over all his cantoned technicals to UNITAF, clearly signaling his intention to play an essentially political game from that time. But on Aideed's side, by mid-February most of the technicals had quietly disappeared from their cantonments to points unknown. He had moved them, along with much of his other military equipment, from Mogadishu toward Galcaio to avoid confiscation. At the time it was enough for UNITAF that the technicals had been peacefully removed from Mogadishu and the main supply routes pursuant to the existing agreement and that it was understood that any technicals spotted after December 26 were open to immediate capture or destruction. The same principle was then applied up-country. UNITAF radio, newspapers, and leaflets spread this information widely, and both Aideed and Ali Mahdi announced it through their radio stations.

Given the limited UNITAF mandate, which deliberately excluded general disarmament, it seemed unnecessary to confront Aideed over the disappearance of stored weapons so long as they posed no threat to UNITAF forces or humanitarian operations and so long as UNITAF was able to confiscate weapons found in the course of its operations without setting off a fight with the faction that owned them. Although always alert for an angle he could exploit, Aideed respected the rules, disowning as "bandits" any from his militia captured or destroyed by UNITAF in Mogadishu, Baidoa, and elsewhere.

SECURING THE PORT AND THE AIRPORT

The military side of the operation proceeded smoothly, as General Johnston moved rapidly to establish UNITAF control of Mogadishu port and airport. Within forty-eight hours of landing, an element of Colonel Greg Newbold's MEU established itself at both locations and organized perimeter security. The first French forces arrived on December 10 and took up positions at Mogadishu's "Kilometer Four" traffic circle, which commanded the main roads between the port, the airport, and UNITAF headquarters. The airport, which had been in use only intermittently, was reopened under UNITAF control on December 9, and the port was brought under UNITAF control the same day. The airport runway was in acceptable condition, but a new control tower, communications reader, and air traffic control were quickly installed. The port itself was initially operating at only 10 percent capacity. Rear Admiral Perkins took over port operations, and began preparing the port for both military and humanitarian relief cargo. By late December, Mogadishu had become the busiest port in Africa, with military ships unloading streams of vehicles and other support and civilian ships unloading relief supplies.[4] There were no serious security problems, although representatives of some NGOs expressed dismay that relief supplies sometimes were held back to allow military equipment to be offloaded first.

---

[4]Over thirty-five days, forty-eight ships were offloaded of 114,000 tons of cargo, including 6,668 vehicles and ninety-six helicopters. Over five million gallons of fuel and 832,000 gallons of water were pumped ashore. Another fourteen civilian ships unloaded 40,000 tons of grain during this period.

On December 9, General Johnston had established UNITAF command headquarters in the gutted ruins of the U.S. Embassy. Like the airport and port, it was in south Mogadishu, near Aideed's headquarters. The building, overrun by an angry mob at the time of Siad Barre's fall, had been stripped of all electrical fixtures and plumbing, though it remained structurally sound. There was no running water and very limited generator-powered electricity. Johnston and his staff bunked down in their offices while his troops dug foxholes and trenches on the grounds outside.

The fact that all installations important to UNITAF, and almost all UNITAF forces, were located in south Mogadishu put them in easy reach of Aideed's headquarters and weapons caches. The same was true of headquarters for the United Nations and most NGOs. This proximity, and the lack of an early UNITAF crackdown, soon gave rise to rumors that the United States favored Aideed, who worked hard to spread and confirm them, telling all who would listen that he had a special relationship with the United States. By the time of the January conference on national reconciliation in Addis Ababa, according to complaints from the UN secretary-general's office to the State Department, many of the Somali participants believed Aideed's claim that the United States was deliberately favoring the Habr Gidr. However, less than twenty-four hours after this complaint was made, UNITAF acted against Aideed's forces by destroying a weapons storage compound that had fired on Marine Corps patrols despite repeated warnings. This put an end, at least temporarily, to rumors of favoritism.[5]

As more UNITAF forces arrived in January, subordinate Marine detachments were established in north Mogadishu, both to provide better protection for NGO facilities and to show Ali Mahdi and others that UNITAF had no favorites. By late February, as more of his weapons caches were discovered and either removed or placed under guard, Aideed was complaining that the greater UNITAF presence in the south was deliberately planned to weaken him vis-à-vis Ali Mahdi. However, UNITAF was careful to balance raids on Aideed's weapons caches with similar raids on those belonging to Ali Mahdi and other factions in the Mogadishu area.

Mogadishu itself, although key locations were secured early, proved the most difficult sector for UNITAF. The capital's population was ten

---

[5]Somali faction leaders, including Abshir, Ali Mahdi, and especially Aideed, proved adept at promoting the impression that they were receiving foreign backing.

times that of any other city, and the forces of Ali Mahdi and Aideed, as well as smaller militias and hundreds of freelance "bandits," were heavily armed with huge hidden stockpiles of arms and ammunition. The economic and political significance of Mogadishu for all Somalis, and its symbolism for national leadership, made it especially important for the national factions and a primary focus for their rivalry.

The concentration of journalists, UN and NGO headquarters staffs, and other foreigners, along with warehouses containing relief supplies, also offered many attractive opportunities for individual acts of robbery and looting even after the organized militias adopted a low profile. The northern sector of Mogadishu, distant from UNITAF headquarters in the south, was very dangerous in terms of crime, especially in the deserted green line area.

UNITAF focused initially on securing such key facilities as the port and airport and protecting food convoys, but avoided as far as possible taking on the police function of patrolling the streets or dealing with common crime. Acting as police was considered likely to put UNITAF in ticklish contact with the local population to the point of risking serious friction and very possibly violence. To avoid this problem while encouraging a return of civil order, Johnston and Oakley sought approval from Washington and the United Nations to establish an interim Mogadishu police force made up of retired Somali police officers. Approval was a long time coming.[6]

EXPLAINING UNITAF TO THE SOMALIS

It was clear from the outset that a major effort, above and beyond meetings of UNITAF and USLO staff with the Somalis, would be needed to explain UNITAF's objectives to the Somali people in a comprehensible way. This would be essential to correct misperceptions and prevent confrontations and might help create a positive long-term political evolution. In the aftermath of the civil war, reliable information was hard to come by, though rumors and propaganda circulated quickly. Aside from word of mouth and local political propaganda, most Somalis got whatever information they had primarily from the shortwave radio broadcasts of the BBC's Somali-language service. Little attention was paid to the Voice of America. Though the BBC's English-speaking head office seemed

---

[6]See chapter 5 for a detailed discussion of the police force.

unaware of it, many of its broadcasts had a decided political slant, often hostile to the United States and UNITAF and in a number of cases simply incorrect. Early on, for instance, the BBC Somali service erroneously claimed that Oakley had met militia leader General Hersi "Morgan" in Bardera—anathema to many Somalis since Morgan, Siad Barre's son-in-law, was associated with serious atrocities under the old regime. Later both the BBC and Reuters disseminated incorrect reports that Morgan had seized Kismayo, implying UNITAF collusion and enraging the suspicious Aideed and his followers.

In Mogadishu, both Aideed and Ali Mahdi used their separate radio stations several hours a day and put out small mimeographed news bulletins, usually containing clever caricatures and political cartoons. It was scarcely the material of informed reporting on developments in the country and abroad, but it was effective political propaganda with little regard for the facts.

Within a week of landing, the U.S. Army and USLO combined to publish a Somali-language newspaper and to run a radio station broadcasting in Somali. A small team of U.S. Army civilians and military from Fort Bragg's psychological warfare unit, working with Somali-American translators, collaborated with USLO political and public affairs officers to compile stories for the newspaper *Rajo* ("hope") and to prepare the hour-long radio program that carried news of UNITAF activities, readings from the Koran, and feature stories of local interest as well as more general world information. The first issues of *Rajo* carried President Bush's December 4 speech and policy statements by Oakley and Johnston; later issues featured stories on rebuilding local government and community structures. *Rajo* and USLO teams traveled throughout the country to find stories illustrating how UNITAF and the local population were working together to improve local conditions. Circulation of *Rajo* in Mogadishu quickly approached 18,000 copies per day, and another 5,000 to 8,000 copies per day were soon distributed by air in the interior. Air-dropped leaflets carried simple pictorial and Somali-language messages—for example, to stay away from an airfield when a Marine landing was due. Millions of copies of different fliers were created and distributed in the first five months.

The UNITAF information operations had a number of successes—perhaps reflected by the fact that when relations between Aideed and UNITAF became tense later, one of his principal complaints was what he claimed to be the anti-SNA slant of *Rajo*. During the brief protest in late February, Somali paperboys delivering *Rajo* were attacked, and Aideed's own radio station and mimeographed bulletins did their best to denounce and discredit *Rajo*. Periodically other faction leaders or Islamic leaders complained; all complaints were carefully reviewed. In a number of cases, erroneous stories were corrected or a new approach to issues adopted. Technical difficulties with the radio transmission to interior regions were a problem since the spoken word is so important in a culture that has relied far more on oral transmission for news than on print.

SECURING BALEDOGLE

Johnston's immediate objective after securing Mogadishu port and airport was to take control of the abandoned Soviet air base at Baledogle, 160 kilometers to the northwest. Advance elements of the U.S. Army's Tenth Mountain Division landed at Baledogle on December 13 and received a warm welcome, including a symbolic handover of weapons. In return the Americans gave sacks of grain to the hungry Somali militiamen. Baledogle's runway, the second longest in Africa, and its isolation from the militias confronting one another in Mogadishu and elsewhere in the interior made it a significant asset—a supplement to Mogadishu for arriving troops and equipment and a jumping-off point for military operations into the interior. From Baledogle Marine and Army units organized and launched the December 17 move by road and helicopter to Baidoa, another hundred miles inland, at the very center of the famine belt.

For the U.S. and Canadian forces based at Baledogle, the primary memory will remain the awareness of the presence, less than a kilometer from the terminal, of huge bunkers full of undetonated Soviet bombs and other ordnance, baking in temperatures so hot that not even the explosives experts knew when a combustion point might be reached and the bunkers explode without warning.

ARRIVAL OF U.S. AND FOREIGN FORCES

Once Mogadishu and Baledogle were secured, U.S. Air Force and charter flights operated night and day to bring U.S. Marine and Army contingents as well as foreign units to Somalia. UNITAF forces reached their peak in January, when coalition forces numbered more than 38,000.[7] They

---

[7]In January 1992, according to statistics provided by the Marine Corps, the UNITAF force reached 38,301, of whom 25,426 were U.S. forces and 12,875 were from other countries.

included the Army's Tenth Mountain Division from Fort Drum, New York, under the command of Major General Steve Arnold, located primarily at Kismayo, south of Mogadishu at Merca, and at Baledogle. The first significant foreign contingents that arrived in December came from France and Canada, followed by troops from Belgium, Italy, and Morocco. Together with U.S. forces and Australians and Pakistanis who arrived in January, they became UNITAF's core components. There were also contingents from Botswana, Nigeria, Zimbabwe, Saudi Arabia, Kuwait, the United Arab Emirates, and six other countries. [8]

In the first days after the UNITAF arrival, however, the forces at Johnston's disposal were sufficient only for basic security requirements in Mogadishu. This situation led to mounting concern by the humanitarian relief organizations. Their staffs in Baidoa and Bardera, as well as in Kismayo 250 kilometers to the south, reported severe intimidation and serious potential violence by gangs of looters and bandits eager to seize what they could in the last days before coalition forces arrived. Neither the Somalis nor the NGOs knew when UNITAF forces would arrive, because of the usual strict requirement for operational security.

This situation created added uncertainty and tension, as well as appeals by the NGOs to Johnston, Oakley, and senior officials in Washington to deploy immediately. The appeals had to be turned down until there were adequate forces both to protect key installations in Mogadishu and to mount large enough operations to deter any resistance to UNITAF or retaliation against NGO workers. At parallel meetings in Mogadishu and Washington on December 12 and 13, the NGO representatives were urged to consider withdrawing their staffs temporarily from field locations pending UNITAF deployment. This had been the practice prior to UNITAF's arrival in country and there was unfortunately no alternative to continuing it until UNITAF was prepared to move inland with adequate force. Even a hurry-up helicopter operation with inadequate preparation and force could easily be more dangerous to the NGOs than waiting. As it turned out, there was some looting and NGO nerves were taut, but no actual violence was directed against the NGOs before the arrival of UNITAF contingents.

---

[8]The countries that sent troops to participate were Australia, Belgium, Botswana, Canada, Egypt, France, India, Italy, Kuwait, Morocco, New Zealand, Nigeria, Pakistan, Saudi Arabia, Sweden, Tunisia, Turkey, the United Arab Emirates, the United States, and Zimbabwe.

PHASE II: MOVING INLAND

UNITAF's operational plan divided southern Somalia into eight humanitarian relief sectors (HRSs), constituting the famine belt where the need to deliver relief supplies was most urgent to prevent further starvation. They included the fertile regions of the Juba and Shebelle river valleys, as well as the scrub brush area stretching from the Indian Ocean on the east to the de facto border with Ethiopia on the west. The southern demarcation line ran from Kismayo to Bardera, and the northern line from Mogadishu to Belet Weyne. The eight zones, each assigned to a separate primary command, were Mogadishu (U.S.), Baledogle (Morocco), Kismayo (U.S. and Belgium), Baidoa (U.S.), Bardera (U.S.), Oddur (France), Belet Weyne (Canada), and Jalalaqsi (Italy). Later, Merca became the ninth HRS, under the U.S. Army's Tenth Mountain Division.

The original sectors had been determined after discussion with OFDA and key NGOs and were intended to provide maximum support for humanitarian relief organizations in the area where documented starvation had been greatest. Still, the total area included less than a third of the country.

Lack of NGO access to the central region around Galcaio because of continued fighting had precluded clear estimates of the humanitarian situation there, but it was not nearly so bad as farther south, since there were far fewer people in that sparse nomadic bush region. UNITAF recognized that from a security viewpoint Galcaio and its environs constituted "a hole in the center" where potential conflict between Aideed's SNA and Abdullahi Yusuf's SSDF forces—as well as the potential for storing, hiding, and moving arms—might destabilize the cease-fire there. However, U.S. policy was firm: Deployment to this central region would be the responsibility of UNOSOM II, to be carried out after that command assumed operational control.

The northeast area of the country, and independent Somaliland, were in much better shape in humanitarian terms and therefore not included in UNITAF's area of operations. This exclusion of major areas from UNITAF responsibility led to military and political problems when the handoff to the United Nations and the buildup of operational capability by UNOSOM II were delayed much longer than expected. However, there were no major explosions of clan conflict outside UNITAF's operational area.

UNITAF's initial operations plan envisaged deployment to all eight HRSs by fifty days after arrival, or approximately the end of January

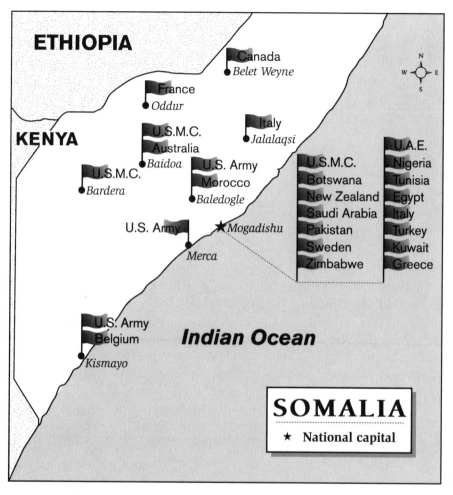

**UNITAF Deployment in Humanitarian Relief Sectors
(adapted from UNITAF map)**

1993. Deployments were in fact completed by December 28, a month ahead of schedule. The accelerated deployment was made possible by the near absence of organized resistance, advance political preparation in each of the sectors, the formidable military reputation established by UNITAF, and tactical intelligence provided by a special field intelligence detachment assigned to UNITAF, combining civilian and military capabilities.

HUMANITARIAN-MILITARY COORDINATION

To develop relations of mutual confidence and understanding between the military and the humanitarian relief community, and to maximize operational coordination, Johnston and Oakley asked UNITAF, with the vital help of OFDA, to establish a Civilian-Military Operations Center (CMOC). In recognition of the UN responsibility for coordination of relief operations and the long-term nature of its mandate, the center was located at UNOSOM headquarters.[9] From December onward CMOC held a daily briefing session attended by nearly 100 participants from the UN agencies, the ICRC, and other NGOs, as well as representatives from UNITAF headquarters and the military commands responsible for each of the HRSs. The objective was to share information on the latest security developments; explain UNITAF ground rules and operational plans; coordinate humanitarian assistance activities, especially the protection for food convoys within Mogadishu and moving to the interior; and provide an opportunity for information exchange, coordination, and cooperation on humanitarian operations generally. This last function greatly facilitated and expanded humanitarian activities and brought about increasing cooperation between civilian organizations and the military forces with humanitarian action capabilities, such as the Seabees and the Army Corps of Engineers. The extensive logistics capabilities of the various military units were able to multiply what would otherwise have been much more limited achievements by the civilians. UNITAF units of Army engineers and Seabees built or repaired 2,500 kilometers of roads, nine airfields able to handle C-130s, eighty-five helicopter pads, and more. They

---

[9]The leadership of CMOC was entrusted to Marine Colonels Kevin Kennedy and Robert MacPherson, who had gained experience with relief activities and civilian agencies during Operation Provide Relief, the U.S. airlift to Somalia that preceded UNITAF. They were joined in the CMOC first by Jim Kunder and Bill Garvelink, and then by Kate Farnsworth of OFDA. The third key participant in what became a sort of humanitarian leadership troika was CARE president Phil Johnston, who was acting as UNOSOM's coordinator of humanitarian operations.

dug scores of wells and, in cooperation with NGOs, rehabilitated schools and clinics, and provided direct medical assistance to thousands of Somalis, partly through a UNICEF-coordinated inoculation program.[10]

CMOC became an effective, innovative mechanism not only for operational coordination, but for bridging the inevitable gaps in perception and nurturing cooperation between the military and civilians. Oakley and other USLO staff gave periodic briefings on political developments. By developing personal relationships with NGO workers and others, UNITAF and OFDA staffs were able to more effectively address the concerns and anxieties of the relief community. Both sides were thus encouraged to seek pragmatic solutions to their difficulties.

The most serious unresolved problem was the extremely complicated, dangerous one of protection for NGO, UN agency, and ICRC personnel and facilities. A particularly vexing dilemma was what to do with the heavily armed private guards retained by most of the relief organizations before UNITAF's arrival. On the one hand, UNITAF believed it could not allow these guards to continue to carry their weapons in public, especially since most were members of one militia faction or another, and a number moonlighted as bandits.

On the other, the relief agencies felt that their guards provided them extra protection, or were afraid to fire the guards lest there be reprisals. This very real risk greatly concerned relief workers. The amount of money earned by Somali guards working for humanitarian agencies, including the ICRC, was enormous in a country where there were no other jobs to be had. The guards usually belonged to whatever militia leader was dominant in the area where the agency was operating and were paid very high wages. One well-known international NGO in Kismayo was paying some seventy guards almost $2,000 each per month plus food. This did not buy loyalty. When word spread that Morgan's militia was attacking the town in late February, the guards all fled, looting the agency com-

---

[10]One of the most striking examples was the rehabilitation of some 200 kilometers of irrigation ditches in the prime growing area south of Mogadishu, where the Shebelle River comes close to the coast before disappearing in the sand. When Oakley visited the Save the Children project in the area in January, he found that the NGO had the plans but could not proceed because the massive gates from the river to the main irrigation canal were inoperable. The U.S. Army engineers quickly repaired the gates, which could not have been done without their heavy equipment. AID's DART team provided local currency from monetized sales of food, and Save the Children employed over 10,000 workers for a period of between three and four months and restored the entire irrigation system.

pound, taking the agency vehicles, and firing at U.S. and Belgian forces as they left town.

Earlier, also in Kismayo, the highly respected UNICEF representative Sean Devereaux had been assassinated by a Somali he had fired. In Baidoa, an ICRC representative was killed during a payroll robbery carried out by former employees. Oakley and Major General Wilhelm went for a first-hand look at the problem and found that the ICRC offices had chosen not to accept the UNITAF offer to all NGOs and UN agencies to guard their premises and payrolls. After review by higher-level ICRC officials, the organization began to rely more on UNITAF for protection.[11]

Despite a great deal of dialogue and study, UNITAF and the relief agencies could not find an overall solution to this problem of protection, one that UNOSOM II also was not able to resolve. The closest UNITAF came to a solution was in banning all armed guards from Kismayo, providing radio contact for emergencies and some direct military protection for humanitarian agencies, and starting local Somali police forces that helped protect relief installations.

EXTENDING UNITAF'S REACH

On December 15, Oakley, along with USLO and OFDA staff, flew to Baidoa, the center of the famine belt, to meet with community leaders—including clan elders, religious figures, women, and local political leaders. The objective was twofold: to defuse potential resistance to the Marine helicopter landing the next day and to lay the groundwork for the revival of local political institutions.

Oakley assured the people of Baidoa that the Marines were coming in peace to help Somalia save itself, not to impose any particular settlement. He reiterated U.S. respect for Islam and its intention to honor local values and traditions. In response to fears expressed by the senior sheikh, a meeting was arranged with a Muslim Marine after U.S. forces arrived; a few days later, the Catholic Relief Service was helping the sheikh repair damaged mosques. UNITAF also helped restore a more normal life by banning the technicals and confiscating arms caches belonging to bandits in the area. To indicate trust and as a bona fide of UNITAF's good faith,

---

[11]Even so, during April and May, ICRC offices in Mogadishu again elected to ignore the UNITAF offer to hold payrolls for protection, with the result that two major payroll robberies were perpetrated in cooperation with employees and the ICRC offices were closed.

Oakley dismissed the heavily armed guards who had accompanied him into Baidoa and returned to the airport without any apparent protection. It was time for Baidoa's traditional community leaders, who had long been suppressed, to take charge again.

Looking hard at the putative local "authorities"—representatives of Aideed's SNA who had been installed as governor, deputy governor and police chief at gunpoint—Oakley stated that leadership would no longer be imposed from outside but chosen by the people themselves using their own local traditions. He observed that Siad Barre had imposed his will and his representatives by force, which had caused the people to rise up and had led organizations like the SNA to fight hard to oust him. Now that peace had been restored, said Oakley, he was sure no Somalis would like to see a return to imposed rule rather than making their own decisions and choosing their own leaders. The SNA representatives sheepishly said nothing. All the others enthusiastically agreed.

NGO workers were also briefed on what to expect when the Marines arrived, and there was a general air of relief, even among some who had earlier been concerned about the ramifications of a military-led relief operation.

The Marines' arrival in Baidoa at dawn on December 16, under the command of Major General Wilhelm, went forward without incident. Colonel Greg Newbold instituted a series of Somali-style "town meetings" with community representatives of all kinds, in numbers that eventually exceeded 200, who were keenly interested in dialogue on security and humanitarian matters.[12] Wilhelm had one of USLO's political officers join his officers in working with local leaders, involving the Somalis systematically in security as well as relief activities. A combined civilian-military humanitarian operations center (HOC) was established, and U.S. Marines and OFDA personnel provided leadership in coordinating inter-

---

[12]Ten days after the arrival of the Marines Colonel Newbold was urged at one of the meetings to stop the marauding of a band of heavily armed Somalis who were operating from a walled compound on the outskirts of Baidoa. He replied by asking the entire group to express its opinion on whether this should be done. The show of hands urging action against "bandits" was unanimous, including representatives of Aideed's SNA faction. Those in the compound surrendered without a fight, and Newbold's men confiscated four technicals carrying heavy weapons plus scores of machine guns, rocket propelled grenades, and lighter weapons. Two days later, Aideed sent Osman Ato to ask Oakley if the SNA could be given back the valuable arms taken at Baidoa from what he admitted had been SNA militia, who also engaged in banditry. Oakley and Ato both found the request amusing, and Ato was not surprised to go back to Aideed empty-handed. After that, in the Baidoa area, the SNA identified its heavy weapons to UNITAF and put them in approved storage sites to avoid confiscation.

national military and humanitarian activities with the local population and
relief agencies. The Somalis of Baidoa responded to appeals for a more
manageable, less time-consuming format than the large unstructured
town meetings. After a few weeks they created a regional council, with
security and humanitarian committees, as their counterpart to the HOC.[13]

Within several weeks the situation in Baidoa turned around. The local
hospitals were dealing with a few gunshot wounds from isolated incidents rather than large numbers of victims of civil war, mass starvation,
and unchecked disease. Markets and streets, once deserted, were again
bustling with activity. Military forces, UN agencies, and the ICRC and
other NGOs were providing food, medicine, and health care; repairing
clinics and schools; and building roads and digging wells.[14] Initial planning began for providing seeds and agricultural instruments for the next
harvest, and herders began to return to their animals. The ICRC had a
particularly effective program of assistance to farmers.

The Baidoa experience became a model for UNITAF deployments in
the other seven HRSs. In each case Oakley or his representative led an
advance team to meet a broad cross-section of the local population and
explain UNITAF's objectives. UNITAF commanders and USLO political
officers encouraged local leaders to come forward, and local and regional
councils sprang up. The great majority of local residents welcomed the
coalition forces, the food situation gradually improved, and child mortal-
ity rates dropped rapidly in all HRSs.

Local representation and cooperation were mixed—better in Baidoa, for
example, than in Bardera and Kismayo, where residents feared retaliation

---

[13]This spontaneous council sprang up from Somali traditions, not in response to foreign
suggestion. It was dominated by members of the Rahanwein clan, who were for the first time
since before the Siad Barre regime in control of their own region. With UNITAF help they
resisted repeated SNA efforts to intimidate them and return the SNA-appointed Habr Gidr officials
to power.

[14]Kathy Newbold, a Marine reserve officer, organized the collection of clothing, books, and
toys from families of the First Marine Division at Camp Pendleton for an orphanage of more than
500 children at Baidoa. The number served later rose to 1,500, from throughout the Baidoa
region. This orphanage and others, as well as several schools and clinics, were rebuilt by the combined actions of the Marines and Somalis. Similar activities took place in all the HRS centers,
often led by U.S. Marine and Army forces but also by Canadians, French, Australians, and other
UNITAF forces. A large school in north Mogadishu was rebuilt by the combined action of a
Marine contingent commanded by Colonel Buck Bedard (responsible for security in the city and
stationed at the old soccer stadium) and the NGO Irish Concern in the middle of Ali Mahdi territory. To the surprise of all at the February reopening (Oakley, Johnston, Zinni, Bedard, the head
of Irish Concern, CNN, and other press) Aideed and his bodyguards showed up and Aideed gave
a speech about his dedication to children and to education, extolling the Marines.

from still-powerful faction leaders. In Kismayo, the SNA and Colonel Jess shrewdly organized the reception to appear responsive to the approach UNITAF had taken in Baidoa. Oakley made clear that he was not fooled and that the recent massacre of another clan attributed to Jess was a matter of grave concern. In Bardera, the effects of recent war and famine were all too evident, and the reception from Colonel Warsame sullen. Yet even in such a difficult town as Bardera, the death rate fell from more than 300 a day in November to five or fewer in February. The relief workers welcomed the enhanced security, humanitarian help and logistics support provided by UNITAF forces. A concern shared by relief workers and Somalis alike, however, was that improvements would be only temporary; they feared that the departure of UNITAF forces and assumption of responsibility by the United Nations would be followed by the return of intimidation and violence from the factions and militias.

MILITARY, POLITICAL, AND HUMANITARIAN COLLABORATION

Johnston, Oakley, and their staffs quickly established a pattern that was to become routine in the next three months, meeting regularly several times a week to coordinate their planning and activities. These meetings were held either in Johnston's or Oakley's office. Usually in attendance were Oakley's military advisor (first Marine Brigadier General Frank Libutti and later Air Force Colonel Rich Mentemeyer and Marine Colonels Mike Hagge and Pete Dotto); Marine Brigadier General Anthony Zinni, who was Johnston's deputy for operations; and John Hirsch, who had been seconded from his position as U.S. consul general in Johannesburg to serve as Oakley's deputy and Johnston's political adviser.[15] Oakley, Hirsch, and Libutti convened a separate meeting each evening at USLO to review the day's activities and look ahead with the entire staff, exchanging ideas on all areas of activity and generating concrete suggestions for military, political, and humanitarian activity. Ideas that were agreed on were then raised with the UNITAF military, the United Nations or the NGO community as well as with the Somalis. Libutti kept the meetings focused on clearly identifiable, concrete achievements,

---

[15]Hirsch had briefly been Oakley's deputy in Mogadishu in 1984, where he remained as deputy chief of mission and chargé d'affaires until 1986. He and other USLO staff were hand-picked for their proven knowledge of Somalia. Zinni had served as chief of staff to the U.S. European commander, General Shalikashvili, and was involved in the combined military-humanitarian Operation Provide Comfort for the Kurds in northern Iraq.

insisting that at least one positive development per day would generate long-term momentum.

The USLO staff, which rotated on short assignments of one to two months, fluctuated between fifteen and twenty-five people. In addition to the military advisor, assigned from CENTCOM, the staff included representatives from OFDA, the U.S. Information Agency, and a support staff of security personnel, communicators, and administrative officers. Additional representatives from Johnston's staff frequently attended the evening meetings at USLO. Representatives from NGOs were frequently present, as were other officers from UNITAF. Often they stayed for dinner and more talk.

Every morning General Johnston's liaison officer arrived for breakfast to coordinate plans for the day's humanitarian and political activities, as did the personnel working on UNITAF's daily Somali-language newspaper and radio station, both called *Rajo*. These early morning and late evening meetings; occasional meetings between Oakley and Johnston; Hirsch's consultations with Johnston and attendance at the daily UNITAF senior staff meetings; and periodic meetings by Oakley and Zinni with the NGO community became the basis for informal but remarkably close, creative, and focused collaboration among the military, political, and humanitarian components of Operation Restore Hope. All concerned came to recognize the synergy and mutual reinforcement that resulted from this collaboration.[16]

NON-U.S. FORCES

Essential to UNITAF's effectiveness was the performance of non-U.S. forces in four critical HRSs. The presence of some 10,000 foreign military

---

[16]The dedicated, committed personnel who worked under extraordinarily difficult conditions to implement Operation Restore Hope included the OFDA group, led first by Jim Kunder and Bill Garvelink and later by Kate Farnsworth. Also on the USLO team were State Department political officers John Fox and Don Teitelbaum; and U.S. Information Agency representatives, starting with Bob Gosende (later Oakley's successor); an outstanding administrative officer, Wayne Bush; and an exceptional secretary, Sheryl Strance. All the USLO staff were experienced in Africa, and many had previous Somalia service. They were extremely talented and highly motivated, and quickly became a cohesive group eager to get into high gear with their respective programs—but also eager to work with one another. Flexibility, cooperation, and interaction were the key attributes of the group's approach. Additional representatives from Johnston's staff frequently attended the evening meetings at USLO. They included Marine Colonels Kennedy and MacPherson and UNITAF military liaison officers. For more on USLO, see Oakley's interview with Ambassador Brandon Grove, Jr., in the April 1993 issue of the *Foreign Service Journal*.

personnel from France, Italy, Belgium, Canada, and Morocco during December helped make it possible for UNITAF to deploy more rapidly than planned. Task Force Kismayo included elements of the U.S. Tenth Mountain Division under Brigadier General Lawson Magruder and an 850-member Belgian paratroop battalion under Colonel Marc Jacqmin. The 2,000 French troops under General René Delhomme did an outstanding job in Oddur, as did the 2,500-man Italian force led by General Rossi, based first at Jalalaqsi and later at Jowhar and parts of north Mogadishu. Early differences with Italy over the location and role of its forces were quietly and quickly resolved by military-to-military talks in Mogadishu and among Rome, Washington, and CENTCOM.[17] The Italian military commanders were much more interested in continuing close, mutually satisfying cooperation with the U.S. military in Somalia than in the ideas of politicians in Rome, anxious to see more publicity for a prominent Italian role in the former colony.[18] The 850-man Canadian unit under Colonel Serge Labbé, operating from Belet Weyne, and the 650-man Australian unit led by Colonel Dave Hurley, which took over from U.S. forces in Baidoa in mid-January, performed admirably. (The deliberate, brutal mistreatment of Somalis in Belet Weyne in spring 1993 by a small group of Canadian soldiers did not become known until after the unit had returned to Canada.)

The Canadians, French, and Australians conducted extensive patrolling in their sectors, to seize technicals and arms caches in remote locations as well as to protect relief activities. The Italians worked closely with U.S. Marines in patrolling Mogadishu as well as protecting relief convoys along some of the basic supply routes to the interior. Belgian and U.S. Army forces coordinated well in Kismayo but had ongoing problems with periodic combat between two Somali factions.

---

[17]Italian political authorities had wanted the Italian contingent to have its headquarters in Mogadishu, in the old Somali naval headquarters next to Ali Mahdi's offices. Johnston pointed out to Rossi that this would cause confusion among Somalis and among other UNITAF forces about who was really in command. The Italian military high command agreed to Jalalaqsi.

[18]To alleviate political pressure from Rome and dispel sensationalist reports in the Italian media that the U.S. was anti-Italian in Somalia and depriving Italy of its due place, UNITAF organized a relief and resupply operation for what had been the country's prime farming area south of Mogadishu. Badly treated by months of civil war, the lower Shebelle area around Merca had become a center of starvation, and the Italians who owned plantations there had all fled. Responding to appeals from Annalena Tonelli, a combined U.S. and Italian operation brought in food and medicine with no opposition from the militias, bandits, and "fundamentalists" who had been plaguing the area. Recognizing the importance of this highly populated, fertile area, UNITAF made it into an additional HRS.

The commanding officers of all non-U.S. forces were notably active, engaging their units in community development projects such as rebuilding schools, building roads, and repairing irrigation canals and tube wells, which went well beyond their official responsibility of escorting the food convoys. The Australians, Canadians, and French worked hard to revive broad community leadership, encouraging the creation of local councils and Somali police units. Following the Baidoa model, they called frequently on USLO political officers and OFDA representatives for help. The Italians worked closely with the United States to encourage the former Somali police to recreate an interim force for Mogadishu of some 3,500 men and women. The Moroccan battalion was given responsibility for Baledogle, taking over from the U.S. Army, as well as for guarding installations in Mogadishu. The Moroccan and Swedish hospitals provided additional medical facilities that remained in place after UNITAF completed its mission. A new Pakistani battalion took over part of Mogadishu from the Marines.

Smaller contingents provided perimeter security at the Mogadishu airport. Botswana, Zimbabwe, the United Arab Emirates, Tunisia, Nigeria, Egypt, Saudi Arabia, and other countries had contributed troops that provided security at selected locations or for specific operations such as feeding programs.

Overall, both U.S. and non-U.S. forces in Mogadishu and the interior conducted themselves with a high degree of discipline and dedication, exercising considerable restraint under arduous conditions. Johnston skillfully managed the disparate national contingents that had joined UNITAF in response to President Bush's appeal, even though there had been no planning for what particular capabilities were needed. As it was, various units arrived when the governments found it convenient, or transportation was provided, with no regard to local needs.[19] Additional complications affected several units that had no common language or training or that were woefully underequipped. Despite the obstacles, Johnston and his senior officers were able to develop a surprising degree

---

[19]In mid-December the Italian ambassador arrived at Oakley's office with news that an aircraft carrying some sixty Italian military personnel and a number of media representatives was headed for Mogadishu via Nairobi. In a subsequent meeting with General Johnston, they informed the Italian ambassador that there were no quarters available except for the tents or foxholes being used by the American military. Nor was there agreement on where the Italians might be stationed. A six-man advance team came to Mogadishu and the other Italians stayed in Nairobi until more practical arrangements were completed.

of cohesion and common purpose, deploying permanent liaison officers from headquarters to the various units and having them appoint liaison officers so that there was continuous communication. There were also weekly meetings with the commanders of all national units at which strategy, plans, tactics, and problems were discussed.

Commanders of national units were allowed considerable discretion in how they carried out common mission objectives, taking into account differences in doctrine, training, and equipment as well as the extent of territory in the HRSs and the degree of imminent threat. This extensive liaison effort with these units, the flexibility accorded component unit commanders, and the prestige enjoyed by the well prepared, equipped, and commanded U.S. forces combined to help overcome the potential command and control problem created by the fact that U.S. command authority over the other forces was de facto rather than de jure; other forces were theoretically able to appeal U.S. commands to their own senior authorities. In practice, this was not a problem for UNITAF. However, it quickly became a major problem for UNOSOM II.

CONFRONTATION IN KISMAYO AND MOGADISHU

The continued volatility of the situation and the suspicion between factions—as well as a genuine personal blood feud born of several previous encounters—were illustrated by a series of violent confrontations between General Morgan and Aideed's ally Colonel Jess between late January and midsummer 1993. Morgan had an estimated 1,000 well-organized men from the former Somali regular army, most from Siad Barre's Marehan clan family, located near the Kenyan border. Jess's disorganized, mostly Ogadeni, Somali Patriotic Movement (SPM) militia were several thousand strong in and around Kismayo.

In a new struggle for control of the city and the port, from which Aideed had ousted Siad Barre's forces a year earlier, Morgan's forces had been moving toward Kismayo when UNITAF landed in December. They moved back to near the Kenyan border, but after the Addis Ababa cease-fire agreement they began again to move south. Despite warnings by the local UNITAF commander, Brigadier General Magruder, on January 24 Morgan's forces attacked SPM units at Bir Hane, only thirty-five kilometers outside Kismayo, where Jess's men had been quietly guarding their heavy weapons in a UNITAF designated compound. Citing the Addis cease-fire agreement, signed but violated by Morgan's Somali National Front (SNF), U.S. helicopter gunships and Belgian armor counterattacked the next day, destroying a number of technicals and artillery pieces and forcing the SNF to withdraw further into the bush.

The January attacks ushered in a month-long game of cat and mouse between the two faction leaders. Jess sought to maintain a power base in Kismayo, Morgan claimed that his men had the right to rejoin their families there, and UNITAF strove to bring both under control. There were numerous discussions among UNITAF officers, USLO political officers, and Morgan, who sounded reasonable and compliant, seemingly reconciled to keeping his forces outside the city. However, during the night of February 22, some of Morgan's men slipped past UNITAF forces by twos and threes into Kismayo, dressed as herders bringing animals to town for export. They recovered hidden weapons and attacked five houses belonging to senior SPM officials. Jess and his militia fled, in some cases looting ICRC and NGO warehouses they had been hired to guard and firing on Belgian soldiers. After this, Oakley and Johnston issued an ultimatum to Morgan to withdraw to Doble at the Kenyan border and another to Jess to canton his men and arms at locations near Jilib.

Although both parties complied, the events in Kismayo precipitated anti-UNITAF demonstrations and violence in Mogadishu, since Aideed's faction was anti-Morgan because of the Siad Barre connection. Both Reuters and the BBC erroneously reported that Morgan had completely taken Kismayo. Some reports suggested that Morgan's forces had overrun the much more powerful U.S. and Belgian forces, implying that the stronger forces must have been complicitous. Others suggested that there had been outright UNITAF-Morgan collusion against Jess, an account promoted by Jess to save face and given some credence by Aideed. Rather than checking out the accuracy of the reports, Aideed and his infuriated supporters mounted angry demonstrations outside the U.S. embassy compound, and the next day there was an attack on Nigerian forces at the Kilometer Four traffic circle and further demonstrations against UNITAF.

The Nigerians were apparently attacked because they were believed to be the weakest of the UNITAF units and the easiest to terrorize. Nigeria also stood in bad odor with Aideed for having granted asylum to Siad Barre. Forewarned by good intelligence and supported by U.S. Marines, the reinforced Nigerians beat off the attack with only two wounded but in four hours they expended a great deal of ammunition, leaving the widespread impression that a large battle had occurred.[20]

---

[20]Despite the appearance of innocence Aideed put on for John Drysdale of the UN, advance intelligence, immediate observation, and discussions with senior SNA leaders made clear that the attack of KM4 was planned in advance.

The attack on KM4 had a severe psychological impact on UNOSOM headquarters, key UN agencies, and several NGOs whose offices were in the immediate vicinity, and on the press huddled in the media hotel right at the KM4 traffic circle. Television and newspaper reports claimed that massive armed opposition to UNITAF had erupted throughout the city, though in fact the entire incident was limited to several hundred Aideed supporters in an area of a dozen blocks. Some members of the UN staff prepared for immediate evacuation, and the NGOs were very nervous.

While the proximate cause of the violence had been the report of Morgan's taking Kismayo, this was only the final straw for Aideed and his lieutenants. Two weeks earlier, SNA representatives from all over the country had met with Aideed to complain angrily about the UNITAF-USLO strategy of empowering local leaders and encouraging the formation of local councils rather than respecting the SNA-appointed entities left from the civil war. They held the United States responsible for deliberately weakening the SNA and criticized Aideed sharply for having told them how well he was managing the Americans.

The subsequent UNITAF arrest of Colonel Jess as he tried to drive from Mogadishu to Kismayo, heavily armed and without permission, added to their anger. Aideed brought Jess to see Oakley to complain, bluster, and threaten, unveiling for the first time his nasty side. When this display failed to move Oakley, who reiterated that the day of gunpoint power had ended, Aideed went away still angry and threatening unspecified retaliation. The events of Kismayo caused him to explode.

Generals Johnston and Zinni, Oakley, and Hirsch consulted on how best to deal with this manifestation of SNA violence. Assessing intelligence and other reports, they concluded that the violence was limited to a small section of the city, despite the panicky cries of alarm from the United Nations, some NGOs, and the media, who felt the entire city was exploding and wanted to be evacuated at once. Additional UNITAF protection had already been provided for UN and NGO buildings and the media hotel. So long as they and UNITAF installations remained safe, the best course of action seemed to be to allow the demonstration to burn itself out, particularly since it was only in Aideed's part of the city. There turned out be no popular sympathy for anti-UNITAF action, even in Aideed territory, despite the frustrations of the SNA leadership, and the people soon became angry at the several hundred SNA militia and the rootless young men doing the demonstrating.

Within two days, order was restored in Mogadishu. Some of the international media even seemed disappointed that events were not leading to another round of the civil war, as had initially been thought. Neither Ali Mahdi in north Mogadishu nor any of the other faction leaders entered the fray, and Aideed recognized that he was in a losing situation. The real message, as Oakley told the press, was that Somalia and UNITAF had proved strong enough to withstand the confrontation without losing their primary focus on reconciliation and reconstruction and without being dragged into renewed factional conflict. After the demonstrations ended, Oakley and Zinni conveyed a private warning to Aideed that he would personally be held accountable for any recurrence. There were no further anti-UNITAF actions by the SNA.

The Framework for Stabilization

*G*radually, a measure of normalcy was restored to Mogadishu. By January, most technicals and other heavy weapons had been moved outside the center of the city to prevent seizure. There were a few skirmishes with those who wanted to test UNITAF, such as an incident in mid-December when three technicals opened fire on patrolling Marine helicopters on the outskirts of the city and were immediately eliminated by Cobra helicopter gunships. Aideed and Ali Mahdi agreed to Oakley's midnight request that they use their radio to denounce as bandits those Somalis who initiated this attack (even though they turned out to be from Aideed's militia). Shortly after Christmas the Murasade subclan of the Hawiye took advantage of the restrictions imposed on Aideed and Ali Mahdi to unleash nightly artillery bombardments in the northeast suburbs in an attempt to regain homes occupied by the Habr Gidr and the Abgal during the civil war. Their weapons were duly located and eliminated by Marine helicopter gunships, and the Murasade leaders were told that they would not be allowed to take back their homes by force.

By mid-January, there were almost no light weapons visible on the streets, the night helicopter patrols had stopped, and there was very little nocturnal shooting. Searches for arms caches in the city were gradually increased, with Botswanan forces participating and impressing the senior U.S. Marine and Army officers with their proficiency and discipline.

Return to a peacetime atmosphere was in evidence elsewhere as well. Casualty figures at the hospitals plummeted, and deaths by gunshot virtually disappeared, although armed robbery was still a problem. It was even possible for UNITAF forces to stage a lively soccer championship, won by the Botswanan team over the Italian, American, and Pakistani teams. The number of street booths and small shops mushroomed, as did the number of people on the streets even after dark. Old habits of Somali sociability returned, repairs of homes and shops damaged in the civil war were much in evidence, and schools and clinics began to reopen.

Except for the minor uprising by Aideed supporters in late February, the strategy of seeking cooperation, avoiding direct confrontation if possible, and gradually increasing pressure on all factions seemed to be working, and the casualty rate on both sides remained low. UNITAF casualties during its five-month deployment were twenty-four wounded, eight killed in action, and ten killed in various accidents. Though the number of Somali civilian deaths inadvertently caused by UNITAF cannot be accurately determined because of the local custom of taking away bodies, there were probably between fifty and one hundred.[1] One Marine was court-martialed and convicted for unjustified use of force on a civilian. In several instances, compensation was paid for genuine accidents, which were also reported by *Rajo* to allay exaggeration and suspicion.

The low number of Somali casualties, compared with the high number of incidents in which UNITAF forces encountered sporadic shooting or stone-throwing, shows how hard and how successfully the UNITAF command worked to instill restraint and discipline in troops of all nationalities. Recognizing this restraint and the high regard for Somali life it represented, the Somalis responded with similar restraint. Only in Kismayo were there instances of what could be termed organized guerrilla warfare or terrorism by Somali factions against UNITAF forces, and they were limited in number, the result of particular grievances by Omar Jess against the Belgians. While there was armed anti-UNITAF violence elsewhere, it came mostly from those engaged in criminal activities.

With deployments completed a month ahead of schedule, UNITAF concentrated its January and February efforts on stabilizing the security situation in the nine HRSs in preparation for the hoped-for handoff to UNOSOM II. The most difficult situations arose in Kismayo and Mogadishu, but generally there was great improvement in the safe movement of food convoys and, in the towns, much improved general safety and public order. However, a precise UNITAF determination of what constituted a stable security environment proved elusive. First, the situation in any particular

---

[1] In one unfortunate incident, a Marine night patrol returned fire coming from a parked truck, only to find that the shooting came from bandits robbing a truck full of civilians, who suffered the casualties. As is customary in Somali society, compensation was promptly paid by UNITAF.

sector changed from day to day. Second, some weapons caches were still hidden in the major cities as well as in the countryside, and although the faction militias were not fighting (except in and outside Kismayo), they were neither demobilized nor disarmed. Third, UNITAF forces could not patrol the entire width and breadth of all sectors, and security tended to be judged by the situation in and around the HRS headquarters location. Forces were initially concentrated in and near the principal cities and then spread out as far as their numbers, the security situation, and the area of the HRS would allow. Finally, remembering Vietnam and the infamous Hamlet Evaluation Program, senior U.S. officers resisted all proposals for simplistic, quantitative measures of security. Instead, responsibility for assessing security was left to the judgment of the HRS commander.

Resumption of relatively normal life in the towns and secure sectors of the countryside did not mean that the situation was normal or that famine had been beaten everywhere. This was particularly true of the large region between Kismayo and the Kenyan border, and also the area west of Bardera to the Kenyan border and north to the Ethiopian border, where there were no UNITAF forces at all and several more or less organized Somali militias remained, as did large numbers of bandits. The U.S. Marines and later the Australians had too few troops to cover the entire HRS in the Bay region around Baidoa. The same was true of the Canadians in the northern part of the Belet Weyne HRS.

On the other hand, French and Moroccan forces were large enough, and their areas of responsibility small enough, that they were able to maintain a stable security situation in the entire HRS of Oddur and Baledogle, just as the U.S. Army was eventually able to do in the Merca HRS. Merca became a sort of living laboratory for UNITAF, with elements of the Tenth Mountain Division drawing from, elaborating on, and developing into doctrine the improvised security, civic action, and humanitarian programs first undertaken by the Marines in Baidoa. Later on, after May 4, Merca was used as the primary location of the Quick Reaction Force, made up of Tenth Mountain Division elements that remained in support of UNOSOM II.

UNITAF and USLO were focused on putting weapons out of circulation rather than on comprehensive disarmament, which would have required a much larger force and generated much greater friction with the Somali population and the militias. Their intervention to ban visible weapons was planned to mesh with NGO action to encourage an embryonic process of building government structures from the ground up. In a number of towns, the combined presence of a USLO political officer with a UNITAF military presence and culturally sensitive, experienced relief workers changed the local political situation significantly. Baidoa had the most success in resurrecting a traditional independent municipal council, which worked with UNITAF on security issues and with UNITAF, the UN, and the NGOs on humanitarian affairs. Progress in this direction was also achieved in Merca, Belet Weyne, Oddur, and, to a lesser degree, in Bardera. The Morgan-Jess confrontation delayed the process in Kismayo, despite the desire of clan elders on both sides to transcend the struggle of the faction leaders.[2] In each HRS local communities were keen to work with the UN and NGO relief agencies to structure food and medical relief.

THE ISLAMIST FACTOR

There was a great deal of publicity and propaganda over the threat of "Islamic fundamentalism." Though the threat did not materialize, UNITAF took the possibility very seriously, and a great deal of effort was devoted to intelligence coverage and political action to deter or detect terrorist attacks. This effort included a high-level U.S. diplomatic dialogue with the government of Sudan as well as information exchanges with Ethiopia and other regional states.

In the beginning, Aideed, Ali Mahdi, SSDF leaders Abshir Musa and Abdullahi Yusuf, and the other faction leaders were keen to tell Oakley and UNITAF commanders of the threat from the Somali National Islamic Front (NIF), which was reportedly receiving substantial support in training, weapons, and money from Iran and Sudan. Each claimed to be ready to take the lead in actively combating these Islamist radicals, with UNITAF help. Aideed, for example, proposed to Oakley that his SNA forces and UNITAF undertake joint military action against the NIF in Mogadishu and other regions. (The offer was rejected.) But most of the intelligence the factions provided was grossly inaccurate or vastly exaggerated; all of it was self-serving.

Leaders of both UNITAF and USLO, acutely aware of terrorist experiences in Beirut and elsewhere, worked hard to check and evaluate all threat information. At the same time, wary of being manipulated by the

---

[2]Agreement among the elders was achieved in July with the help of UNOSOM II, putting an end to the intermittent but persistent low-level conflict between Morgan and Jess for several months. Tensions remained volatile, however, and renewed fighting broke out in early 1994.

Somali faction leaders and determined to avoid being sucked into an unnecessary confrontation with Islamic groups or developing an anti-Muslim image, they declined all suggestions of an active anti-Islamist crusade. Instead, Oakley met periodically with the long-established mainstream Somali Higher Islamic Council. Reports of the meetings were carried in *Rajo*, both in print and broadcast. The *Rajo* radio station always began its daily broadcast with appropriate verses from the Koran, and, together with the newspaper, carried a great deal of additional Islamic information.

In Mogadishu, NIF and other Islamist radical activity remained almost solely in the form of propaganda, with leaflets and public meetings, all very critical of the U.S., the UN, and UNITAF. There were frequent rumors of planned Islamist terrorist attacks, but none took place during the period of UNITAF deployment.

In the interior, humanitarian protection operations brought UNITAF personnel into direct contact with an Islamist-dominated area only once, when the NIF warned Major General Arnold's Tenth Mountain Division against entering Merca. When the U.S. unit moved in nevertheless, the NIF evaporated rather than confront it; some militia left for other locations and some stored their arms and coexisted peacefully with UNITAF. Indeed, the Islamist administration of Merca, before UNITAF's arrival, had been much less corrupt and abusive of the local population than those in any of the towns occupied by other militias.

There was also a sizable concentration of NIF militia north of Bardera at Luc, near the Ethiopian and Kenyan borders, a location to which many Somali refugees in Kenya wished to return. There were reportedly heavy weapons there but the Marine unit responsible for the Bardera HRS had insufficient forces to expand up to Luc. Had they done so, it seems unlikely that a major clash would have ensued, partly because of the overwhelming superiority of U.S. military force, but also because of the disorganization and weakness of the NIF at that point.

In the north there was much greater interest, organization, and commitment to the Islamist cause. The north had had close religious links with Sudan for more than a century, and there was some active Sudanese financial support as well as organizers and propaganda for NIF cells. UNITAF received reliable reports of some non-Somali Muslims intermingling with Somali NIF members in the north. There had earlier been some major battles between the SSDF forces of Abdullahi Yusuf and NIF forces in the northeast. In Hargeisa during February, several Somali women were stoned to death for adultery at the instigation of a local NIF leader who wished to demonstrate the power of Islam, though popular reaction proved decidedly negative. Generally speaking, however, even in the north, militant Islam was strong only where there was a local political and leadership vacuum.[3]

REFUGEE RESETTLEMENT

In the disorder left by war and famine, USLO and UNITAF found themselves drawn into the issue of refugee resettlement even though it was not explicitly part of their mandate. On January 28, UNHCR representatives based in Nairobi came to Mogadishu for the first time in more than a year to discuss with Oakley and UNITAF the pressing problems of the quarter million refugees in squalid camps on the Kenyan side of the border. They wanted UNITAF to deploy to the three main border-crossing points (at Mandera, El Waq, and Doble) to support the resettlement of refugees in the lower Juba valley and the area to the west between Bardera and Luc. At their meeting, Oakley urged the development of a coordinated effort, under UNHCR leadership but involving NGOs, which would include the provision of seeds and tools for agriculture, an initial food distribution, and plans for resettlement and job creation as well as the security and transportation support. Under the plan, UNHCR would have primary responsibility for organization, but UNITAF would be ready to provide initial assistance. Oakley explained that deployment to the border was not part of UNITAF's mandate and that coalition forces were too few to undertake the additional responsibility. However, other possibilities could be explored, such as providing security and demining the roads, at least for part of the route.

During the next month, UNHCR began to open offices in southern Somalia to prepare for the initial phase of refugee resettlement. In mid-February, Oakley and Generals Wilhelm and Zinni met with High Commissioner Sadako Ogata in Bardera to hold further discussions about how UNITAF could help. To deter bandits who might prey on them in the

---

[3]From June 5 through October 3, when U.S. forces were attacking the SNA, Islamic militancy increased significantly, assisted by more significant involvement by Libya, Iran, Iraq, and particularly Sudan. The Islamist network began to invoke rhetorical parallels with Bosnia, where Christians were killing Muslims, and some newspapers in Morocco, Egypt, and Pakistan criticized their governments for participating in UNOSOM.

remote region, Wilhelm offered the possibility of helicopter support to provide surveillance of relief convoys as refugees returned to the Luc area.

In further conversations Oakley and Ogata agreed that security must be improved on the Kenyan side of the border and that Kenya should be urged to cut off assistance, official or unofficial, to General Morgan's insurgent forces. Oakley, Ogata and UK minister of development assistance Linda Chalker met separately with Kenyan president Daniel Arap Moi in late February, urging him to go beyond hortatory calls for the return of refugees to Somalia to a more constructive approach in which Kenya would play a role by patrolling its side of the border. While Moi never acknowledged any Kenyan support for Morgan's forces, he was well aware of the contacts that his defense minister, an ethnic Somali, had with dissident Somalis under Morgan's command. Moi asked for help in weapons transport and communications so the Kenyan army could do a better job, as well as unsuccessfully requesting UNITAF patrols of the Kenyan border. After these meetings Kenya's assistance for Morgan decreased.

By mid-March, the Tenth Mountain Division was ready to provide assistance in rebuilding roads, houses, and schools as well as to work with local elders in Luc and elsewhere on security issues and the return and resettlement of refugees. Though heavy rains suspended the construction programs, and the Tenth Mountain Division was assigned other duties, UNITAF, after initial reluctance, had shown readiness to play a major supportive role in the resettlement effort.

ESTABLISHMENT OF AN INTERIM POLICE FORCE

Reestablishment of a Somali police force was key to improving security in Mogadishu and other cities. The Somali police, in contrast to the army, had a longstanding reputation for fairness, and most police officials had not been co-opted by Siad Barre. Indeed, many senior police officers had retired to their homes when the civil war started, deliberately avoiding taking sides. When, in mid-December, USLO took soundings on whether an interim force could be established, it quickly became evident that the personnel were available if funding for uniforms, food, minimal radio communication, and some vehicles could be located.

How to go about supporting the revival of the police force was a delicate problem. General Johnston originally was reluctant to have UNITAF become involved in responsibility for and oversight of what ought to be an indigenous Somali institution, a function that was not in the UNITAF mandate. However, he and Oakley soon came to share a pro-police view when it became clear that establishment of such a force would serve several purposes. It would eliminate the need for UNITAF troops to serve as police, not only freeing them for other duties but avoiding confusion about their role and reducing friction with the local population, thus minimizing casualties on both sides. A police force would also enable Somalis to deal with ordinary criminal activity (as distinct from organized looting and robbery) and give them some responsibility for their own affairs. Finally, it would create jobs and provide income to several thousand otherwise unemployed Somalis.

While all this made good sense to UNITAF and USLO, problems arose when the idea was broached with the UN. Kittani argued that it was premature to establish an interim force since it would prejudge the outcome of the UN's nationbuilding efforts. He and UN headquarters believed national institutions had to be established first, including a national police force, and local police authority could be devolved afterward. Kittani was particularly concerned that the interim police would be perceived by the faction leaders as partisan and that policemen would regard themselves as entitled to be part of the national force. The UN would neither confer legitimacy on an ad hoc force nor undertake any commitment that the participants would be part of a future national force. UN humanitarian affairs coordinator Philip Johnston was a supporter of the police idea and proposed detailed plans to make it a major element of the UN program. This was largely on his own initiative, and when he sought to locate and coordinate financial and material resources for the project, he was ordered to desist and told this was not the UN's role. The United States government was also originally cool to the police proposal; both CENTCOM and the Joint Chiefs saw it as "mission creep," and the State Department worried about being accused of violating congressional prohibitions on aiding foreign police forces.

USLO and UNITAF nonetheless proceeded with contingency planning, raising the issue with the Aideed–Ali Mahdi joint security committee and later conducting more detailed discussions with a committee of former senior police officers from south and north Mogadishu. The officers said they were ready to resume active duty, but only if they were not in any way under the authority of Aideed, Ali Mahdi, or any other faction or clan leader. In January the joint security committee told Oakley that it approved the idea, recognizing that Somalis needed to start doing things for themselves. Security committee members said they would support an autonomous, neutral executive committee composed of the senior police officers if USLO and UNITAF would protect the police committee against political pressure or reprisals from the faction leaders and UNITAF would find them material support as well as providing liaison officers and protection from militia attacks. However, UNITAF would have no official responsibility for the police. This was agreed on by Oakley and Johnston and communicated to CENTCOM, the Department of Defense, and the Department of State; none raised objections.

Oakley personally negotiated with Ali Mahdi and Aideed to get them to accept the list of names put forward for the police executive committee, which was balanced between individuals from their subclans and other influential Mogadishu subclans. General Johnston started identifying informal sources of assistance and appointed Zinni to supervise the operation. The WFP, appreciating the need for an honest police force, promised to help supply each policeman and his family with food rations for a time as the force went into operation.

The Somalis worked closely with a U.S. team headed by Lieutenant Colonel Steve Spataro, the Army's provost marshal, who had extensive experience in military police operations. Together with Oakley's military advisors Colonels Mentemeyer and Hagge, and Lynn Thomas of UNOSOM, Spataro drew up a detailed plan for the vetting of some 2,500 policemen. They also outlined the logistical requirements for the reopening of police stations, the allocation of police officers by district, and the initial stages of reviving a judicial and penal system. The elements of the USLO-UNITAF plan were coordinated with and approved by the Somalis at each stage. When U.S. Marines started to suffer casualties patrolling the streets of Mogadishu and the hazards of combining military duties with policing became abundantly clear, Washington became more supportive of the police force idea. Although neither the State nor Defense departments provided resources for the police force rebuilding, UNITAF and USLO were permitted to proceed with what they were doing. Requests were made to other governments—Italy, Germany, and the Netherlands—to provide the support that the Bush administration felt the United States could not provide because of legal and political constraints.

By mid-January, the first police patrols were on the streets of Mogadishu. They were quickly detailed to augment or replace UNITAF troops outside the port, the airport, and UNITAF headquarters as well as to improve the traffic flow on the main roads and reduce bottlenecks at major intersections (one of which was colloquially known as "Kamikaze Corner"). Similar small interim police forces were quickly established in most of the HRSs and contributed to the return of relative normalcy in Baidoa, Merca, Bardera, and Oddur.

The Italians were very supportive and agreed to earmark part of their WFP contribution for the police program. Food purchases were intended, as far as possible, to come from Somali farmers, not from imported humanitarian aid stocks. The Italians agreed as well to provide uniforms and such policing equipment as nightsticks and whistles.

The base of support for the police improved during the next few months, as the WFP was joined by some NGOs in providing food. The head of the UN Development Program (UNDP), William Draper, visited in mid-February and promised funds for salaries. UNITAF was able to provide surplus vehicles and radios left over in Saudi Arabia from Operation Desert Storm.

By late February, UN headquarters, at U.S. urging and following the UNDP decision, agreed to contribute funds for the operation of the interim police force for at least six months. The contribution was subject to approval from the Italian, Dutch, and German police experts who had been asked by UN headquarters to plan for creation of a major national force. When they arrived, they agreed that the interim force should be continued, but without any commitment that its members or senior officers would become part of the eventual permanent national force.

The UN experts found the Mogadishu interim force hard at work, among other things assuring crowd control at thirty-five newly opened dry feeding stations which were providing rations to almost a million people per week. UNITAF forces, including some from Morocco, Zimbabwe, Botswana, and the United Arab Emirates, worked closely with the police to provide more heavily armed protection against attack by militias or bandits.[4] Both UNITAF and the NGOs agreed that both these aspects of protection were crucial if feeding programs were to operate without being mobbed (which UNITAF could not have prevented) or looted (which the police could not have handled at this stage).

---

[4]There was a UNITAF military contingent located at each police station in Mogadishu providing vital communications, logistics, psychological, and, if necessary, military support. This enabled the Somali police to stand up to the SNA and others.

The police had been issued some light weapons for protection of the stations and use in joint patrols with UNITAF in dangerous areas but had received very little new training and could not be considered a force capable of confronting organized militia. They were good at crowd and traffic control and static guard duty. The police also patrolled with UNITAF, and on numerous occasions individual police had to take on heavily armed bandits, suffering a score killed and wounded. Efforts by Aideed, Ali Mahdi, and other faction or clan leaders to dominate the Mogadishu police force had little effect.

The police were proud of their work and status and popular with the men and women in the street. At one point in early February the police in Mogadishu worked with the joint security committee to end armed confrontation over property and negotiate the peaceful return to members of the Murasade subclan of several hundred houses that had been seized from them. In the interior of southern Somalia, another thousand former police had been constituted by UNITAF into a dozen local forces, most successfully at Baidoa, Merca, Belet Weyne, and Oddur. In Bardera and Kismayo serious clan problems with the police required correction. In the northeast and northwest (Somaliland) forces of about 1,500 had been organized without UNITAF or UN help.

By the time of the UNITAF pullout, the beginnings of a court and prison system were in place in Mogadishu, Baidoa, and a few other locations, staffed by individuals who had resumed their former professions as lawyers, judges, and police. The Somalis who organized it decided to rely on the pre-Siad Barre criminal code of 1962-63, revised and published in 1968, and UNITAF had helped reprint the old manuals for police and judges. The UNITAF judge advocate general and his staff provided some rudimentary guidance. A request had gone to Italy for more professional assistance, since most of the criminal code was derived from Italian practice. There were also, following longtime Somali precedent, Islamic courts operating in many locations. As in the past, the two court systems existed with little friction, partly because the jurisdiction and concerns of each were mutually understood.

By May 4, when the United Nations took over official responsibility for Somali peacekeeping from the United States, there was an interim police force of more than 3,000 operating in Mogadishu's eighteen districts, using police stations repaired by UNITAF and the Somali police engineering unit and sharing space with the UNITAF units responsible for each district.[5]

EFFORTS TO REBUILD CIVIL SOCIETY

To curtail the power of the fighting militia leaders and encourage the development of greater pluralism as Somalis rebuilt their nation, USLO led efforts to find and encourage groups that had gone underground during the civil war. Bob Gosende and Frank Strovas, the two USIA representatives, took the lead, with John Hirsch, in establishing contact with professors from the Somali National University, and with IIDA, the leading Somali women's organization. Meetings were held every week or so at the Conoco compound, with women or professors or journalists meeting sometimes separately, sometimes all together. The professors told a remarkable story of preserving a small area on the campus where they and their families lived, and of having brought whatever books they could salvage from the university library, destroyed during the civil war with most of the other buildings, to their homes for safekeeping. The professors represented the remnant of intellectual life and were an essential resource for the revival of Somali politics and culture.

The women of IIDA were remarkable for their courage, candor, and perseverance. In their first meeting with Oakley, they pointed out that women and children had taken the brunt of the suffering during the civil war and that it was women who had cared for the sick and dying. Nonetheless, despite their role in keeping Somali society and family structure together, women had been kept politically powerless by Somali men. A postwar revival of Islamic fundamentalist education—funded by

---

[5]After May 4, the UN provided very limited resources to the fledgling police and judiciary. Preoccupied with other problems, both UN headquarters and UNOSOM II chose to await completion of the experts' report on forming a national justice system. The existing interim system dwindled because of sporadic salary payments, an end to military liaison and assistance previously provided by UNITAF, and a drop in morale, as well as the confrontations with the SNA before the report was finally published in late August. A meeting was held at UN headquarters in mid-September to solicit help for the re-creation of the police and judicial functions. This meeting produced very little in the way of concrete results and UN activity was not much increased or accelerated despite the urging of UNOSOM II. Only after the United States decided to withdraw its forces by March 31 did the police program become serious. Thanks to money, personnel, and prodding by the United States, funds and experienced personnel were finally available for UNOSOM II's justice division. Hundreds of vehicles were delivered and a serious training program begun. However, there was not enough time to train and deploy more than a handful of police before the deteriorating security situation paralyzed and then ended the program.

groups in Sudan, Iran, and Saudi Arabia—was, they asserted, trying to deny women the right to work and to impose a strict dress code, even though this was not part of Somali tradition. With help from UN agencies, IIDA was actively engaged in creating job opportunities for women, reopening schools and clinics, and (by providing sleeping mats and other household articles) helping nearly destitute families resume more normal lives. The U.S. Department of State also approved self-help grants to assist IIDA.

In February, IIDA convened a conference of nonaligned intellectuals— men and women neutral to the factions—that drew up a platform of democratic proposals for presentation to the planned national reconciliation conference. In early March, IIDA and UNOSOM together, with U.S. encouragement, convened a national women's conference in Mogadishu. Women from all sections of Somalia participated, the bright colors of their traditional dress belying their recent suffering and deprivation, and lending an air of hope for the future. At USLO's urging, the UN invited representatives from the women's and lawyers' groups to attend the meetings in Addis Ababa, and present their views. It was a first step in institutionalizing the participation of popular representatives of independent groups and individuals in the process of rebuilding the country.

Another group, mostly lawyers from north and south Mogadishu, was urging the creation of a constituent assembly to draft a new democratic constitution for Somalia. They were concerned especially with continuing human rights abuses, and argued strongly for the reestablishment of a legal and penal system to deal with abuses. In Kismayo, for example, Colonel Jess's militia had murdered more than a hundred intellectuals and professionals shortly before UNITAF's arrival. Notwithstanding international press coverage, the killers were still at large.

THE ADDIS ABABA ACCORDS

While Oakley and Johnston continued to concentrate on stabilization and informal political development at the local and regional levels, Boutros-Ghali and Kittani headed for Addis Ababa to convene the UN preparatory conference on national reconciliation. In December, Kittani, with strong U.S. support, had devoted much effort to pinning down who would attend, especially Aideed and his SNA colleagues. The UN was eager for their participation, though not at the price of giving them a veto over its work. But there was considerable question about what would happen if Aideed did attend, especially after he indulged his anti-UN attitude by staging a protest against Boutros-Ghali when he visited Mogadishu on January 3, en route to Addis. Oakley told Aideed that he absolutely must attend, that he must recognize that the U.S. would soon leave while the UN would have an ongoing operation in Somalia, and that he should stop exaggerating his suspicions of Boutros-Ghali. At the last moment, Aideed agreed to go, saving face by a UN change in nomenclature to describe the conference as "preparatory."

The January 5–6 session and its aftermath proved more fruitful than expected, laying out a number of useful proposals the Somali parties agreed to for disarmament and reconstruction. These agreements, however tenuous, nonetheless constituted an important step forward. It was notable that the Somali participants, including Aideed, Ali Mahdi, and their representatives, remained in Addis Ababa for four days after Boutros-Ghali's departure, clearly intent on reaching preliminary agreement on a cease-fire and disarmament package. They were uncomfortable with the formalities of the UN-sponsored conference, but encouraged by President Zenawi, they concluded several limited agreements and planned to hold a full-scale follow-up conference in March.

Cease-Fire and Disarmament

The January 15 agreement signed by the Addis conferees called for a verifiable, countrywide cease-fire, supervised by a UNITAF and UNOSOM monitoring group; the cantonment of all heavy weapons in designated compounds; the demobilization of militias at designated transition sites; and the disarming of all other "armed elements." The cease-fire meant that Morgan's forces should stay near the Kenyan border, where they were on January 15—a provision promptly violated to the detriment of security in the Kismayo area. The Somali signers asked the international community to provide upkeep for the militias at the transition sites and then to assist them and the other armed elements by providing skills training and resources for reintegration into civil society. There was no effort to attach financial costs to these proposals, but clearly the magnitude of such an ambitious program would be very great.

Most Somali factions appeared ready to take the disarmament process seriously, in large part because they understood the U.S. expectation that the process would move forward. At General Johnston's insistence, the UN organized and convened early February follow-up meetings in

Mogadishu with representatives of all the factions, who were asked to identify specific cantonment and transition sites and to establish a timetable for implementation.

Since UNITAF deployment was confined to southern Somalia, simultaneous disarmament throughout the country was out of the question. Instead the plan, drawn up by the Somalis and Colonel Pete Dotto, proposed a phased approach starting in the south and moving progressively north. Demobilization, training, and the establishment of a cease-fire monitoring group were identified as issues that UNOSOM II would have to deal with.

Dotto also held discussions on demobilization, jobs, and training for Somali militia with NGOs and UN agencies, although there was very limited practical experience available in their ranks, and they made no specific commitments. The discussions were to prepare the way for UN operations, not to assert UNITAF responsibility.

UNITAF commander Johnston made it clear to the UN that his forces were ready to start implementing the plan but only if the UN were willing to assume formal responsibility. Johnston, Oakley, and the commanders of other key UNITAF national contingents (Italy, France, Canada, Belgium, and Morocco) held a meeting on the proposal at UNITAF headquarters in mid-February and were disconcerted to hear Shaheen and Kittani flatly reject any UN responsibility for cease-fire or disarmament, saying that the UN role had been suspended so long as UNITAF was in the field. This policy was eventually changed, weeks later, by UN headquarters. But valuable time had been lost, U.S. forces were preparing to depart and reluctant to take on more disarmament, and the UN was equally reluctant to assume it, even though they had finally acknowledged nominal responsibility.

The Humanitarian Conference

The issue of where to hold the humanitarian conference scheduled to follow the preliminary Addis Ababa meeting gained importance, as did the question of when to hold the next political conference. There was some sentiment for convening the humanitarian conference in Nairobi, where most of the donor government representatives were based. Oakley, UN under secretary-general Jan Eliasson and UNOSOM humanitarian operations coordinator Phil Johnston, however, felt it was important to hold the two conferences back to back in Addis Ababa. This approach, they felt, would make clear that political reconciliation and economic reconstruction were inextricably linked, that progress could occur only in a climate of security, and that broadly representative participation was essential for reconciliation. The nonfaction Somalis present for the humanitarian conference would stay on for the political meeting.

Ambassador Kittani (who was in New York for medical treatment until mid-February) was reluctant to proceed with the conferences. Aideed had refused to attend the small planning sessions called for at the January Addis Ababa meeting, and the UN feared he would either not attend or disrupt the next. UN headquarters was also reluctant to invite Somalis other than the faction leaders and their lieutenants to a conference on national reconciliation. Encouraged by the United States, the UN eventually decided to go ahead and obtained agreement in principle on broad representation from the various factions, including Aideed's. Though some of the faction leaders assumed they would be able to control or manipulate the selection of participants, they were chagrined to find that they were not allowed to dictate this part of the arrangements. Their agreement in principle was the extent of their role. The limits made Aideed and some other faction leaders suspicious of the process.

In preparation for the humanitarian conference, Philip Johnston and his small, hardworking staff drafted a "1993 Relief and Rehabilitation Program for Somalia," incorporating elements of the old Hundred-Day Plan and looking forward to rebuilding Somalia's infrastructure and economy rather than focusing only on short-term relief needs. At Johnston's insistence, there was extensive preliminary consultation with Somali NGOs, traditional leaders, and women's groups. In the plan Johnston developed ten "building blocks" that the Somalis, working in "core groups," had identified as essential for development. The priority areas included the reestablishment of local administrative capacities, including national and local police; attention to special needs of Somali women; creation of job opportunities and reestablishment of primary education and vocational training; expansion of agriculture and enhancement of livestock; return of refugees and displaced persons; development of a food security system; and increased access to basic health care, potable water, and sanitation services.

When UN under secretary-general Eliasson opened the humanitarian conference in Addis Ababa on March 13, 190 Somalis were present, representing a broad cross-section from all regions of the country, including clan elders, religious leaders, and women's groups as well as the fifteen political factions. Extensive behind-the-scenes work by the USLO and UNOSOM staffs had been instrumental in bringing about this turnout.

Most participants recognized that peace and real security were the bedrock requirements for rebuilding their country. The women were particularly eloquent. As Eliasson said, "Women and children [have] been the main victims of the cruel war and their cry of anguish was a moving reminder of our shortcomings. Their courage and determination earned them a role in the national reconciliation conference."[6]

Donors and participants were keenly aware of the pitfalls that lay ahead. Eliasson sought donor commitments of $166 million. Pledges of approximately $130 million were made, but a number of donors indicated that actual payment would depend on political progress by the Somalis as well as on the successful deployment of UNOSOM II and the achievement of a stable security environment. Eliasson subsequently expressed disappointment that less than 15 percent of the pledges had actually been made available. Even if the 1993 program were fully funded, he noted, it would represent only 10 percent of the $1.5 billion projected for UNOSOM II peacekeeping in the next twelve months. He warned that military operations would be perceived as an end in themselves rather than as a means to ensure security for rehabilitating Somalia's infrastructure and forging national reconciliation.

The National Reconciliation Conference

The National Reconciliation Conference, held immediately after the humanitarian conference, was disrupted as it got under way by renewed fighting in Kismayo between Morgan and Jess.[7] When UNITAF sent the Quick Reaction Force to quell the fighting, Aideed, suspecting another anti-Jess, anti-SNA move, prevented the conference from going forward until an investigatory team—including himself—went to Kismayo to determine what had happened. Again, Aideed was posturing to improve his power position, and when he had made his point the conference was allowed to resume.[8]

---

[6]Statement to the Economic and Social Council, UN headquarters, July 21, 1993.

[7]The meeting was chaired by a new UN special representative, Guinean ambassador Lansana Kouyate, who had been picked to succeed Kittani but became deputy representative under Howe. Howe had just arrived in Mogadishu and spent only a day at the Addis meeting. Kouyate's skillful, Africa-wise diplomacy played a major role in reaching agreement.

[8]At the conference Aideed continued to make clear his preference for a political system in which the five major factions would hold the real power, rather than one which equated them with the small factions with much less power and support. He went along with the final agreement but obviously did not see it as binding and planned major changes in the implementing process.

It had two major results—a renewed commitment by all fifteen factions in attendance to implement the nationwide cease-fire and disarmament plan, and agreement on a broad framework for a new political dispensation, its core to be a seventy-four-member Transitional National Council (TNC). The TNC would be the bridge to a long-term political solution, subsuming existing regional structures and creating a temporary national government.

The participants stated their intention to implement the voluntary disarmament program by June. Although this timetable was to prove as unrealistic as earlier agreements, it nonetheless demonstrated formal Somali commitment to the earlier agreement, increasing pressure on the faction leaders to turn in their heavy weapons and demobilize their militias. It further cleared the way for international undertakings, led by the UN, to provide the assistance the Somalis needed to implement their agreement, but no such help was forthcoming.

The Accords also envisaged a two-year transition period during which, it was hoped, the focus of the international community would be turned to rehabilitation and reconstruction of economic infrastructure while the Somalis developed representative institutions based on their own traditions. The TNC was to be the top level of a three-tiered provisional government. Regional and district councils would be established, together with central administrative departments, the forerunners of government ministries. The seventy-four seats on the TNC would be allocated so that each of the eighteen regions would have three representatives. Each of the fifteen factions would have one representative, and five additional seats would be reserved for Mogadishu councils, given the city's large population. Each regional representation was to include at least one woman among the three members—a marked departure from Somali tradition, made in recognition of the critical role played by Somali women in providing community as well as family leadership during the civil war and as a response to the women's assertiveness, which had been encouraged by UNITAF and the UN.

These agreements, like previous Somali undertakings, left open the issue of implementation. Determining membership on the TNC, the geographic definition of the regions, and the future of the north were all left to the future. In behind-the-scenes negotiations with Lansana Kouyate, the UN deputy representative, the factions tried to sew up the fifty-four regionally allocated seats, in effect cutting out independent regional players and undermining the concept of local selection. The effort failed, and it remained unclear how local representatives would finally be selected.

Nor was a timetable established for the startup of the TNC. The Addis Ababa Accords expressed desiderata rather than concrete programs, and would require further hands-on work by the United Nations with the Somalis, as well as greater trust and confidence among the participants.[9]

The most significant gap in carrying out the Addis Ababa Accords pertained to disarmament. Operation Restore Hope's strategy for maintaining a stable security environment during the transition counted heavily on effective and timely follow-up. The accords were clearly far from self-enforcing: UNITAF's mandate did not cover nationwide enforcement, the UN was unwilling and unable to accept the responsibility, and the NGOs had neither the cohesion nor the resources required to do so. The factions, each watching and waiting for the other to disarm, were either too suspicious and frightened to do so or, in some cases, had no real intention of doing so. They feared both serious attacks from their enemies and the loss of future power and position, and Aideed's SNA prepared to challenge the UN peacekeepers as soon as U.S. forces had departed.

---

[9]Though a charter committee of faction representatives was set up to work this out, it was eventually blocked by Aideed's insistence on a dominant role for the SNA. There was a provision for UN mediation of disagreements over the establishment of local councils, but the precise nature of the UN role was unclear. This uncertainty led to considerable difficulty with the SNA when UNOSOM later took an active role in promoting local and regional councils. Aideed denounced the councils as illegal, claiming that they were imposed upon Somalis in violation of the Addis Ababa Accords. In fact, his protest was due to the limited SNA influence over the councils. Some other faction leaders also felt that their interests had been slighted by the emphasis on regional and district selection of council members, but stopped shcrt of calling for their dissolution. The Security Council came to endorse the accords, transforming them into Western-style binding agreements rather than guidelines for future negotiations, the usual Somali approach to such agreements. This, of course, severely hindered Aideed's objective of revising the accords during the implementation process.

From UNITAF to UNOSOM II

6

*1*993 began in Somalia with visits from two foreign dignitaries—visits very different in appearance and evidencing different perceptions of the task remaining. Outgoing U.S. president George Bush arrived for a three-day visit on New Year's Eve, to draw attention to the U.S. commitment to helping Somalia save itself and to express his appreciation to U.S. forces for their role in the unprecedented humanitarian intervention. Speaking to troops in Baidoa on January 1, Bush reiterated his intention to bring U.S. forces home as soon as possible and to turn the operation over to a UN peacekeeping force. President-elect Clinton, he assured the troops, supported this approach.

A Mogadishu stopover by UN secretary-general Boutros-Ghali on January 3, en route to the Addis Ababa conference, did not go so well; it cast doubt on how rapidly and well the United Nations would make the transition. Aideed seized the opportunity to orchestrate a large, though mostly nonviolent, anti-UN demonstration, accusing the United Nations—and Boutros-Ghali in particular—of planning to impose a trusteeship on the Somali people. The demonstration prevented Boutros-Ghali from reaching UNOSOM headquarters, located in a narrow cul-de-sac quickly made impassable by the crowds. The demonstration reportedly terrified many members of the secretary-general's party already inside UNOSOM headquarters, surrounded by a mob they feared was coming over the walls to tear them limb from limb. (In television footage available later, the demonstrators seemed largely to be going through the motions for the cameras, but this was decidedly not the feeling inside.)

At a hastily convened airport press conference, the secretary-general maintained his composure, deliberately downplaying the significance of the demonstration and calling it unrepresentative of broader Somali opinion. Privately, however, Boutros-Ghali was angry and very concerned. He felt humiliated by Aideed and feared that the demonstrators would create an impression that the United Nations had lost control, thus making it harder to find troop contributors. He also appeared to view the Somalis as incapable of assuming responsibility for their own affairs and ready to rise up en masse against the United Nations should it take over from UNITAF. The visit further reinforced his view that much remained to be done before the United Nations could consider taking over, and left him with lingering personal resentment of Aideed.[1]

In a characteristic performance, Aideed, having made his point with the demonstration, went on to the UN conference on Somalia in Addis. He did not want to miss the opportunity to advance his political goals, despite his dislike of the United Nations, and he mixed politically useful anti-UN posturing with cooperation where it served his interests.

U.S. AND UN PERSPECTIVES

Drastically different U.S. and UN perspectives on UNITAF and UN roles in Somalia had been evident during talks between Acting Secretary of State Eagleburger and Boutros-Ghali in late November. They were sharpened with the exchange of letters between President Bush and the secretary-general in December. Ensuing tensions over the transition to UNOSOM II arose when the differences were not resolved; the hitches in the transfer cannot be understood without taking them into consideration.

The United States believed its discussions with the secretary-general had made amply clear that American forces would operate only in southern Somalia; that the creation of a benign security environment pertained only to providing security for UNITAF forces, the relief convoys, and the humanitarian relief personnel; and that in the near future a large,

---

[1]Brian Hall's description of Boutros-Ghali's understanding of the situation is informative: "Boutros-Ghali seems not to have realized that his background would also be a major problem in Somalia. 'I think he made a bad mistake in not saying that because of his background and experience and the part of the world he's from, he should step away from Somalia,' says a long-time observer of the United Nations who spoke only on the condition of anonymity. He cites a UN tradition of not putting peacekeepers or negotiators in a situation where there would be conflicting national interests. 'You had Pérez de Cuéllar and Giandomenico Picco running between Iran and Iraq. Well, that's not a bad combination—Peru and Italy. If you've run foreign affairs in Egypt, if you have strong opinions about the Horn of Africa, you should step away.'" (See "Blue Helmets," *New York Times Magazine*, January 2, 1994.)

conventional UN peacekeeping operation would take over, with limited U.S. participation.[2]

This flexible application of UNITAF's mandate, the U.S. military leadership believed, would help lay the foundation for expeditious planning for the transition to UNOSOM II. Other troop contributors concurred. Timely planning could ensure that the UN force, armed with the Chapter VII mandate, would have strong U.S. support during the transition, enhancing its ability to defeat challenges by the faction leaders. Most UNITAF forces would remain as part of UNOSOM II, and U.S. forces were prepared to play a major role in assisting and supporting it.[3]

In contrast, the UN headquarters view, repeatedly expressed by the secretary-general, was that the UNITAF mission should be much more extensive than the United States envisioned, with an ambitious disarmament program, broader geographic extent, and longer duration. The UN Secretariat felt that only the United States could carry out the kind of comprehensive disarmament and stabilization that would enable a UN peacekeeping force to operate effectively when U.S. forces departed. There was considerable apprehension that without such action the security situation would deteriorate quickly. The faction leaders would again use violence to seek personal advantage, and the UN national reconciliation and economic reconstruction programs could not be implemented. The secretary-general did not want even to start planning the transfer until the United States had accepted his broader construction of the mission.[4]

ARMS CONTROL AND DISARMAMENT

At the heart of these differences lay the issue of disarmament and arms reduction. President Bush had stated U.S. policy clearly: "First, we will create a secure environment in the hardest hit parts of Somalia so that food can move from ships overland to the people in the countryside now

---

[2]In a letter replying to Boutros-Ghali, President Bush said, "I want to emphasize that the mission of the coalition is limited and specific: to create security conditions which will permit the feeding of the starving Somali people and allow the transfer of these security functions to the UN peacekeeping force."

[3]The original U.S. proposal had been that for a number of weeks the two commands would operate side by side, with UNOSOM II having a broader geographic area of responsibility. It would gradually have taken over from UNITAF, sector by sector; the delay, however, made this impossible.

[4]See the secretary-general's report of December 19, 1992, "The Situation in Somalia," S/24992.

devastated by starvation. And second, once we have created that secure environment, we will withdraw our troops, handing the security mission back to a regular UN peacekeeping force."

This U.S. position was pragmatic in both concept and practice. Any UNITAF disarmament program was to be limited and specific. The Oakley and Johnston strategy of seeking cooperation from the faction leaders included obtaining their agreement to the cantonment of heavy weapons—especially the technicals—and then enforcing it, as well as ensuring that there was no armed interference with humanitarian operations. This policy, extended throughout the HRSs in conjunction with UNITAF troop deployments, had three short-term benefits. It reduced the level of confrontation with the faction leaders and minimized the risk of casualties, it put heavy weapons out of circulation, and it quickly broke through obstacles to the delivery of food and medicine in south-central Somalia, allowing humanitarian operations to proceed. Had UNITAF pursued a policy of full-scale disarmament, it would have needed a much greater force for the mission and would almost certainly have become embroiled in a series of local clashes, both small-scale and with large militias such as the SNA, SNF, and SSDF.

The secretary-general, however, felt that this approach was insufficient. Boutros-Ghali said that a disarmament program must ensure "that the heavy weapons of the organized factions are neutralized and that the irregular forces and gangs are disarmed." To do so would require establishing or consolidating cease-fire agreements with the leaders of all organized factions and disarming the lawless gangs. UNITAF, and any successor, "should do all [it] can to induce individuals to hand in their weapons."

Boutros-Ghali also contended that UNITAF's disarmament program should be countrywide. In his December 8 letter to Bush, he observed that the need for a nationwide disarmament program "should be apparent from the outset. It is true that the quantity of suffering is greatest in the areas where it is planned to deploy the unified command's forces in the first phase. But qualitatively the situation is just as bad elsewhere, especially in the north."[5]

U.S. officials at all levels explained repeatedly that this kind of program was not in UNITAF's mandate. Eagleburger, at that time secretary of

---

[5]Ibid.

state, told the secretary-general bluntly that only the United States would decide how to use its forces and when to bring them home, but publicly the administration played down its irritation with the United Nations.

UNITAF forces, General Johnston emphasized, would seize arms caches reported or discovered in their area of operations—a commitment fulfilled in Mogadishu, Baidoa, Bardera, and Kismayo. UNITAF would also do its best to see that weapons were not carried or used where its forces were present. But it would not conduct systematic searches of houses or every car on the road. In an interview at the time, Oakley noted that even in countries with functioning legal and penal systems, it is extremely difficult to control the availability of weapons. How, he asked, could disarmament of this magnitude—"house-to-house, hut-to-hut searches"—be carried out in the lawless conditions prevailing in Somalia?[6]

The UNITAF command felt strongly that it was vital to avoid serving as a police force—a task that Johnston and Oakley believed should be entrusted to the Somalis themselves. They wanted to avoid unnecessary confrontation between the military and civilians and to take a gradual approach to arms control and weakening the forces of faction leaders. As for deployment to the center and the north, the U.S. position remained unyielding: This would be the function of UNOSOM II. (As some U.S. officials noted privately, UNOSOM I had never been deployed to these areas even though the Canadians and Belgians had been prepared to proceed.)

If UNOSOM II commanders arrived prepared to undertake a well-planned disarmament program, U.S. and other UNITAF forces would assist. Although this stance was made clear to UN representatives in Mogadishu, and UNITAF was actually doing contingency planning for the possibility, it appears that this point was not fully grasped at UN headquarters. They continued to believe the United States would accept no role in *any* disarmament activity once UNOSOM II came into being. If UN pressure on the United States were kept up, UNITAF might eventually agree to do the job.[7] This misapprehension seems to have been an important factor behind the delay in planning. Until late April, Boutros-Ghali continued to argue that it was premature and dangerous for a UN peacekeeping operation to take over as long as UNITAF's mission (as he defined it) had not been carried out.

---

[6]Press conference, Mogadishu, December 13, 1992.

[7]Kofi Annan, interview with John Hirsch, New York, July 19, 1993.

The differences also meant that the United Nations never drew up a plan for disarmament, demobilization, and the reintegration of Somali militias into civilian life, though it had prepared such plans for Namibia, El Salvador, and other UN peacekeeping operations and had considerable experience with what was required for success. There was no such planning for Somalia, despite the secretary-general's insistence on the importance of disarmament. When UNOSOM II arrived in mid-March, and even after it took full control on May 4, no detailed plan had been prepared, even though the Somali faction leaders themselves had developed an initial approach during their Addis meetings.[8]

PLANNING FOR THE TRANSITION TO UNOSOM II

When Boutros-Ghali visited Mogadishu in January, Johnston briefed him and Kittani in detail on UNITAF's progress and outlined in broad terms U.S. recommendations for the planning process. In effect, Johnston proposed that UN and U.S. military planners in Mogadishu start work at once to develop a detailed handoff plan, to be presented to the secretary-general and the Security Council as soon as the decision to proceed had been made. Johnston emphasized the priority of the United Nations' designating a force commander and providing him with a planning staff, noting that prompt planning would enable UNITAF to provide maximum support to UNOSOM II. After this discussion, Johnston thought Boutros-Ghali had agreed to the establishment of a UN "technical team" to start planning, and was deeply disappointed when this proved not to be the case.

No planners were sent out from UN headquarters, although Ambassador Brandon Grove, Jr., of the State Department, who was heading the Somalia Task Force, and Rear Admiral Frank Bowman of the Joint Chiefs of Staff were told in early January that they would arrive "right away." UN and U.S. delegations in New York discussed the transition require-

---

[8]Only at the fourth humanitarian conference in Addis Ababa, November 29 to December 1, 1993, did the UN put forward preliminary ideas for a disarmament plan covering all of Somalia. (There had been a skeleton UN Development Program plan for Somaliland.) This was thanks to the insistence of Under Secretary-General Eliasson and UNDP with strong American support. Only in the secretary-general's January 6 report to the Security Council (S/1994/12) did Boutros-Ghali acknowledge that a weaker UNOSOM II, after withdrawal of U.S. and other forces, would be obliged to pursue voluntary disarmament, although his own continued preference was for a stronger, longer UNOSOM II with a continued mandate for "coercive disarmament." In fact there had been very little coercive disarmament even during the UNITAF period (although there had been quite a bit of both voluntary and "encouraged" disarmament relating especially to heavy weapons) and almost no disarmament of any kind between May 4, 1993, and January 6, 1994.

ments weekly, but did not address the same issues as the on-site planning would have raised.

The situation in Mogadishu was further complicated by Kittani's prolonged absence for medical reasons and General Shaheen's leave and subsequent hospitalization in Kenya; even when both were present they were not authorized to proceed. Unwarranted assumptions and expectations at UN headquarters also led to disappointment. Under Secretary-General Kofi Annan, for example, thought the Americans' limited definition of disarmament would be expanded once UNITAF forces came up to full strength and that the United States could then be persuaded to carry out disarmament in the center and the north. Annan expected "more aggressive" disarmament beyond the stated geographic limit of the U.S. undertaking; he was disturbed that the United States thought there were no significant arms caches in Galcaio, the famous "hole in the center," and therefore was not willing to go there.[9]

The United Nations came to believe as well that the United States was following a "policy of extrication," planning the departure of U.S. forces even before all of them had arrived, without any concern for what would occur on the ground or what it might mean for a follow-on force.[10] This impression was fueled in part when some White House officials repeated to the press that the United States hoped to be out of Somalia by January 20, even though both Cheney and Powell had explicitly ruled out such planning as premature.

Johnston could not develop a plan for force replacements until UNOSOM II participants could be identified and dates set for their arrival and deployment. Both the secretary-general and the United States were approaching prospective participants. It was expected that Italy and France would remain in UNOSOM II, but the Australians and Canadians then participating in UNITAF had indicated they would depart in May and June, respectively. Continued Belgian participation was uncertain. Efforts to bring additional Pakistani forces hinged on a waiver of legislation barring U.S. military assistance to Pakistan, and the participation of a promised Indian brigade of 4,500 was also uncertain. The Pakistani

---

[9]In fact, doing so was considered by both Bush and Clinton, because they were aware of sizable arms caches. However, both decided not to extend the geographic limits of UNITAF, although they would probably have assisted a well-planned UN operation there. The issue of unilateral UNITAF action in central Somalia was debated and decided against in the NSC Deputies Committee during early January.

[10]Annan interview.

forces arrived in April, bringing their total to more than 4,000, but they were accompanied by little equipment. Discussions in New Delhi seemed to be going nowhere as the Indians raised a number of political and financial issues, underlying which was deep unease about involvement in internal conflict in a Muslim country.

The first three months of 1993 were difficult for Johnston and his staff; while day-to-day operations were proceeding reasonably well, they felt they had made little headway in organizing the transition. They did not consider that their request to begin planning with their UN counterparts implied an intention to leave precipitately; instead, they repeatedly underscored their interest in a professional handoff that would ensure a successful launch for UNOSOM II and prevent the many problems that had plagued its predecessor.

The United States continued to press hard for a decision on a force commander and a start to serious planning. In February Boutros-Ghali designated Lieutenant General Cevik Bir, a respected Turkish officer well-known in NATO circles. The United States promptly named Army Major General Tom Montgomery to serve as his deputy. Notwithstanding these appointments, however, the planning process in Mogadishu remained stalled. According to Jonah, the UN Secretariat was not given authorization to start the planning process on the ground until late March—despite the earlier undertaking to begin in January.[11] Bir and Montgomery, after an initial visit to Mogadishu on February 23–24 (at the height of the Aideed-inspired demonstration against UNITAF), returned to Somalia only in mid-March, still without a command staff.

THE UNITED STATES, THE UN SECRETARIAT, AND THE SECURITY COUNCIL

Beyond U.S.-UN misperceptions, however, other issues had to be resolved. In organizing the transition, Boutros-Ghali understandably wanted to know what commitment the new U.S. administration would make to UNOSOM II. This question was answered in general terms when the new secretary of state, Warren Christopher, in his first meeting with Boutros-Ghali in February, reaffirmed the Clinton administration's intention to participate.

Boutros-Ghali also hoped that the political process set in motion by the Addis Ababa conferences would move forward sufficiently to provide

---

[11] Jonah interview.

a more promising context for UNOSOM II, and wanted to see what results came from the March conference before accepting the handoff. His concerns were shared by some members of the Security Council, cautious about instituting another peace enforcement operation. The large-scale UN peacekeeping operations in Bosnia-Herzegovina and Cambodia—as well as ongoing operations in Angola, Mozambique, and elsewhere—had already overtaxed the limited planning capacity of the small peacekeeping staff and badly overdrawn its budget.

As long as UNITAF was in the field, the United States was picking up more than 75 percent of its cost. Once UNOSOM II was established, the operating costs would fall under the UN peacekeeping account, which was badly in arrears, and for which the U.S. share was only 30 percent. Moreover, the U.S. military establishment had an outstanding logistics capability, which it was providing to most of the UNITAF forces, and the United Nations was justifiably apprehensive about how to provide adequate logistical support when UNITAF came to an end.

The United States intended from the outset to provide substantial ongoing support for UNOSOM II—a point made at the time Operation Restore Hope was announced, and reiterated by the Clinton administration. Admiral Bowman, of the Joint Chiefs staff, told the UN Secretariat in February that the United States would contribute a 1,300-man Quick Reaction Force (QRF), capable of responding to security emergencies in the interior. The Marine Expeditionary Unit that operated in the Indian Ocean–Persian Gulf area would be made available if required. The United States would also undertake to leave behind much of its logistical equipment for the startup period, although it recommended that logistics be turned over to a civilian contractor as soon as possible. On the military front, the United States would provide the deputy commander, General Montgomery, as well as other senior officers for Bir's staff. The total number of U.S. military remaining would be about 4,000.[12]

---

[12]An important factor in the original Bush decision, supported by the secretary of defense and the chairman of the Joint Chiefs, was that combat forces for the Quick Reaction Force would remain under the operational control of a U.S. general, who would in turn report for this purpose to CENT-COM. Although this arrangement satisfied U.S. military and congressional concerns over putting U.S. forces under foreign command, it created confusion in the command and control of UNOSOM II, among other things by setting a precedent which other national units could follow in refusing to accept UNOSOM orders unless approved by their own headquarters. By the time of the October 3 clash between U.S. Army Rangers and the SNA, even Congress was confused about where U.S. forces were getting their orders. Many were under the impression that the UN was commanding U.S. combat forces and had ordered them into dangerous actions. The administration made no public acknowledgment that this was not the case, nor that U.S. combat forces had been ordered into action by U.S. commanders on a mission approved by the president as commander-in-chief.

At the same time, a search was under way to find a successor for Kittani, who had indicated from the outset that he would serve only for several months. When the secretary-general asked the United States to propose a candidate, it was clear that he was intent on ensuring continued U.S. involvement. Admiral Jonathan Howe, who had worked on the Somali situation and Operation Restore Hope as deputy national security advisor for President Bush, was proposed and promptly accepted.[13]

On March 3, Robert Oakley completed his stint as the American special representative in Somalia. The high personal profile he had maintained as a political advisor and negotiator with the Somalis had been productive in the early days of Operation Restore Hope. The United States had come to be regarded by the Somalis and the international community alike as the de facto arbiter of the Somali political situation, though the mandate in fact belonged to the United Nations and both the Bush and Clinton administrations were careful not to take it on. By stepping down just before Howe took on the job as the secretary-general's special representative, Oakley made clear the U.S. message to the Somalis that it was the United Nations that had the long-term responsibility to lead the international effort to help them rebuild. His departure was also intended to signal to UN headquarters that the United States believed its humanitarian mission had been achieved and that it was time for the United Nations to replace the United States on the military as well as the civilian side.[14]

The transition from UNITAF to UNOSOM II began in earnest when Bir and Montgomery returned to Mogadishu in mid-March. Bir and Johnston worked side by side for six weeks, deciding on the deployment of UNOSOM troops in the nine HRSs. With Johnston's help, Bir assembled about half his headquarters staff of officers from the major contingents already present (Italian, French, Belgian, and U.S.) that would serve under his command. Though there had earlier been some consideration of a handoff phased over a matter of weeks, Bir and Johnston decided that because of the delays, it would be better to turn over command in toto on a date to be agreed.

---

[13]As reported by *Los Angeles Times* correspondent Stanley Meisler, "From the secretary-general's point of view, the operation (UNOSOM II) had been fashioned to U.S. specifications." (*Los Angeles Times*, April 4, 1994.) Patrick Sloyan of *Newsday* reported that Howe was the personal choice of National Security Advisor Tony Lake. (*Washington Post*, April 5, 1994.)

[14]Although there was no overlap in Mogadishu, Howe and Oakley met several times in Washington to discuss the situation in Somalia.

On March 26 the Security Council adopted Resolution 814, calling for the replacement of UNITAF forces with a UN peacekeeping force that, for the first time in UN history, was established under Chapter VII of the UN Charter.[15] The resolution established two objectives for the United Nations: to provide for the "consolidation, expansion, and maintenance of a secure environment throughout Somalia" and for "the rehabilitation of the political institutions and economy of Somalia." U.S. ambassador to the UN Madeleine Albright, speaking to the Security Council, pronounced that this resolution meant "an unprecedented enterprise aimed at nothing less than the restoration of an entire country."[16]

After Howe arrived, he tried to convince Johnston and Zinni to keep UNITAF forces in Somalia at least until the beginning of June, and again raised the question of deployment to Galcaio and the north. Howe shared the secretary-general's concern that there had not been enough disarmament. Failing to make headway with Johnston, he used his close contacts with high-level U.S. military and civilian officials in Washington to seek administration approval for enlarging and extending UNITAF's mandate. Johnston, supported by Hoar, insisted that UNITAF had fulfilled its mandate and contended that to stay longer would imply a different mission for which new presidential approval and additional resources would be required. This position was sustained by the Joint Chiefs of Staff and approved by the White House despite last-minute lobbying by Howe and Boutros-Ghali in late April.

THE BEGINNING OF UNOSOM II

With the U.S. departure, the new UNOSOM II command felt considerably more vulnerable—a perception shared in New York. Indeed, according

---

[15]This resolution and the secretary-general's report on which it was based had been expected by the United States since mid-February. However, the promised report kept meeting with delays as Boutros-Ghali tracked the military and political situation in Somalia and the attitudes of other Security Council members and attempted to obtain as much of a U.S. commitment in material, financial, and political support as possible before finally accepting UN responsibility. At times the U.S.–UN dialogue on this resolution resembled bargaining in a bazaar. In the end, the United States provided more support than had been planned, and the secretary-general agreed that the UN should take over from the U.S.

[16]US-UN Press Release 37-(93), March 26, 1993. Thus the theories of enhanced UN peace-keeping in the late 1980s and 1990–92, including the ideas in Boutros-Ghali's "Agenda for Peace," such as "nationbuilding" and "peace enforcement," were put into practice. As Albright said later, this offered a means for the international community to rebuild "failed states." (Televised appearance on ABC's "Nightline," August 12, 1993.) As it turned out, the resolution of the Security Council was one thing, implementation on the ground something else.

to some UN headquarters staff, they were taken by surprise when informed by telephone on May 4 that the Marines had actually departed—evidently there was still some expectation that Howe might persuade the United States to stay.[17]

The military side of the transfer was flawed in several respects. A large number of the anticipated forces had not arrived by May 4. In fact many, such as the Indian brigade and 1,500 Germans, did not arrive until the late summer or fall. Units already present lacked adequate equipment—Pakistani forces had no armor; helicopters were in short supply throughout the forces. Essential planning for military action on issues such as disarmament had not been done, and logistical, engineering, intelligence, and psychological warfare resources were inadequate. Moreover, the close, informal coordination among military, political, and humanitarian activities was no longer present. The new UN organization was much more bureaucratized, broken down into clearly separate functions.

Still, by May 4 UNOSOM II had enough forces on the ground to carry out Phase I of its mission, taking over from UNITAF in Mogadishu and the nine HRSs in southern Somalia.[18] Although not up to expected full deployment of 28,000,[19] the major contingents were on the ground when the handoff took place. The 4,000 U.S. troops—including the 1,300-strong Quick Reaction Force from the Tenth Mountain Division—were available, as were the major contingents from Italy, France, and Belgium. With a 4,000-man Pakistani brigade replacing 2,600 U.S. Marines, Bir actually had more troops in Mogadishu than Johnston had had in the preceding month. The largest gap was in the Kismayo-Bardera corridor and over to the Kenyan border, where the yet-to-arrive Indian brigade was supposed to deploy.

The military side of UNOSOM II was thus in relatively sound condition, but the atmosphere of anxiety about its unpreparedness was heightened by uncertainty about how to carry out the mandate of Resolution 814. This was the first peace enforcement operation ever, and neither the Security Council nor the secretary-general had provided precise guidance

---

[17]Elizabeth Lindenmayer, UN Peacekeeping Operations office, interview with John Hirsch, New York, November 11, 1993.

[18]The four phases of UNOSOM II's military operations are set forth in paragraph 79 of the secretary-general's March 3, 1993, report (S/25354). They were phase I, transition from UNITAF; phase II, consolidation and expansion of security; phase III, transfer to civilian institutions; and phase IV, redeployment.

[19]The 28,000 consisted of 20,000 military and 8,000 civilian and logistical support.

to Bir. There had been no consultation and agreement among the troop contributing governments on precise rules of engagement, command and control issues, or coordination of the political and military functions. It was unclear who had authority to order the use of force except in self-defense. Both Bir and Howe, therefore, tended to look to UN headquarters for decisions, and Boutros-Ghali's style was to retain close control, while the Secretariat's decision making remained notoriously slow. Moreover, there was a fair amount of conceptual carryover from traditional peacekeeping, and when the confrontation came, there was no clear idea of how to deal with Aideed because of the implicit contradiction between his threat of force and the disposition of UN forces to go to great lengths to avoid using it.

Whatever Bir's problems, the situation was considerably more difficult on the civilian side. Howe had inherited a small, exhausted, and demoralized staff at UNOSOM headquarters and an even skimpier, equally demoralized staff in the interior. He immediately asked for U.S. and UN assistance in analyzing needs and identifying organizational and personnel requirements, and a high-powered personnel management team was sent out from Washington.[20]

An earlier study conducted by the Secretariat had recommended that 2,800 UN civilians be recruited to carry out the many tasks enumerated in Resolution 814. This projection was soon scaled back, but it took until the end of the year for both UNOSOM and UN headquarters to realize that the "trusteeship" concepts of that unwieldy resolution were far beyond their capabilities. The system moved almost as slowly in Somalia as elsewhere, despite Howe's high level of energy and management expertise. While struggling to sort out its priorities, the United Nations was pleased to accept the U.S. offer to second staff temporarily from State, USAID, and CENTCOM, even though it irritated other potential contributors and gave the United States an awkwardly high profile. But events quickly outran UN efforts to upgrade UNOSOM's staffing and improve its organizational structure, and the coordination problems that had plagued Sahnoun and Kittani remained.

---

[20]The UN found out about this team, which included no Secretariat personnel, just before it arrived in Mogadishu. The incident illustrates the duality of Howe's role, in which he retained close relationships with the U.S. administration while serving as the secretary-general's special representative. Eventually this duality created confusion in Washington and New York as well as among members of the Security Council, troop contributors, and Somalis about which party Howe was acting for.

The bureaucratic barriers between political, humanitarian, and military operations and planning, which UNITAF had worked hard to abolish, returned with a vengeance to the UNOSOM II staff. The military were no longer used to support and supplement humanitarian operations or to help with the police and other functions. Political decisions were usually kept separate from military considerations and military commanders. The humanitarian side was neglected and close contact with the NGO community was lost, particularly since the CMOC disappeared once UNITAF departed. At the same time, UNOSOM II introduced a much less austere living environment for its personnel. UNITAF had neither built nor renovated living facilities, using tents and abandoned buildings. U.S. forces had only field rations. UNOSOM II brought in prefabricated housing and rehabilitated numerous buildings for officers and others. Ultimately, this contributed to the greater isolation of the forces from the Somalis than had been the case during UNITAF.

Additional important complicating factors in a dangerous environment were the interrelated practical issues of uncertain command and control of the various national contingents in Somalia and uncertain, slow communication and command relationships between UNOSOM and UN headquarters. These problems had been clearly identified in many earlier peacekeeping situations, but they were even more troublesome for the Somalia mission, confronting an unfamiliar situation that UNOSOM forces felt was apt to explode at any moment.[21] The problems added to the widespread perception that UNOSOM was not properly prepared or equipped, as well as to the perception among the Somalis, particularly the SNA, that the operation was probably weak and could be pushed around.

---

[21]It had been relatively easy for Johnston to make rapid decisions and maintain operational security on UNITAF use of force, and he was able to obtain a high degree of cohesion from other national contingents. This was decidedly not the case with Generals Bir and Montgomery, Admiral Howe, and UN headquarters. Unlike the U.S. military, which had very recently completed Operation Desert Storm, and was trained in dealing with such situations, UN civilians and military had no experience working together in combat. Nor was there any UN or other common doctrine or training which prepared either Bir or the UNOSOM II forces for a coordinated response to the many problems which arise in combat.

Challenge and Confrontation

*I*t was virtually inevitable that a test of strength between Aideed and the UN forces would occur early on. Among other factors, there was a widespread Somali perception that UN-led forces would be weaker than UNITAF, even if most of the units stayed the same, and even with strong U.S. military support.[1] USLO and UNITAF officers had tried hard to dispel that belief, with only limited success. Before the transition, General Johnston and new U.S. special envoy Bob Gosende discussed with Admiral Howe and Generals Bir and Montgomery the likelihood that Aideed would challenge the new operation. These discussions were inconclusive, although there was agreement that the SNA and others were likely to test UNOSOM's resolve and capabilities.

To make matters worse, Aideed and his followers had also concluded that UNOSOM II was biased against them. Not only did Aideed have a long-standing distrust of Boutros-Ghali, he believed that Howe had deliberately attempted to embarrass him and harm his political prospects by

---

[1]The departure of the heavily armed, aggressively patrolling Marines from south Mogadishu obviously had a much greater psychological effect on the Somalis, especially the SNA, than the continued presence of a QRF from the Tenth Mountain Division. Australian and Canadian battalion-sized units left in May and June, but some 4,000 Italians, 1,500 Germans, and 1,500 more Pakistanis arrived during June through August, bringing UNOSOM II military forces up from a low of 14,000 to about 25,000. The German unit was essentially for logistics and engineering, not for combat, and was protected by Italian UNOSOM units in the Bay region. Chancellor Helmut Kohl fought and won a major political and legal battle to obtain constitutional court approval to send German army units out of the NATO theatre and use them for peacekeeping. This deployment to Somalia was a major breakthrough in terms of German military participation in international activities.

renouncing UNOSOM support for a Mogadishu peace conference that Aideed had convened in mid-May to discuss the situation in central Somalia and by refusing to accept the peace agreement concluded there. When the United Nations provided transportation for rival faction leader Mohamed Abshir and others to attend a parallel UN-arranged conference, Aideed was particularly affronted, believing that the United Nations was implying significant recognition of Abshir as a political player. UNOSOM leaders, for their part, thought that Aideed had tried to dupe them into supporting an event intended to promote his political ambitions. When, as a means of political pressure, some of the participants from other clans were detained by SNA militia in the Olympia Hotel, UNOSOM concluded that Aideed's ambitions could never be satisfied by genuine power sharing and compromise. They concluded that he should be politically marginalized rather than engaged in continued high-level dialogue.[2]

The uncertainties affecting UNOSOM contributed to a general feeling of unease, and surprisingly, although some acknowledged concerns about Aideed's reaction to the handoff, few understood how strongly he might react to being marginalized.[3] After the handoff to UNOSOM II, day and night patrolling by the Pakistanis in south Mogadishu was sharply reduced, partly because of a lack of equipment and personnel. Their doctrine and training were different from those of the Marines whom they had replaced, and there was also uncertainty about what kind of support they could expect from UNOSOM command in the event of a confrontation. The reduction sent a message of irresolution that Aideed, already convinced that UNOSOM II planned to continue paring down his military power, took as an opportunity. Having managed to slip much of his heavy weaponry back into Mogadishu, he went on the offensive, making

---

[2]For a detailed account of the two conferences, see Walter Clarke, "Testing the World's Resolve in Somalia," *Parameters*, Vol. 23, No. 4 (Winter 1993–94). There are also SNA communiqués and press releases that reveal how much this episode worsened Aideed's attitude toward UNOSOM. Interestingly, the arrangements worked out by Aideed were respected by the major subclans and the four factional militias, which cooperated to avoid conflict in the region from Galcaio to Bossasso even during the period between June 5 and October 7. Clarke's assessment is shared by the independent investigating commission established in response to Security Council Resolution 885.

[3]Given Aideed's well-known vision of himself as the man who saved Somalia from Siad Barre and the man destined to assume national leadership, his equally well-known capacity for devious violence when opposed, and his demonstrated hostility to earlier attempts to marginalize him and the SNA, UNOSOM and the United States should have better appreciated the dangers along the path they had chosen. UNOSOM and the U.S. were taken by surprise, politically and militarily, and had inadequate resources to deal with the problems that arose.

the SNA presence prominent on the streets and using his radio station to launch a series of scorching attacks on UN interference in Somalia's internal politics.

The UN command in Mogadishu and New York debated its response to Aideed and began to consider various military options. In Mogadishu, rumors were rampant that his radio station, Radio Mogadishu, would be seized, and UNOSOM had, in fact, decided to close it.[4] On June 4 UNOSOM informed Aideed, through a subordinate, that it intended to dispatch teams to inspect and inventory his weapons depots the next day. This action was backed by the United States, which had come to see Aideed as the chief enemy of the implementation of Security Council Resolution 814. The idea was to hold the SNA to the agreement reached at the Addis Ababa conference and in follow-up discussions with UNOSOM, tightening controls that the SNA had increasingly come to test and flout.

Fighting broke out on June 5, after a Pakistani patrol actually entered Radio Mogadishu, located at one of six weapons storage sites under inspection. Although the patrol completed its inspection and withdrew, a hostile crowd had gathered. Within ninety minutes angry crowds were assembling at other locations in south Mogadishu. In midmorning the SNA, taking cover behind stone-throwing women and children, ambushed a group of Pakistani soldiers on October 21 Road. SNA militia and angry crowds elsewhere in the city confronted the Pakistani patrols, which were caught by surprise.[5] By early afternoon, with the Pakistani teams pinned

---

[4]The local political subtleties that caused Aideed to interpret this action as partial to Ali Mahdi, whose station was not seized, were not fully appreciated by UNOSOM, which saw itself as responding to Aideed's inflammatory broadcasts on what claimed to be an official Somali radio station. (The UN accepted Ali Mahdi's claim that his radio station was private.)

[5]It will never be certain who initiated which actions, for what purposes, on June 5, or what the circumstances were which contributed to the incidents. UNOSOM reported to UN headquarters that these were deliberate, well-planned ambushes, while the SNA claimed it was responding to Pakistani provocations. The UNOSOM view prevailed, and was accepted virtually without question by the UN Security Council, which had little time for fact-finding between the attack on June 5 and the June 6 vote. Information on the ambush of the Pakistani soldiers and other of Aideed's activities is available in greater detail in the UN secretary-general's reports S/26022 (July 1, 1993) and S/26738 (November 12, 1993).

Additional information is contained in the report of the independent investigatory commission, which appears in the *International Documents Review* of May 23–27, 1994. The report notes that a mid-level SNA official was given an "ultimatum" on the evening of June 4 that an inspection would take place the next day, using force if there was resistance. The SNA official warned strongly against this but UNOSOM decided to proceed without further discussion with Aideed. The UNOSOM force commander was out of town, most of the QRF was in Kismayo, and the Pakistanis claimed afterward that they had been taken by surprise. Although deputy UNOSOM force commander Montgomery made preparations for potential armed resistance by attaching

down, elements of the U.S. Quick Reaction Force and the Italian armored units were brought in to end the fighting. When it ended, twenty-four Pakistanis were dead and scores injured.[6] The bodies of many of the victims were mutilated or subjected to other degrading treatment.

Meeting in urgent session on Sunday, June 6, the UN Security Council unanimously adopted Resolution 837, which expressed grave alarm at the premeditated murder of UN peacekeepers, "launched by forces apparently belonging to the United Somali Congress (USC/SNA)." The Security Council authorized that "all necessary measures" be taken against those responsible for inciting such attacks, including their arrest and detention for prosecution, trial, and punishment. The SNA was named in the resolution and thereby became the enemy of UNOSOM and the U.S. military, although Aideed's name was dropped after appearing in an early draft resolution.[7]

The resolution did not demand military action, but given the rapidly evolving Mogadishu situation, there is no question that it implied a go-ahead for the military steps subsequently taken against Aideed and his senior associates. The United States was among those urging the strongest action against those who deliberately attacked UN peacekeepers, imagining the repercussions for other peacekeeping operations if a decisive response were not forthcoming.[8]

---

twenty-two armored personnel carriers to the Pakistani patrol going to inspect the weapons storage sites and discussed dangers with the Pakistani commanders, no one anticipated such a violent reaction and few understood that the SNA had worked itself into seeing any interference with the radio station as a casus belli. The report considered the June 5 inspection highly provocative and unwise, though it did fall within the mandate of Security Council Resolution 814. It found that the SNA had initiated the attack on the Pakistanis, but discovered no "conclusive evidence" that the SNA attacks were "preplanned and premeditated," although this was the information provided by the UN Secretariat to the Security Council before it voted for Resolution 837 and was the firm conviction of UNOSOM and U.S. military and political leaders.

[6]The exact number of casualties on June 5 has been disputed since the event; these figures are drawn from S/26022.

[7]Security Council Resolution 837 was proposed by Pakistan and originally named Aideed personally. The U.S. had his name removed, on the grounds of inadequate evidence, but pushed hard for identifying the SNA. The wording of the resolution and its interpretation by the UN in both New York and Mogadishu were fully supported by the U.S. The Department of Defense and the Joint Chiefs did not express their views at the top levels on this extremely important turning point in policy.

[8]From conversations with both senior and midlevel officials directly involved with Somalia, it is evident that there was no real appreciation of how much of a change of policy and mission this was for UNOSOM II and the United States forces associated with it. Nor was there a realistic appreciation of just how tough it would be to successfully take action called for by the Security Council against the SNA in the back alleys of south Mogadishu. There was obviously an unwarranted initial assumption that the SNA, with only light arms, would not be difficult to deal with.

Events following from the June 5 ambush quickly produced new command and control problems for UNOSOM II. The French had begun to check quietly with Paris, pointing to the fact that the U.S. Quick Reaction Force reported to Montgomery and then to CENTCOM, rather than being under the operational control of Bir and Howe. French units followed orders from Paris to return to Baidoa rather than remain in Mogadishu after a June 17 operation against an SNA enclave, despite being told by Bir to remain. After four Italians were killed in a July 2 ambush, the Italian military command, in disagreement with the new anti-Aideed policy and already reluctant to place forces under Bir's direct command, indicated that it would instead take orders from Rome.[9] The French and Italians also alleged a lack of adequate consultation, planning, and advance notification by UNOSOM of military operations in Mogadishu. Italian units in the city refused to participate in actions against the SNA and were publicly accused by some UN and U.S. officials of collaborating with Aideed's forces to the point of deliberately refusing to come to the aid of a Pakistani unit under attack in proximity to Italian forces.[10] UN Under Secretary-General Kofi Annan publicly rebuffed the criticism of UN policies by the Italian commander, General Bruno Loi, and called for his replacement. The flap was eventually resolved, but the deeper issue of how to assure effective command and control of a multinational force persisted.[11]

Over the next four months the confrontation between Aideed, the United Nations, and the United States escalated steadily. In the ten days after the June 5 ambush, there were numerous clashes as UNOSOM sought to collect heavy weapons held by SNA forces in south Mogadishu and confronted large anti-UN demonstrations by pro-Aideed crowds, mostly women and children.[12] These incidents frequently led to armed clashes, with UNOSOM accusing Somalis of initiating ambushes and the SNA accusing UNOSOM of deliberately shooting women and children. There were scores of casualties among the peacekeepers and hundreds

---

[9]In fact this operation was planned and executed exclusively by the Italians, who decided not to inform UNOSOM. Its failure was apparently attributed to the UN in order to ease Italian political and military embarrassment, much as the U.S. did after October 3 and 4. By so doing, authorities in Rome seriously aggravated tensions with UNOSOM and tilted even more toward the SNA.

[10]This action was particularly ironic because at the outset of UNITAF Aideed and the SNA had been critical of Italy as biased against them and favoring Ali Mahdi.

[11]Loi finished his tour of duty, and the Italians moved out of Mogadishu.

[12]Pakistani, Moroccan, Malaysian, Nigerian, and other UNOSOM forces took the lead, but the QRF was called on more frequently for help as tensions escalated. Its involvement was approved by CENTCOM, the Joint Chiefs, and the White House; operations were under U.S. orders and command, coordinated with UNOSOM.

among the Somalis, and Aideed and the SNA used their mastery of media relations well during this period, portraying themselves as victims and the United States and United Nations as villains.

There were contacts between Howe's advisor, John Drysdale, and Aideed on June 7 in which Howe's idea of an independent inquiry, in accordance with Security Council Resolution 837, was raised. Aideed rejected the idea of any inquiry initiated by UNOSOM. According to Drysdale, for a period Howe was "ambivalent on whether to have Aideed arrested or not."[13]

On June 17 Moroccan peacekeepers took heavy casualties in a battle with SNA forces, initiated by a UNOSOM attack on Aideed's enclave in south Mogadishu. The Moroccans lost their battalion commander, and there were numerous other UNOSOM casualties. The same day, Admiral Howe issued a warrant for Aideed's arrest and detention, offering a $25,000 reward for his capture. This infuriated Aideed and effectively ended any remaining hopes for reviving dialogue between UNOSOM and the SNA.[14] The subsequent effort by American University professor Tom Farer, asked by Howe to conduct an inquiry into the events of June 5, obviously stood no chance of being accepted by the SNA or of causing them to reconsider their hostility toward UNOSOM.[15]

During late June and early July, UNOSOM attacked several SNA weapons storage compounds and other facilities. The attacks did considerable damage to the SNA but did not end its aggressive resistance or anti-UN propaganda. At the same time, however, Aideed, the SNA, and members of the Habr Gidr were arguing among themselves about how to proceed. Some SNA and Habr Gidr leaders, in conjunction with Ethiopia and Eritrea, attempted to arrange for Aideed to go into exile in some

---

[13]See John Drysdale, *Whatever Happened to Somalia* (London: Haan Associates, 1994), pp. 191–194.

[14]Howe asked in mid-June for U.S. Rangers to capture Aideed; Montgomery supported the request informally and was confident that they would succeed once they arrived and went to work. He did not believe the QRF was properly trained for the mission. The request initially was not approved in Washington, and only in late August did the Rangers and Delta Force get to Mogadishu, primarily because of Howe's persistent urging.

[15]Farer's report concluded that there was "compelling evidence" that Aideed had authorized the June 5 attack on UNOSOM; that the attack violated the Somali Penal Code and international law, thereby making "Aideed and his senior colleagues liable to prosecution before an international tribunal or the criminal courts of any state"; that the June 13 SNA attack on Pakistani UNOSOM forces was "consciously designed by persons associated with General Aideed's political faction"; and that statements made by SNA-controlled media before June 5 "do not constitute criminal incitement." (From an unpublished report submitted by Farer to Admiral Howe, pp. 108–109.)

African country, pending a full investigation of what had occurred on and after June 5. Aideed himself asked for the appointment of a commission of inquiry, in a letter to former U.S. president Jimmy Carter.[16]

On July 12, after several weeks of escalating tension, the Quick Reaction Force used helicopter gunships in a raid on Aideed's command and control center in an effort to seize arms, documents, and communications equipment as well as to attack high-level SNA leaders (possibly including Aideed) believed to be inside. This operation was planned and recommended by UNOSOM but approved in advance up the entire U.S. chain of command to the White House, as well as by UN headquarters. Without warning, the helicopters blocked all chances of escape, firing some sixteen missiles.[17] UNOSOM later acknowledged between twelve and twenty Somali casualties; the SNA said more than seventy had died—many of them elders and political leaders holding a meeting.[18] After the Quick Reaction Force withdrew, an angry Somali crowd surrounded the journalists who had arrived to cover the story; four of them were killed and their bodies displayed for television cameras.

The change in the atmosphere was evident; the effect of the raid irrevocable. Any question of SNA accommodation with the United States or United Nations was overtaken by the impact of the carefully planned attack, which affected Somali attitudes as much as the attack on the Pakistanis had influenced attitudes within UNOSOM.[19] The attack also

---

[16]It is possible that had the UN established the commission at that time, thus leaving the question of Aideed's guilt to the outcome of its investigation, the attempt to get him to leave Somalia would have succeeded. However, despite the support of the presidents of Ethiopia and Eritrea, the idea met with little sympathy in Washington and New York. U.S. officials were of the opinion that there was no hope for the exile idea after the escalation of hostilities in the summer, even though the idea was kept alive even after the change of U.S. policy announced in October. The independent investigatory commission noted that after July 12, the SNA "closed ranks and Somalis appear to have stopped giving information to UNOSOM II." (*International Documents Review*, May 23–27, 1994.)

[17]According to the independent commission, the July 12 operation "was intended to eliminate the SNA command center and its occupants. *Therefore no warning was given in advance*" (emphasis added). This was confirmed by UN and U.S. officials. The operation was intended to cripple the SNA leadership. It merely caused a brief period of disarray before the SNA regrouped with new leaders.

[18]Some U.S. sources say at least forty bodies were counted; others, including Major General Montgomery, insist there were no more than twenty. The ICRC had figures of 54 killed and 161 wounded.

[19]An account in the *Washington Post* quotes "American and UN officials, and Somalis sympathetic to Aideed," as saying that Aideed, in the wake of the July 12 attack, "made a calculated decision to kill American soldiers." SNA spokesman Abdi Abshir Kahiye is quoted as saying that after the airstrike "there was no more United Nations, only Americans. If you could kill Americans, it would start problems in America directly." (Keith B. Richburg, "In War on Aideed, UN

caused a number of non-Habr Gidr Somalis to sympathize, and even join forces with, the SNA, as well as substantially increasing Aideed's support among those Habr Gidr who had not previously been with him.[20]

The SNA continued to step up the pressure. On August 8 it exploded a remote control device under a Humvee, killing four U.S. soldiers, and the feeling of siege deepened. When six more Americans were wounded by a landmine explosion on August 22, President Clinton ordered Delta Force commandos, Army Rangers, and a helicopter detachment airlifted to Mogadishu. Though acting in support of the UNOSOM II mandate, they operated under separate U.S. command, reporting to Major General William Garrison of the Joint Special Operations Command, who reported to CENTCOM directly. Their orders were to capture Aideed and senior SNA officials whenever the opportunity arose. Montgomery was to be informed but had no authority over the operations. In effect, the Rangers and Delta Force became a posse with standing authority to go after Aideed and his outlaw band.[21]

Over the summer there were drastic changes in Somalia. UNOSOM activities were almost entirely directed at the military struggle with the

---

Battled Itself," *Washington Post*, December 6, 1993.) In conversation with USLO political officers and UNITAF representatives during early 1993, Hersi Morgan had made similar threats. There is no doubt that the militia leaders had studied not only Operation Desert Storm but Vietnam and Lebanon to understand the domestic political impact of American casualties.

[20]A ten-person U.S. interagency assessment led by Ambassador David Shinn reviewed the overall situation in Somalia from July 20 to 27. The team concluded that UNITAF and UNOSOM II had made great progress "in restoring Somalia to the community of nations." The grim humanitarian problems had been largely resolved, banditry reduced, and "with the important exception of south Mogadishu, organized militia attacks have ended." However, the team report observed, "it should come as no surprise that such a complicated and previously untried Chapter VII operation like Somalia should encounter numerous obstacles and difficulties." Among those identified were that "problems in south Mogadishu are having an impact on UNOSOM's ability to do its job throughout the country." Disarmament and establishing a police and judicial system were top-priority recommendations, and the secretary-general promised $6 million for the purpose, but there was virtually no UN action on the ground.

"Pacification of south Mogadishu" was another urgent priority for the team, which found that UNOSOM had no real plan for political reconciliation other than bringing about Aideed's demise. It suggested that the U.S. pursue the idea of getting Aideed into house arrest in a third country, followed by an independent investigation. There was no positive response from the U.S. administration or the UN to this proposal, and the suggestion of more determined military effort to neutralize Aideed was the one followed. An unclassified, sanitized version of the report, shared with major troop contributor governments and the UN, was made available to the authors.

[21]For a fuller account, see Patrick J. Sloyan, "How the Warlord Outwitted Clinton's Spooks," *Washington Post*, April 3, 1994. Sloyan reports that Joint Chiefs chairman Colin Powell dropped his objections: "We have to do something or we are going to be nibbled to death." He also reports Hoar's reservations. The State Department was strongly in favor of the use of greater force against Aideed.

SNA, and humanitarian operations were significantly reduced. International and Somali support for UNOSOM diminished greatly, and tensions among Somali clans and factions increased. The UNOSOM confrontation with the SNA became almost an obsession, bolstered by Aideed's skillful manipulation of media attention. As he evaded capture, and his organization survived repeated attacks, the media focused on Aideed's self-portrait as SNA David versus UN-U.S. Goliath. Fewer and fewer patrols took to the streets; a new road, primarily for military traffic, was built from the airport and port to bypass south Mogadishu en route to the interior. Most expatriate NGO personnel evacuated to Nairobi, as did the UNOSOM humanitarian coordinator. OFDA officials estimated that relief activities in Mogadishu were reduced by as much as two-thirds, in the interior perhaps by half. The NGOs and the media were inclined to hold UN and U.S. policy responsible for the return to violence and the growing neglect of humanitarian activities, which UNOSOM had been created to protect and assist.[22]

Although there was little armed conflict between them, there was an acute polarization of the Hawiye clan and of the fifteen political-military factions. The SNA had become more militant, more disciplined, and better organized from necessity; almost all the important Habr Gidr, including tribal elders, rallied around it. As the casualties in their south Mogadishu population base mounted into the thousands, the Habr Gidr began to fear that their subclans were being targeted for physical as well as political elimination. Hundreds of them, as well as some from sympathetic Ogadeni subclans, moved from central Somalia to reinforce the SNA militia.[23] Aideed began to take on an almost mythological stature, even among Somalis who did not care for or support him, through his appeal to powerful traditional and nationalist identifications. The SNA mounted a skillful propaganda campaign to enhance this image.[24]

On the other side of town, Ali Mahdi and other Hawiye leaders assembled a large coalition of political factions that came to be called the Group of Twelve (G-12). It was not as solid as it sometimes appeared, nor was Ali Mahdi its uncontested leader, but it served as a rallying point for

---

[22]There was little realization that UNOSOM was trying to carry out with some 18,000 troops a much wider mandate than UNITAF had with almost twice that number or that the fighting with the SNA had caused so many UN casualties in Mogadishu.

[23]According to Ethiopian and Somali sources. This phenomenon was underestimated and not well appreciated by the UN or U.S. at the time.

[24]For a fairly typical SNA communiqué, see the SNA press release of August 3, 1993.

anti-SNA forces, throwing its support behind the United Nations as the best bet for defeating its political enemy Aideed. However, outside of a few pro-UN demonstrations, the G-12 did little to build an alternative political organization, preferring to stake its future on outside intervention.

Outside Mogadishu, there was a surprising absence of organized violence between clans or factional militias. Even in the sensitive Galcaio region, the Aideed-negotiated "peace agreement" among the SNA, the SSDF, and the SNF held firm. In Kismayo, clan elders negotiated an agreement that kept clashes from breaking out between the forces of archrivals Morgan and Jess. Drawing inferences from the localized agreements, and realizing that political progress at the national level was still out of the question, UNOSOM decided to shift to the bottom-up approach. Starting late in July, Howe and his staff began to work hard to facilitate the establishment of the district and regional councils agreed to in the Addis Ababa Accords. The councils remained subject to their share of controversy—although Aideed had signed the accords, the SNA was generally hostile to the councils because it was not in a position to control them politically. The G-12, for the most part, supported the UNOSOM effort, though its leaders also had some concerns about the implications of strong local leadership and independent councils.

EVOLUTION IN U.S. POLICY

As casualties continued to mount over the summer, members of the U.S. Congress became more and more uneasy about the aggressive military path taken by UNOSOM II. Reports that the famine crisis had ended added to their reluctance to keep U.S. forces on the ground.[25] By mid-August both the political and the military concerns were felt acutely by General Hoar at CENTCOM as well—he suggested an end to the ongoing military approach, and did not endorse Howe's request for the Rangers and Delta Force. Joint Chiefs chairman Powell had also expressed reservations over the aggressive pursuit of the SNA, though he eventually, albeit somewhat reluctantly, approved the decision to dispatch the 400-man Task Force Ranger after an SNA mine caused more casualties. The chairman had recommended to Defense Secretary Les Aspin that a

---

[25]On August 10, as U.S. forces continued to fight in the streets of Mogadishu, UN ambassador Albright said they would "stay as long as needed to lift the country and its people from the category of a failed state into that of an emerging democracy."

full-scale review of Somalia policy was urgently needed, and Aspin was considering how to proceed. However, the events of August 22 and the prospect of continued attacks on U.S. forces convinced Powell to approve Task Force Ranger as a stopgap measure to end SNA attacks.

In a major policy speech on August 27, Aspin called for a narrower, more realistic approach to what might be achieved in Somalia, implying a more limited nationbuilding mission. He called for additional efforts to set up a local police force and urged the United Nations to develop a detailed plan pulling together its economic, political, and security activities into an overall strategy. Most important, he called for the United Nations and the OAU to "act now to bring the parties back on the peace track."[26] It was during this period that Aspin disapproved Montgomery's request for tanks and armored personnel carriers, reportedly concerned that U.S. forces were already too deeply involved in offensive military action and wanting to avoid still deeper involvement.[27] Still, despite the reservations at CENTCOM and the Pentagon, the policy and the orders to the Rangers and Delta Force remained unchanged.

There was increasing criticism from the media, NGOs, and even anti-Aideed Somalis of the mounting Somali death toll and the use of helicopter gunships against targets in heavily populated areas of south Mogadishu. A series of incidents between September 5 and 15 resulted in hundreds of Somalis killed and wounded as well as dozens more Nigerian, Pakistani, and Italian UNOSOM casualties. The Rangers and Delta Force undertook a series of raids and began to arrest scores of Somalis, including not only some senior SNA officials but also many uninvolved Somalis and even some foreign relief workers.[28]

---

[26]Remarks at the Center for Strategic and International Studies, Washington, D.C., August 27, 1993.

[27]Montgomery's request, as he explained to the Senate Armed Services Committee in a hearing on May 12, 1994, was prompted by the changed UNOSOM II mission, brought on by confrontation with the SNA, mandated by Resolution 837, and supported by both Boutros-Ghali and the Clinton administration. Montgomery concluded that in view of the ongoing low-intensity conflict and danger to U.S. forces in Mogadishu, he needed more than a dozen tanks and other armored vehicles to protect U.S. forces stationed in the city. The request was not to strengthen the attack capability of the QRF. Montgomery told the committee that for the original mission as he and Bir conceived it, "the forces that were provided at the outset in March pursuant to Resolution 814 were adequate for the mission that was envisaged." However, at that time, he said, no one foresaw open combat with the SNA.

[28]Those arrested by mistake were mostly released, although sometimes this took weeks. Those believed to be SNA members were held.

As the ante rose and the American public became increasingly uneasy, Clinton was beginning to consider a change of policy. On September 13, after the signing of the Israel-PLO agreement, he and former president Jimmy Carter discussed Somalia at length. Earlier in the month, Carter told Clinton, he had received a letter from Aideed in which the SNA leader portrayed himself and his SNA followers as under attack in an unjust war. Aideed had appealed to Carter to "prevent an impending disaster" and reiterated his willingness to accept the findings of a commission of inquiry into responsibility for the June 5 attack. In his discussion with Clinton, Carter urged an end to the United Nations' military option, and recommended fresh efforts to find a political solution. Carter also spoke with Secretary of State Christopher and came away convinced that Clinton shared his view and would put a prompt end to the use of U.S. force against the SNA.[29]

In the meantime UNOSOM, supported by the Security Council and the Secretariat, continued to pursue Aideed. On September 14, in a press briefing at UN headquarters, Admiral Howe painted a positive picture of UNOSOM's tactics and achievements, particularly outside Mogadishu. He stoutly defended the use of force against "perpetrators of crimes against the United Nations . . . beginning with the June 5 attack by the SNA," and said that it was "hard to avoid civilian casualties" and "very difficult to estimate what the casualty numbers are on the other side." On September 22, the Security Council unanimously adopted Resolution 865, reaffirming previous resolutions on Somalia, commending UNOSOM II for its activities, and setting a target of March 1995 for national elections. By omitting any suggestion of a change in the policy of pursuing Aideed, the Security Council effectively endorsed its continuation. The resolution had sixteen operative paragraphs, of which twelve referred to the secretary-general and specific goals he and UNOSOM were to undertake in Somalia, notably political reconciliation and "nationbuilding." Although it also called on the Somali people to show "the political will to achieve reconciliation, peace and security," the resolution clearly treated them as secondary players in finding solutions to their country's problems.

Responding to growing concern over the reliance on military muscle to deal with Aideed and the SNA, the United States decided to convey to Boutros-Ghali its view that the United Nations should shift to a more

---

[29]See Sidney Blumenthal, "Why Are We in Somalia?" *The New Yorker,* October 25, 1993, for an account of the Carter-Clinton discussion.

political approach. During the week of September 20, a "non-paper"—an informal memorandum—explaining this view in detail was prepared; it was personally presented to the secretary-general by Secretary Christopher. According to press and other reports, Boutros-Ghali was entirely unpersuaded.[30] He reportedly told Christopher that the policy in force, stemming from Resolution 837, should continue. Boutros-Ghali provided a strongly worded rebuttal to the American memorandum, warning the United States against withdrawing its forces and affirming that the United Nations had no choice but to pursue Aideed militarily. When Aideed's militia shot down a U.S. Army helicopter on September 25, killing three soldiers, Congress adopted a nonbinding resolution calling on President Clinton to seek its approval by November 15 for keeping U.S. forces in Somalia. In a September 27 speech to the UN General Assembly, Clinton alluded obliquely to concerns over events in Somalia but suggested no change of course.

The issue finally came to a head October 3, when U.S. Rangers launched another attempt to find the elusive general. In a surprise helicopter raid on the Olympia Hotel in central Mogadishu, the Rangers captured twenty-four SNA suspects, including several of Aideed's key aides.

As the Rangers were evacuating the SNA prisoners, however, SNA militia, using rifle grenades and automatic weapons, shot down two U.S. helicopters. In the subsequent rescue effort, the Rangers and Delta Force found themselves pinned down in a huge firefight; QRF and other UNOSOM forces headed to the scene to try to get the trapped soldiers out. As the battle continued, more SNA and volunteer Somali fighters joined the fighting. When it ended, 18 U.S. soldiers had been killed and 78 more wounded, with Somali casualties estimated between 500 and 1,000 killed and wounded in what had become one of the costliest battles of any UN peacekeeping operation. The capture of Chief Warrant Officer Michael Durant dominated headlines, and the degrading treatment of a U.S. soldier's body, dragged through the streets of Mogadishu, shown repeatedly on American televisions, fueled public outrage and revulsion.[31]

---

[30]*Washington Post*, September 30, 1993; *New York Times*, November 1, 1993.

[31]For detailed accounts of the battle and surrounding events, see the two-part series by Rick Atkinson in the *Washington Post*, January 30–31, 1994, and "How the Warlord Outwitted Clinton's Spooks" by Patrick J. Sloyan, in the *Washington Post* on April 3, 1994. For an account of the events' effect on the policy discussion in the administration, see "Mission in Somalia," a four-part series by Sloyan in *Newsday*, December 5–8, 1993, and "Somali War Casualties May Be 10,000," *New York Times*, December 8, 1993.

The bloody clash sent shock waves through the United States, arousing anger and incredulity that at the same time the country was asking the United Nations to back off from confrontation, its own forces, under direct U.S. operational control, were actively engaging in military attacks.[32] For ten days, once-remote Somalia electrified Washington. Though Clinton resisted calls from many members of Congress for an immediate withdrawal of U.S. forces, he recognized a major crisis of confidence in Somalia policy. On October 5, he sent National Security Advisor Anthony Lake, Secretary of State Christopher, and Secretary of Defense Aspin to meet with congressional leaders on Capitol Hill to discuss Somalia policy. According to press accounts, the meeting was a disaster, making the administration appear confused and directionless. Even its supporters called for urgent presidential action to get matters under control.

On October 6, Clinton convened an urgent policy review with the vice president, key cabinet members, and senior civilian and military staff. Former special representative Oakley was invited to join the review, which concluded with agreement on a new policy approach, a set of implementing proposals, and selection of a date for the withdrawal of U.S. forces. Clinton personally ordered the acting chairman of the Joint Chiefs of Staff, Admiral Dave Jeremiah, and General Hoar to stop any further action by U.S. forces against Aideed, the SNA, or other Somalis except in self-defense. That evening UN ambassador Albright and Hoar communicated the president's decision to an extremely unhappy Boutros-Ghali. On October 7, Clinton publicly announced a major change in course, strongly defending overall U.S. policy but acknowledging that it had been a mistake for U.S. forces to be drawn into a UN decision "to personalize the conflict" in response to Aideed. He outlined plans for a new policy and its implementation, first in a two-hour meeting with congressional leadership and later in a televised address to the American people. The simultaneous reappointment of Oakley as special envoy was intended to

---

[32]President Clinton professed to be surprised and shocked by the battle and its aftermath. In a May 12, 1994, discussion with family members of Rangers killed in the incident, he is described as having been "dismayed on October 3 that the raid was launched after he had decided that there should be a diplomatic solution." See Michael R. Gordon, "U.S. Officers Were Divided on Somali Raid," *New York Times*, May 13, 1994. However, despite repeated concerns expressed to the White House by Congress and the military, and despite Clinton's apparent reservations, there was no revocation of the Rangers' orders.

signal the administration's intent to focus U.S. policy once again on political reconciliation—involving all Somali factions.[33]

In his address Clinton argued that with the humanitarian crisis under control, the political aspects of the Somali problem outweighed the military. But he emphasized the prudence of keeping U.S. forces there until March 31, 1994, with reinforcements for enhanced protection, in order to give the United Nations, and Somalia, "a reasonable chance" and to show that the United States "will have lived up to the responsibilities of American leadership in the world . . . addressing the new problems of a new era." Clinton was deeply concerned that, with a precipitous departure of U.S. forces, "[our] leadership in global affairs would be undermined at the very time when people are looking to America to help promote peace and freedom in the post-Cold War world."[34]

On October 13, the president submitted to Congress, at its request, a detailed report on U.S. policy in Somalia, explaining that "the U.S. military mission is to assist in providing a secure environment to enable the free flow of humanitarian relief. . . . The U.S. military mission is supportive of but more limited than the overall UN mission." The report provided precise numbers of U.S. forces involved in the operation, and assured the Congress that "all U.S. troops are under U.S. command. The logistical troops are assigned to the UN Force Command for operational control only."

Clinton described the "recently modified U.S. policy in Somalia" as incorporating three decisions. First, there would be "additional troops and equipment" sent in primarily to protect U.S. forces already there, though Clinton did not "[rule] out any military options." Second, regional African leaders would be encouraged to work with the Somalis for a lasting political solution. Third, the United States would withdraw its forces no later than March 31, 1994, in the meantime assisting the United Nations "in deploying additional forces from other nations."[35]

---

[33]The subsequent decision to replace Gosende as head of USLO with Ambassador Richard Bogosian was made for similar symbolic reasons, aimed at the Somali people generally and the SNA in particular. Gosende had become identified with the policy of pursuing Aideed, and removing him clearly signaled the change in policy.

[34]"Remarks by President Clinton on the Situation in Somalia," October 7, 1993. The speech does not explicitly acknowledge U.S. approval of previous policy toward Aideed, nor does it acknowledge that U.S. forces were at all times under U.S., not UN, command.

[35]"Report to the Congress on U.S. Policy in Somalia," October 13, 1993.

THE NEW DIPLOMATIC MISSION TO SOMALIA

When Oakley returned to Mogadishu on October 9, his primary objectives were to obtain the release of American helicopter pilot Michael Durant and Nigerian soldier Umar Shantali, to consolidate the cease-fire, and to attempt to get a new political process under way. In earlier telephone conversations with Under Secretaries-General Kofi Annan and James Jonah, Oakley had explained the nature of his mission and the importance of the realigned U.S. policy, not only for the survival of UNOSOM but for sustaining long-term U.S. support for UN peacekeeping.

In Mogadishu, Oakley met first with Howe, and then with Bir and Montgomery, to explain the shift in policy and its implications and to confer with them on how best to proceed. The UNOSOM leaders were understandably upset at both the heavy U.S. casualties of October 3 and the sudden U.S. decision to abandon the use of military force in pursuing Aideed and the SNA. U.S. military commanders shared the feeling of being let down by the sudden reversal of course after so much military effort had been expended in following the policy directives received from CENTCOM and the Pentagon. They were dubious that the SNA was sincere about maintaining its unilateral cease-fire, and that Aideed could be trusted to play by the rules. Howe noted that his proposals to the SNA for a political dialogue and an official cease-fire had met with no response. He was also unhappy that the secretary-general had not informed him of the U.S. policy change—instead he had found out from Oakley.[36]

Oakley also met with Somali political leaders from various Mogadishu factions, including second-echelon figures associated with Aideed and Ali Mahdi. He avoided meeting the two main rivals in order to downplay their personal importance and to emphasize the need for less rivalry and violence on all sides. To Ali Mahdi's associates, Oakley explained that the United States recognized the importance of the G-12 alliance as a political entity, and urged them to pursue an inclusive political process as a better means of achieving their objectives and helping Somalia. He made

---

[36]Both Major General Garrison, commanding Task Force Ranger, and Major General Montgomery had received orders from Hoar to stand down and no longer pursue the SNA. This led to a common decision among UN forces in Mogadishu to avoid confrontations with the SNA and strengthen the de facto cease-fire. It meant that most patrolling stopped and several checkpoints in SNA neighborhoods were abandoned. Subsequently, while Oakley was still there, Under Secretary-General Annan arrived and provided Howe with the view from New York. Annan, Oakley, and Howe were able to start discussions on how best to implement the abrupt change in policy brought about by Clinton's decision. Annan was extremely helpful in this situation.

it clear that since they could no longer rely on others to eliminate the competition, the G-12 must stop acting as onlookers and engage more fully in the effort to pull together all sensible Somalis.

In a meeting with SNA representatives, Oakley and Zinni (who had returned to Somalia with him) recalled the UNITAF period of mutually beneficial dialogue. They stressed the importance of Clinton's decision to depersonalize Somalia policy and explained that while it meant no more U.S. manhunts, Aideed should not think he could openly engage in political activity. They then discussed the need for the unconditional release of the American and Nigerian prisoners held by the SNA. Oakley's point regarding the prisoners was brief and direct: The United States had learned the hard way about hostage situations and had a very firm policy; it would not agree to any trade or precondition for release. Any attempt to haggle over the matter might lead to an armed rescue attempt by the soon-to-be-strengthened U.S. forces. If such an action met with armed opposition from the SNA, much of south Mogadishu could expect to suffer badly.

Releasing the two men right away, however, and reinforcing the cease-fire would help restore goodwill for the SNA. After a great deal of reflection, and fierce internal debate within his faction—particularly with the angry relatives of the SNA prisoners held by UNOSOM—Aideed agreed to release Durant and Shantali on October 14, while Oakley was still there, adding that the SNA would continue to respect its unilateral cease-fire.[37] The news was communicated to Oakley by the SNA delegation at a second meeting that day, and shortly thereafter Aideed came out of hiding long enough to make a brief appearance on CNN and announce the release to the world.

Aideed's decision to release the prisoners without any quid pro quo was exceedingly difficult. Thousands of casualties in south Mogadishu in the summer and fall had been among his followers and kinsmen, and

---

[37]The meeting took place at the Conoco compound, where Oakley had had his office from December 1992 to March 1993, on the same street as Aideed's headquarters and other SNA installations. Given the continued deep-seated SNA fears of being attacked or arrested, there was no other means of gaining their confidence. Security was provided by the SNA. Oakley and Zinni felt very much at ease, although UNOSOM and USLO security officers were very nervous.

Representative John Murtha (D-PA), chairman of the House Appropriations Subcommittee on Defense, also visited Mogadishu on October 14, where he explained forcefully to Howe, other UNOSOM leaders, and the U.S. military commanders the importance of supporting the new policy direction. Murtha looked carefully into the question of whether there was solid justification for March 31 as the date for the withdrawal of U.S. forces.

feelings were running very high. The families of the killed and wounded, and those of the Somalis still in prison, saw absolutely no reason to be considerate of the United States or its citizens.

Oakley's mission was also to drum up the regional support needed in light of UN reservations about the U.S. policy changes. On October 17, he stopped in Addis Ababa to consult with President Meles Zenawi. Ethiopia and Eritrea had been designated to represent the OAU in mediating Somali political reconciliation, the "African solution to African problems" that Clinton hoped to encourage. Both countries had experienced diplomats in Mogadishu, with whom Oakley had worked during his earlier mission to Somalia. They had credibility with most of the Somali leaders, who were impressed by the degree of political reconciliation achieved in Ethiopia after years of repression and civil war and were watching how civil institutions were being rapidly created or rebuilt.

After his October 18 return to Washington, Oakley privately briefed key congressional leaders, who welcomed the steps being taken to implement the new policy. During the same week, Secretary of Defense Aspin and Under Secretary of State Peter Tarnoff testified on Somalia before various committees. As Representative Lee Hamilton (D-IN) later described it, the debate over Somalia was the most controversial foreign policy issue faced by the administration in 1993. Senator Robert C. Byrd (D-WV), who had originally demanded a pullout of all U.S. forces by December 1, ended up as author of a consensus bill transforming the president's October 7 statement of policy into law, and providing that U.S. forces would remain in Somalia through March. After March 31 no money could be spent to support U.S. military operations in Somalia, except for the small force protecting U.S. civilians. The peak of the president's political crisis over Somalia had passed.[38] The substance of the new policy had been endorsed by Congress, though developments on the ground were being watched very closely.

---

[38]At the October 6 leadership meeting and subsequently, several senior congressional leaders on foreign policy and military matters opposed setting a specific withdrawal date. However, they recognized that anti-Somali feelings were running so high that had Clinton not fought for his March date, Congress would almost certainly have adopted the Byrd date. This would have been disastrous for Somalia, the UN, and for U.S. foreign policy. It would also have put U.S. decision-making on peacekeeping use of U.S. forces into the hands of Congress rather than the executive branch, a development the administration, like its Republican predecessors, had fought hard against on several occasions. The rapid pullout Byrd demanded would almost certainly have caused the other troop contributors to follow suit rather than agree to stay, as they did once the situation had calmed.

IMPLEMENTING THE NEW POLICY

The administration proceeded to implement the new policy, first by urging the United Nations to create an independent commission to investigate the events of June 5 and their context, an idea that now had wide support. Until the commission's investigation was complete, the arrest order for Aideed would be suspended. Second, the arrival of additional U.S. forces, including AC-130 gunships, a light infantry battalion, an armored battalion task force, and two Marine Expeditionary Units, was accelerated. Additional military forces had begun to arrive and completed their deployment in mid-November. They would provide additional protection against any attack and would also "keep the pressure on those who cut off relief supplies and [attack] our personnel." Third, the United States urged the United Nations to hold its planned humanitarian conference on Somalia as soon as possible, to reinforce the incentive of financial and other assistance for reconstruction in stable areas, and to allow for informal political discussions by Somalis in attendance. Clinton raised the matter personally with OAU chairman President Hosni Mubarak of Egypt and obtained his support.[39]

After considerable negotiation, the Security Council on November 16 adopted Resolution 885, which established an international commission and suspended the call for Aideed's arrest. In effect the Security Council agreement endorsed the Clinton policy and accepted that the exclusion of the SNA from political negotiations and the use of force against it were no longer viable options.[40] The three-man commission of inquiry arrived in Somalia in mid-December and promptly issued a statement recommending the release of all remaining prisoners.[41]

---

[39]To enhance the administration's ability to implement the new policy quickly, National Security Advisor Anthony Lake approved a new coordinating structure for Somalia, cochaired by Richard Clarke of the NSC and James Dobbins, the new Somalia coordinator at the State Department. They reported to the NSC Deputies Committee. There were daily and weekly interagency meetings and frequent visits to the United Nations for discussion with senior Secretariat officials. Oakley joined this team for discussions with senior UN officials before and after each of his visits to the region.

[40]Resolution 885 authorized "the establishment of a Commission of Inquiry . . . to investigate armed attacks on UNOSOM II personnel." The Commission was announced on November 24. The Honorable Matthew Ngulube, chief justice of Zambia, served as chairman, with Lieutenant General (retired) Emmanuel Erskine of Ghana, former force commander of the UN Peacekeeping Force in Lebanon, and Lieutenant General Gustav Hagglund, chief of the Finnish Defense Staff. The executive director was Winston Tubman of the UN Legal Office. Its report was submitted to the secretary-general in late February 1994 and published in *International Documents Review*, May 23–27, 1994.

[41]More than 700 Somalis had been arrested by UNOSOM and U.S. forces between June 6 and October 7, often without grounds other than suspicion of SNA sympathy. By October 7 only about

Supplementing these actions was the U.S. decision to press vigorously for an accelerated program to organize regional Somali police forces, pledging some $25 million in surplus U.S. military equipment, plus $2 million for salaries and $8 million for a long-term interagency training team. With the departure of U.S. and other Western peacekeeping forces, a working Somali police force would be all the more essential.[42]

In addition, the United States began to help the United Nations, in New York and Mogadishu, to plan for the departure of U.S. forces. This included asking other governments to maintain their forces already in Somalia or to participate for the first time, as well as looking at logistics and other requirements after March 31. The United States also helped UN headquarters and President Meles Zenawi plan for the conference in Addis Ababa, set for the end of November, encouraging other governments to make specific commitments of development assistance and urging the Somali factions to send senior representatives. Four persons were invited from each of the eighteen regions and three from each faction, with an additional twenty Somali development experts invited individually by UNOSOM.

On November 12, the secretary-general reported to the Security Council, noting a number of positive changes in Somalia, especially outside Mogadishu, where agricultural life had returned to near normal, harvests were good, and many schools had reopened.[43] Progress was being made

---

seventy, including three senior SNA members, were still being held. The total gradually diminished to eight by December. The three senior officials—Osman Ato, Mohamed Awali, and Omar Salad Elmi—were held separately on a small island off Kismayo. On several occasions their continued detention came close to provoking renewed attacks. Aideed, the SNA leadership, and the families and friends of those detained protested, saying that the U.S. and Nigerian prisoners had been released on October 14, the cease-fire was being respected, and there was no excuse for the continued detention. This disagreement further exacerbated tense U.S.-SNA relations. When the prisoners fell ill in mid-December, the SNA and Habr Gidr were on the verge of breaking the cease-fire. At the last minute, after a conversation between General Hoar and General Montgomery, the three were moved to a hospital in Baidoa and allowed family visits. Finally, on the advice of the UN legal advisor, Boutros-Ghali ordered the release of the eight remaining prisoners in early January. (Earlier recommendations to free them had been made by the United States, the Security Council, and the independent commission, as well as Howe and Bir.)

[42]The administration thus decided on, and Congress accepted, invoking provisions for the presidential determination of an exception to the legislative prohibitions against official U.S. assistance to foreign police. The same provisions had been used by the Bush administration for Panama and El Salvador, but not for Somalia. Before October 6, the Clinton administration had also been unwilling to provide more support.

[43]As part of the UN effort to accentuate the positive, there was a push by UNOSOM II from August through October to help establish district and regional councils. This help included Howe's trips to the interior, and a visit by Boutros-Ghali to Baidoa that was publicized as an example of how well things were proceeding politically and of the renewal of economic and social life

in establishing the district and regional councils. Boutros-Ghali noted, however, that Somalia remained fragile, greatly dependent on political developments, and still without a functioning government, police force, or judiciary. He discussed the obstructionism of the SNA and outlined three options for the UNOSOM II security role after March 31: a force of more than 30,000, which would carry out coercive disarmament; a medium-sized force of about 19,000, to seek voluntary disarmament; or a minimal force of some 5,000 to protect vital installations. Although any of these forces would have continued to operate under Chapter VII authority, the secretary-general reluctantly recognized that UNOSOM II's mandate and operations would have to be scaled back.[44]

THE SNA CONSOLIDATES ITS POSITION

In Somalia, Aideed and the SNA were exultant over President Clinton's new approach and immediately declared a unilateral cease-fire in response. The SNA moved to capitalize on its image of having withstood the United States and the United Nations by demanding dissolution of all the district and regional councils created with UNOSOM assistance. By doing so, Aideed and his political strategists hoped to reverse the local political gains made by their rivals and to block any attempt by UNOSOM to recognize a TNC that their opponents might dominate. The SNA also refused to cooperate with UNOSOM on security or other issues, at least until all SNA prisoners were released. At the same time, by praising Clinton's decision to change policy and signaling willingness to work bilaterally with the United States, the SNA was acting very much like a government, displaying organizational effectiveness and political acumen.

From the SNA's perspective, the district and regional councils were a serious institutional obstacle to Aideed's long-term ambitions. It argued that under the Addis Ababa Accords, UNOSOM had no right to interfere or be involved in any way in creating local government structures. The SNA's real objection was that few of the councils were under its control.

---

away from the violence and obstructionism caused by the SNA in Mogadishu. A Somali observer from Baidoa reported that at the time of the visit UNOSOM occupied a well-finished four-story building (the Summer Palace), with dozens of vehicles and lots of office equipment, while the much-touted regional and district councils were in partially ruined buildings without any vehicles, equipment, or furnishings, which began to arrive later. Boutros-Ghali also made a November airport stop at Mogadishu, apparently to show that the UN would not be scared off by Aideed.

[44]Report of the Secretary-General, S/26738, November 12, 1993.

(Council control had been a major issue for the SNA ever since a Rahanwein-dominated council sprang up in Baidoa during January and the SNA-appointed governor was ousted by popular pressure.) Even while the SNA was fighting off military pressure in south Mogadishu during September and October, it had been organizing local groups to contest council leadership in Brava, Merca, and Qorioley, south of Mogadishu, and in Baidoa. (This opposition often involved armed intimidation as well as political action. Indeed, most Somali factions, and certainly the SNA, saw no distinction.)

THE FACTIONS LOOK TO THE FUTURE

By mid-November, the SNA's opponents, spurred on perhaps by a spirit of self-preservation and unhappy that they could no longer count on the United States and the United Nations to marginalize the SNA, had organized to fight back. Though the G-12 alliance was having serious internecine difficulties, it presented a cohesive external image. There was a lot of talk about the G-12's putting an end to the SNA by its own military means, and various G-12 factions were importing new weapons. In regions removed from SNA power, such as the lower Juba area and the center and northeast (Galcaio and Bossasso), local leadership had already taken advantage of the SNA's problems to organize and consolidate political control. General Morgan's Somali National Front had become the dominant force in Kismayo and parts of the lower Juba. In the center and northeast, a coalition led by the SSDF's Mohamed Abshir and Abdullahi Yusuf (a sometime ally of both Aideed and Morgan) seemed to have gained a strong political position. The political understanding reached during the May talks in Mogadishu held, allowing the local representatives of the SNA, SNF, and the SSDF to cooperate peacefully and maintain security in the region despite clashes between the groups elsewhere.

Oakley had made a second trip to Mogadishu, Addis Ababa, and Asmara in late October, anticipating that the Security Council would soon adopt the proposed resolution on an independent investigation, Aideed's status, and the SNA prisoners, thus enhancing the possibility for forward movement and political reconciliation. When this adoption was delayed, Oakley's talks with the SNA delegation became very difficult. Without movement on the issues of Aideed and the prisoners, the SNA representatives were under orders to take an unyielding line, against the better judgment of some of them, even on such issues as SNA participation in the humanitarian conference, the resurrection of the Mogadishu police force, and the creation of a joint security committee for Mogadishu. Some put about the lightly veiled threat that "undisciplined and angry" elements might undertake violent action against the United Nations or the United States. Oakley focused his arguments on the need for continued SNA restraint and promised to take up the prisoner issue directly with President Clinton.[45] In discussions with the UNOSOM II leadership, and with commanders of the national military forces making up UNOSOM II, Oakley found them willing to play a more active role in opening and patrolling major roads leading from Mogadishu's port and airport to the interior, provided the U.S. forces were ready to participate actively. Unfortunately the greatly reinforced U.S. units did not implement the directive for this sort of proactive operation, remaining instead in their bases. As other UNOSOM units followed this example, U.S. leadership suffered a serious blow.[46]

By Oakley's third visit, in mid-November, the situation was somewhat clearer. The Security Council had adopted Resolution 885, which eased tensions within the SNA and the danger of attacks on U.S. or UN personnel. Plans for reopening main roads and reoccupying key checkpoints had been quietly dropped to reduce the risk of more American casualties and the consequent domestic political reaction. Some of the G-12 leaders were beginning to think more of waging a political struggle than of going to war with the SNA.

Oakley saw Aideed, who was eager for the meeting and had arranged for it to take place at his temporary headquarters, providing an SNA security escort for Oakley and his party, who proceeded without U.S. military protection. There was in-depth discussion of cooperation with the United Nations on security, revival of the police force, plans for the humanitarian conference, and long-term prospects for political reconciliation. Aideed made a great point of his regained affection for the United States, though he continued to criticize the United Nations severely.[47] Oakley reminded Aideed that all of Somalia needed the United Nations,

---

[45]He did so, and the president agreed that the Somali prisoners should be released after due consultation with and approval of the UN secretary-general and key Security Council members.

[46]After reconsidering the probability of casualties to U.S. forces, absent an agreement with the SNA, the administration quietly signaled U.S. commanders in the field not to take any unnecessary risks.

[47]En route back to the UNOSOM compound, Oakley's party drove through the weekly rally of thousands of SNA supporters—all of whom were suddenly cheering the United States.

explained that the new resolution meant a new UN policy that accepted the SNA, and urged him to meet and cooperate with UNOSOM even if he still did not wish to meet with Howe. Though Aideed was not persuaded, neither did he appear committed to a military effort to take over the country.

Thus the stage was set for another round of the contest over political power, even as the particulars of the institutional political design agreed on at Addis Ababa were called into question. There were too many variables to form a clear idea of what might transpire between November and the end of March 1994, much less after U.S. forces departed. Would there be a peacekeeping force at all after the end of UNOSOM's mandate in May 1994? If so, what would its mandate be? Would there be a return to clan and faction war, or would the struggle be primarily within peaceful political channels? Would the SNA decide to launch major military operations to achieve Aideed's ambitions, and if so could it succeed? Would there be a strong enough coalition of other factions and clans to deter any such SNA effort, at least once it moved away from the SNA's south Mogadishu power base? The November 1993 humanitarian conference in Addis Ababa was intended to engage some of these questions, but no one expected to find easy answers for Somalia.

HUMANITARIAN CONFERENCE LOOKS TO THE FUTURE

The fourth humanitarian conference, which opened in Addis Ababa November 29, was a tribute to the persistence of UN under secretary-general Eliasson, who had overcome resistance within the Secretariat to the date, venue, and agenda.[48] He chaired the meeting, encouraging a fundamental change in the international community's approach toward Somalia. President Meles Zenawi stated flatly that the Somali leaders had one last chance to save their county from devastation and death; they could choose to come together for a political settlement or continue to fight over possible future power. If they continued to fight, Somalia would be abandoned by its neighbors and the international community, and the eventual victor might find he had inherited nothing but disaster.

---

[48]During late October and November there was a behind-the-scenes struggle at the UN between those who favored a more prominent role for Ethiopia and Eritrea and those who felt this would favor Aideed and the SNA as well as reducing the potential influence of Egypt, which held the OAU chair and had long had a special interest in Somalia and the Horn.

U.S. delegation head Richard McCall of USAID set the tone for the other donors by saying that while they had been willing to run great risks to save hundreds of thousands of Somalis from starvation and disease, the time for rebuilding Somalia had come. "Before we move into this critical next stage, the United States will need to receive tangible assurances that the Somalis are ready to make much greater efforts to work together and with the international community." The United States had set aside $100 million for development assistance to Somalia in 1993–94, but only for regions that could provide reasonable security for donor personnel and that had working civil institutions to ensure the success of an aid program. These regions would receive help and not be held back by other, less stable regions.

This view was reflected in the statements of other donors and incorporated in the final declaration of the conference. The donors' judgments were reinforced by the March 31 deadline for withdrawal of U.S. and other peacekeeping forces, forcing Somalis to face their future. The combination of tangible international support for reconstruction, offered on the basis of local responsibility, and evident international determination to leave Somalia to its own devices if necessary, had a pronounced impact on the Somalis present.

These tough realities were not lost on those faction leaders—most notably Aideed, Ali Mahdi, Omar Hadji Mohamed (Somali National Front) and Aden Gabyou (Somali Patriotic Movement)—who were reluctant to come to Addis Ababa for political discussions. Many important leaders were already there, including General Morgan, SSDF leaders Mohammed Abshir and Abdullahi Yusuf, and USC leader Mohamed Kanyare Afrah. The chance that a deal might emerge from the political discussion taking place among this group, and with representatives from Ethiopia, the United Nations, the United States, Italy, and the European Community, was another factor motivating the holdouts to reconsider, because of the threat that a deal might be cut without their participation. By December 1 they had all responded positively to Meles's urging that they come to Addis Ababa.

As the conference proceeded, the United States and the United Nations sent aircraft to pick up the latecomers. Aideed's distrust of the United Nations and serious fears for his personal safety—as well as his eagerness to be again in the international spotlight—were such that he would travel only on a U.S. aircraft, creating a fleeting controversy in the United States, and angering Egypt and some of his Somali rivals who interpreted the arrangement as a U.S. endorsement of Aideed's political ambitions rather than as logistical assistance for facilitating political dialogue.[49]

The impasse in political discussions reflected the continuing power struggle among the faction leaders. But it had the benefit of having them all understand the position of the international community. There was much jockeying for position between the G-12 and Aideed's SNA. Aideed refused to talk with an eight-man negotiating group designated by the G-12, and Ali Mahdi was unwilling to meet Aideed. Both sides eventually changed their minds and agreed to talks between groups of eight representatives each. Thanks primarily to the efforts of Abdullahi Yusuf, a ten-point communiqué was hammered out by the two sides, though it was ultimately rejected. The basic issue in dispute was the composition of the TNC, which the SNA wanted altered to regain ground lost in the creation of the district and regional councils.[50] Ali Mahdi and his fellow Abgal representatives returned to Mogadishu, pressing unsuccessfully for immediate creation of a TNC without the SNA. Aideed stayed in Addis Ababa for more informal political talks, later moving to Nairobi. The Addis Ababa meeting had served its purpose in jumpstarting political dialogue between Somali rivals. This dialogue also improved the attitudes of major troop-contributing countries and Security Council members,

---

[49]Oakley took the initiative to arrange transportation for Aideed, sending Colonel Pete Dotto, who had been a liaison with the SNA during UNITAF and so was trusted, to accompany him on the flight. Even then, Aideed was extremely reluctant to expose himself, fearing assassination and showing the effects of four months as a hunted man. Although not informed in advance of the use of a U.S. aircraft, Clinton responded to criticism by saying that he supported Oakley's decision. Responding to a query from the State Department, Oakley compared the abrupt change in treatment accorded Aideed to the abrupt change in policy toward PLO chairman Yasir Arafat. In the pursuit of peace, Oakley argued, it is sometimes necessary to come to terms with those previously considered enemies.

Despite the implication by Michael Kelly in "It All Codepends" (*The New Yorker*, October 3, 1994) that former president Jimmy Carter played an important role in Aideed's decision to maintain the cease-fire and go to Addis Ababa for talks with other faction leaders, Aideed never referred to Carter in discussions with the U.S., UN, and African officials who were urging him to go. The only references to Carter in talks with Oakley and other U.S. officials during the period between October 1993 and February 1994 were in connection with the UN investigating commission.

[50]During the course of numerous discussions with Somali leaders, Howe, Kouyate, and Oakley heard Aideed say he would not insist on the dissolution or even the modification of all councils, acknowledging that some of them had been selected without UN interference and were genuinely representative. However, an expanded TNC seemed essential. UNOSOM acknowledged that a few of the councils were not fully representative and should probably have their membership revised; it agreed to refrain from pressing so hard for the creation of more councils in controversial areas. Some of the G-12 were ready for an expanded TNC and also had doubts about certain of the existing councils. Thus the formula on councils agreed on at Addis Ababa in March 1993, the implementation of which had became a key element of UNOSOM strategy, was no longer regarded as inevitable. The change was a welcome initial sign of political realism and flexibility.

particularly since there were no major clashes in Mogadishu or else-where, and the focus remained on politics.

On January 6, 1994, the secretary-general provided another update to the Security Council, in which he recommended scaling back UNOSOM's mission, focusing on the need to encourage cooperation between the Somali factions, and reinforcing the objectives of the humanitarian con-ference to provide assistance only to the stable areas.[51] At that time he also highlighted the SNA's culpability for blocking political progress and noted its opposition to the United Nations and preference for the Inter-governmental Authority on Drought and Development (IGADD), an orga-nization of East African states, as mediators. He also noted the positive attitude of the G-12 toward political reconciliation and the United Nations. Fifty-three of eighty-one district councils and eight of thirteen regional councils had been created with the help of UNOSOM. The report rejected the SNA criticism of alleged UN interference in the selection process, noting that the G-12 was "fully satisfied" and suggesting the early nomination of the TNC.

At the same time, the secretary-general adopted a new theme: "The main focus of UNOSOM II's activities in the period ahead will be on promoting Somali initiatives." Regarding the use of UN military force, the secretary-general concluded that his preferred option, continuing UNOSOM II's mandate for coercive action if necessary, would not be feasible given the response of troop contributors. Therefore he recommended "voluntary disarmament," with the emphasis on forces "to protect ports, convoys and refugees." Success for UNOSOM II in these circumstances would depend on the "cooperation of the Somali parties."

The Clinton administration continued to work in parallel with the secretary-general in urging major troop contributors to retain their forces as part of a reoriented UNOSOM II, even after U.S. forces withdrew on March 31. For some countries, such as Egypt and Pakistan, the provision of additional equipment such as armored personnel carriers was key to their agreeing to stay. As the situation evolved, these two major contrib-utors, the Italian 4,000-man force, Malaysia, and Zimbabwe decided to remain, thus providing for a respectable force.

This evolution in approach was reinforced when top UNOSOM II mil-itary commanders Bir and Montgomery were replaced by Malaysian gen-eral Aboo Samah Bin-Aboo Bakar and Zimbabwean general Michael

---

[51]See the Report of the Secretary-General, S/1994/12.

Nayumbua. Howe was recalled to New York early for consultations preparatory to final departure, and his deputy, Ambassador Lansana Kouyate, who enjoyed a better rapport with the Somalis, was named acting special representative on February 3.

At the same time, the imam of the Herab, traditionally the most powerful and respected moral authority of the Hawiye clan, undertook a major initiative. Seeing that the greatest single obstacle to hopes for peace came from intra-Hawiye feuds, the imam called an all-Hawiye conference, deliberately excluding both Aideed and Ali Mahdi but including elders of their Abgal and Habr Gidr subclans. The conference unanimously recommended an early rapprochement of the competing factions and enjoined the political leaders to get on with reconciliation. Although the injunction was in no way binding, it exerted the pressure of moral authority on the faction leaders.[52]

The international community also sought to keep up the pressure and show its readiness to support the new approach. A February donors meeting in Nairobi fine-tuned the Addis Ababa action plan by establishing a separate Somali Aid Coordinating Body (SACB), with the UN Development Program responsible for its secretariat. The role of UNOSOM II was deliberately downgraded, reflecting the concern of donor governments and NGOs that it had undertaken too intrusive a role. U.S. representative McCall took the lead, together with the European Union representative, in clarifying how the donors would work in providing assistance for reconstruction. The UNDP was designated as the lead agency with a continued watching brief by SACB representatives in Mogadishu and Nairobi.

Oakley's fifth round of consultations with Somali political leaders, UNOSOM officials, and regional heads of state also sought to encourage early movement to a transitional government and to avoid new confrontations. He learned that the Somalis were indeed pursuing informal talks on reaching a political compromise. Aideed had recognized the United Nations' change of leadership in Somalia and indicated his renewed readiness to cooperate with UNOSOM.[53] Oakley urged him to

---

[52]During the February talks, Oakley heard Aideed and Ali Mahdi each claim that the other was really the inspiration for the imam's action. Even in Somali politics where the gun is so powerful, it does not overpower public opinion. There was clearly a growing desire for early reconciliation.

[53]At a February 16 meeting in Nairobi, Aideed gave Oakley a categorical guarantee that the SNA would take no action to jeopardize the safe withdrawal of U.S. forces and said he would

meet with Kouyate to review the political situation and to cooperate with UNOSOM on security issues, including police, liaison between the militias and military forces, and protecting NGOs. Oakley also encouraged the SNA to participate in the rehabilitation program. Within two weeks, Aideed had incorporated these recommendations into his own agenda, even meeting relatively harmoniously with Kouyate.

The regional leaders, Kouyate, and Oakley agreed that outside parties should use their influence to urge the Somali factions to move more quickly with their own informal negotiations. Oakley reiterated the need to reverse the trend of rising, though largely spontaneous, violence before most of the NGOs and other donors gave up on Somalia. Egypt, however, still held that circumstances favored Aideed unjustly and that a conference or some other external political action was needed to redress the balance.

Over the next month frenetic jockeying for position continued among the Somali factions. Aideed moved between Nairobi, Kampala, Addis Ababa, and Asmara, meeting Somali leaders (except for leading G-12 representatives), regional representatives, and Kouyate and giving the impression of being virtually a chief of state. Members of the G-12 went to Cairo for talks and moral support, in an effort to counter Aideed, at the same time maintaining close contact with Kouyate in Mogadishu. The March 7 "Cairo Communiqué" of the G-12 called for a new Transitional National Salvation Council (TNSC) which would adopt legislation, form and supervise the provisional government, and establish public institutions within three months.[54]

On March 10, Aideed broadcast a major radio address in Mogadishu, stressing his qualifications for national leadership and calling for "an all-inclusive, broad-based government of national unity." He praised "the world" for having "agreed to change the mistaken policies pursued by UNOSOM" and cited Security Council Resolutions 865 and 897 as evidence of new international approval. He called for cooperation with the international community, including UNOSOM's military and civilian

---

send written orders to his organization in Mogadishu. The SNA leaders there confirmed to Oakley that they had received and would carry out the orders. Periodic intelligence reports of planned SNA attacks proved incorrect; there was no organized violence against the departing forces, despite several incidents that the SNA itself found provocative and that resulted in the deaths of Somali civilians.

[54]Cairo Communiqué on Consultations among the Somali G-12 Political Organizations, Cairo, March 1-7, 1994. Although explicitly making a place for Aideed on the new TNSC, these provisions would have reduced his and the SNA's influence to minimal proportions and foreclosed the possibility of his playing a role in the provisional government.

components and NGOs, "who agree with us that the Somali people have the exclusive right to solve the future of their country."

On the ground, U.S. forces were accelerating their withdrawal with Marines from the amphibious force coming ashore to provide protection as the last remaining army units pulled out. The Pakistani contingent was reinforced with U.S.-supplied M-60 tanks and Cobra helicopter gunships so it could create a new QRF for UNOSOM. In response to continued intelligence reports predicting impending attacks on U.S. forces, careful security precautions were taken and troops were evacuated by sea rather than by air.

As Aideed had promised, there was no organized SNA interference or violence directed at U.S. forces. However, banditry, looting, and some spontaneous violence were on the rise in Mogadishu and the interior. NGO compounds were looted in Baidoa, Belet Weyne, and elsewhere. The Italian embassy in Mogadishu was attacked by a large band of armed looters. Outside Kismayo, there were small-scale clashes between Jess's SNM and Morgan's SNF. The intelligence community saw this as the beginning of the full-scale civil war they kept predicting when U.S. forces withdrew, but unrest remained at modest levels.

Instead, by March 14, key Somali leaders, including Aideed and Ali Mahdi, gathered in Nairobi for direct talks mediated by Kouyate. On March 24, after intermittent signs that the talks would collapse, Aideed and Ali Mahdi, on behalf of their allies, signed a joint statement recommitting to a cease-fire and the formation of an interim government. A preliminary meeting in Mogadishu established procedures and criteria for a planned national reconciliation conference that would elect a president, vice president, and prime minister; complete and review the formation of local authorities where needed "as a basis for regional autonomy"; and establish an independent judiciary. The agreement was difficult to achieve and due almost entirely to the patience, persistence, and persuasiveness of Kouyate, though it was evident at the time that there were many unresolved political undercurrents and a long way to go before the faction leaders would be ready for a serious reconciliation.

On March 25, the last U.S. forces were withdrawn and the Marines returned to their ships offshore. The Marine amphibious force stayed off the coast in case violence ashore became great enough to warrant the evacuation of the roughly 1,000 American civilians and military personnel remaining in Somalia. The largest remaining UNOSOM II military contingent as of March 31 was Pakistan's, followed by those of India, Egypt, Zimbabwe, Morocco, Malaysia, and Botswana.

For the United States, fifteen months of unprecedented military support for a humanitarian operation was coming to an end. Public, congressional, Somali, and international reactions to the American role had gone from the highest praise to the fiercest criticism. The initial phase, Operation Restore Hope, had stopped the mass death and clan war with very few casualties, though the later confrontation with Aideed had proven very costly, with thirty Americans killed and 175 wounded. A powerful, sometimes angry political debate had wrestled with the proper American role in UN peacekeeping. Under heavy congressional pressure, the Clinton administration had modified its earlier policy on the issue, falling back substantially from its admittedly overambitious vision of assertive multilateralism and rebuilding failed states. Congress set additional limits on U.S. participation in UN peacekeeping, cutting requested funds and legislating restrictions on the use of U.S. armed forces.

For the United Nations, the experience had been equally difficult, with hard lessons about the realities of peace enforcement and the use of Chapter VII, the difficulties of command and control, and the limitations of UN involvement in the internal affairs of other nations. Sixty-eight UN peacekeepers had died, and 262 were wounded between May 4, 1993, and March 25, 1994. Yet the experience was not over. Some 20,000 UNOSOM forces remained, with a new, limited mandate accepted by all Somali leaders. The opportunity to restore stability in cooperation with the Somalis was still there. The UN political strategy was for Kouyate to keep working to persuade the parties to stop their jockeying for position and convene the conference agreed to in March. Although he had excellent relations with all of them and worked hard, the priority for most factions remained one of strengthening their hands by seeking alliances or realigning internal factional politics. Militarily, UNOSOM II continued the "hunkering down" it had inherited from the combined U.S.–UNOSOM II force.[55] There were several UN casualties, notably Indian forces in isolated incidents outside Kismayo and five Nepalese killed when they got into the middle of a fight between two factions in Mogadishu.

---

[55]Curiously, as UNOSOM II drew more and more into a self-protective shell, with fewer military or civilian personnel venturing out of their compounds, the number of civilian personnel and the amount of equipment, especially vehicles and prefabricated housing, continued to increase. By October 1, the civilian total was 799, an all-time high. By that date, the UNOSOM military had all been moved to Mogadishu, Kismayo, and Baidoa. There were hundreds of housing structures and thousands of vehicles for the civilian side, located mostly in Mogadishu.

UNOSOM WINDS DOWN

The future of Somalia itself remained uncertain as its people waited to see whether the fragile peace could sustain their survival and even nurture a more prosperous future. Prospects of establishing national and regional institutions intermittently brightened and dimmed as faction leaders continued to maneuver for political position, with sporadic flare-ups of low-level violence. The patience and support of Somalia's international supporters and donors stretched thin, as they watched to see what would happen next.

During this period, the preparatory meeting was repeatedly postponed, while interclan tensions and factional rivalries caused sporadic minor conflicts, mostly in Mogadishu but also in Merca, Kismayo, and other locations.[56] Aideed was among those who wanted to postpone the national conference until regional agreements could be reached and his own faction strengthened. The G-12 was more eager to meet. A serious regional undertaking to stop fighting and create a degree of stability in Kismayo and the lower Juba was eventually concluded in early June with Osman Ato, Hersi Morgan, Abdullahi Yusuf, and a number of clan elders leading the way. All significant elements of Somali clan and factional powers except Omar Jess and the Ogadeni were in agreement. The Ogadeni subsequently held their own meeting, removed Jess from leadership, and joined the broader agreement.

Using a combination of politics, alliance building, and military force, the SNA strengthened its position in the northeast and Somaliland, as well as in the area around Belet Weyne and Merca. However, the situation in Mogadishu remained unresolved and became steadily more tense and violent, with heavy fighting near the airport in June between the SNA and the Hawadle subclan and appeals by Ali Mahdi for a war to remove Aideed. By mid-July almost as many technicals were back on the streets as before the arrival of UNITAF, and elements of the SNA had begun to deliberately ambush UN convoys and call for the departure of the United States and UNOSOM. Experienced Aideed watchers concluded that he had reverted to his earlier attitudes and tactics and that these were not minor incidental events.

---

[56]The SNA regained control of Merca by military action in late March and April 1994, upsetting hopes of holding the conference at that time.

At the end of May the UN Security Council expressed its concern over the deteriorating situation, extended the UNOSOM II mandate until September 30, and called for another review at the end of July. This review was undertaken by the UN Secretariat and the secretary-general reported to the Security Council that the dangerous security situation made it impossible for UNOSOM II to carry out its mission.

At the same time the secretary-general decided to drastically reduce UNOSOM forces, the United States closed down USLO, by then staffed by only twenty persons and a protective force of fifty-eight Marines. Throughout the previous year, USLO had provided strong support to UN efforts to promote political reconciliation, managed U.S. civil assistance programs, assisted the international humanitarian effort, and maintained close liaison with NGOs and all American citizens in Somalia. The Departments of State and Defense announced on August 26 that USLO would be closed and all official Americans removed by mid-September, though some USLO personnel would maintain a watching brief from Nairobi.

As the last U.S. forces left Somalia in September, it was clear that UNOSOM was entering a last and dangerous phase. Its overall strength was diminishing as units left without being replaced. The UN Secretariat and the troop contributors were having difficulty agreeing on a precise withdrawal plan, primarily because of uncertainty over how to withdraw without destabilizing whatever tenuous political balance there might be. They were also concerned to avoid possible confrontation, killing, and looting.[57] The continued and increased fighting among Somalis, the growing hostility of some factions toward the United Nations and the United States, and the absence of any movement toward political reconciliation created a situation in which further productive action no longer seemed feasible. Moreover, pinned down by the priority for self-defense, UNOSOM was able to provide less and less protection to the dwindling NGO community. The Somalis had been given every opportunity and assistance to resolve their differences and start rebuilding their country but had instead turned the other way, back toward violent struggle for personal political and factional advantage.

---

[57] Late in July, a Zimbabwean unit of 150, preparing to withdraw from Belet Weyne, were detained by an SNA force of several hundred. The confrontation lasted for a week, during which UNOSOM II headquarters failed to respond to the Zimbabweans' repeated requests for help. At that point, the badly outnumbered, outgunned Zimbabweans decided to surrender and the SNA stole their weapons.

Attacks on peacekeepers intensified. In August and September, two ambushes in Baidoa killed ten Indian peacekeepers in the space of ten days. By the end of September, UNOSOM forces were stationed only in Mogadishu, Baidoa, and Kismayo. UN efforts at political reconciliation had again been frustrated by the unyielding rivalry between Aideed and Ali Mahdi. The secretary-general and the UN Security Council set March 31, 1995, as the final date for withdrawal of UNOSOM forces. A committee of Security Council members, including the United States, visited Somalia and discussed the situation with key Somalis and regional African representatives and concluded that there was no sensible alternative but to withdraw military forces.

Intensive planning for the withdrawal was carried out by the UN Secretariat, UNOSOM, and national contingents. In the United States, the Clinton administration, urged by General Shalikashvili, chairman of the Joint Chiefs of Staff, decided to assist militarily with the withdrawal, thus acknowledging the U.S. role in persuading several governments to remain after it left, and ensuring that its weapons and equipment would be evacuated. Italy and France volunteered to assist the Egyptian, Pakistani, and Bangladeshi units in the final departure. CENTCOM and the Pacific Fleet Marine force were again assigned responsibility for the U.S. mission and on February 8 assumed command of all forces participating in the withdrawal.

Outside Mogadishu, Somalia was relatively calm. Grain harvests were up to 75 or 80 percent of normal, livestock exports were continuing, there was no famine. Fragile, ad hoc regional understandings between clans, subclans, and factions were holding in and around Kismayo, Bardera, Baidoa, Galcaio, and the northeast. Some NGOs were still operating, despite sporadic attacks by bandits. In Mogadishu, the political struggle among major factions was echoed by occasional armed clashes as they appeared to be positioning themselves for combat over the port and airport after foreign forces departed. It was not clear whether this would result in more large-scale civil war, as in 1990–92, or whether popular sentiment for peace would contain the struggle. However, it was clear that despite a massive international effort, the stabilization and reconstruction of Somalia would be a long time in coming.[58]

---

[58]Richburg, Keith, "Somalia Slips Back to Bloodshed," *Washington Post*, September 4, 1994; Secretary-General's Report to the Security Council S/1994/977, August 17, 1994.

Reflections

*P*eacekeeping in Somalia, as anywhere, proved complex and difficult. The first phase, UNOSOM I, was ultimately an inadequate effort launched with only limited support from the Security Council and the Secretariat. Its failure in the face of humanitarian disaster exacerbated widespread international dissatisfaction with the shortcomings of traditional peacekeeping, and prompted the Bush administration to take the initiative in launching Operation Restore Hope.

With surprising rapidity and few casualties, Operation Restore Hope succeeded in allowing humanitarian operations to proceed, bringing famine under control, and ending, at least temporarily, clan conflict. The success of this powerful twenty-four-nation operation had an energizing effect, not least on the new Clinton administration, which was eager to see a more dynamic, effective UN. However, while Operation Restore Hope encouraged growing hopes for a more assertive UN, it also raised unrealistic expectations and increased the already excessive demands on the organization. The Security Council had become so busy that it had little time or capacity to plan and oversee the implementation of a large number of peacekeeping operations involving more personnel, equipment, and more complex political-military problems than in the past.[1] The Secretariat was badly understaffed, underfunded, and poorly organized for effective conduct of peacekeeping operations. The similarities of UNOSOM II to the successful Operation Restore Hope—even though some of them were superficial—obscured some of these inadequacies.

---

[1]The number of resolutions adopted by the Security Council between mid-1992 and mid-1994 was five times the number adopted between 1986 and 1988.

It was therefore not surprising that policy and operational decisions initially made by the Bush administration for UNITAF were expanded for UNOSOM II by the Clinton administration, the Security Council, and the secretary-general. The changes, however, were not clearly thought through in terms of their potential difficulties and prerequisites for success. The UN Security Council and the secretary-general, with U.S. support, began to impose their judgments about what would constitute acceptable political evolution and to set up an intrusive administrative structure supported by military force. When challenged by Aideed and the SNA, the United Nations responded by designating them the enemy, politically and militarily. The outcome was devastating, for Somalis and the peacekeepers, for U.S. foreign policy, and for peacekeeping itself.

When the announcement of the U.S. withdrawal from Somalia came in October 1993, followed by the *Harlan County* episode in Haiti and difficulties in Bosnia and elsewhere, the backlash hit. Reflecting on the Somali situation, UN under secretary-general Kofi Annan observed bleakly: "I don't think the member states have the stomach for this type of operation. It's going to be a very long time before the United Nations as an organization takes on a peace enforcement mission and manages it itself."[2]

Despite this outcome, none of the four phases of Somali peacekeeping can be simply labeled "success" or "failure." In fact, in light of their mixed records, the Somalia operations provide an excellent opportunity for analysis, for assessing what worked and did not, and why.

POLICY AND PLANNING

Where UNOSOM I was a traditional UN peacekeeping operation, both Operation Restore Hope and UNOSOM II were experiments launched at a time of intense thought about how peacekeeping could be enhanced to deal more effectively with the increasing number of internal crises affecting the post-Cold War world.[3] Indeed, the Security Council and the secretary-

---

[2]In Stanley Meisler, "Kofi Annan: The Soft-Spoken Economist Who Runs UN Peacekeeping Forces," *Los Angeles Times*, June 21, 1994.

[3]Thirteen new peacekeeping operations were instituted between 1989 and 1992, the same number as the total instituted between 1945 and 1989. In 1989 there were 8,000 UN peacekeepers; by 1994 there were almost 80,000. However, at the same time that the Security Council authorized more and more peacekeeping operations, there was clear recognition that major improvements were needed if the United Nations was to be successful in carrying them out. This concern for enhancing UN capabilities led to an extraordinary summit meeting of the Security Council on January 31, 1992, which asked Secretary-General Boutros-Ghali to prepare an "analysis

general, with enthusiastic support from the United States, decided perhaps more by accident than design to make Somalia into a sort of laboratory for applying the new theories of UN peacekeeping. The concepts of nationbuilding, the reconstruction of "failed states," and "assertive multilateralism" were all applied in Somalia. The second UN peacekeeping operation there was vastly different from the first, and from UNITAF—more politically intrusive and more willing to use military power to enforce its goals.

But actually applying these concepts to Somalia proved much more difficult than theory would have anticipated. Problems arose in part because the later phases of the Somalia mission encountered the uncertainties and unforeseen complications that attend new ventures of any kind. In part, however, difficulties arose from a lack of clarity and consistency in the policies of both the United States and the United Nations, and from a lack of agreement between them on what the Somalia operation was intended to accomplish and how.

The U.S. role in Somalia went through several phases, some never fully articulated, which culminated in confusion about objectives and policy. There was only limited interest in Somalia before President Bush ordered Operation Provide Relief in August 1992, although the United States had been providing large amounts of food for more than a year. Subsequently there was a great deal of attention from the Bush administration, leading up to the president's December 4 announcement launching Operation Restore Hope.

Between the Operation Restore Hope landings in December 1992 and February 1993, however, little high-level consideration was given to the longer-term issues of peacekeeping in Somalia. The pragmatic Weinberger-Powell doctrine of intervention, designed to achieve limited, specific objectives with the support of overwhelming force if needed, had been well understood by the Bush team. But by mid-January, that team was leaving Washington. The incoming administration was occupied with

---

and recommendations on ways of strengthening . . . the capacity of the United Nations for preventive diplomacy, for peacemaking, and for peacekeeping." The secretary-general's report, "An Agenda for Peace," published in July 1992, addressed these issues, raising, among other things, the possibility of peace enforcement military operations "under the authorization of the Security Council and . . . under the command of the secretary-general." During 1994, however, both the secretary-general and the Clinton administration concluded that a more modest approach was needed. PDD 25, issued in May 1994, reflected the U.S. view. The secretary-general's "Supplement to the Agenda for Peace" (UN Document S/1995/1, January 3, 1995) highlighted "areas where unforeseen, or only partially foreseen, difficulties have arisen."

many issues more important than Somalia, and as the reins of government were handed over to President Clinton, the transition team took only a cursory look at the situation. At that moment things seemed to be proceeding rather well. Starvation had been stopped, and the factional fighting that was its immediate cause controlled, with few casualties on either side. A political process was beginning in Somalia, and public support for Operation Restore Hope was strong domestically and internationally.

While the United Nations had not formally committed itself to accepting the handoff from UNITAF, and the timing was still undecided, no one in Washington foresaw that there would be major problems in the transfer. An NSC-led policy review in mid-February gave priority to the issues paramount at the moment—the selection of a new UN special representative and the extent of continued U.S. involvement in the coming UN-led operation. The administration wanted to see a more active global role for the UN, with greater U.S. support and participation, particularly in peacekeeping and nationbuilding. This approach was naturally applied to Somalia, the first case that presented itself, but its implications for the potential need for greater military force were not really examined. The assumption that the United Nations could manage with what was in the pipeline and that U.S. forces should be brought home as originally planned was not challenged. This acceptance is understandable, given the new administration's relative unfamiliarity with these matters and pressure from the armed services to withdraw, accentuated by the prospect of large cuts in the defense budget and the U.S. absorption of many of the costs for UNITAF.

Boutros-Ghali was eager to nail down U.S. participation in UNOSOM II, and concluded that appointing an American as special representative would do so. The reciprocal benefits seemed sensible to the Clinton administration, which saw a way to show support for the United Nations and to facilitate the transition from U.S. leadership to a UN operation. Placing Americans in UN command positions also seemed a good way to satisfy the need for keeping U.S. combat forces under direct U.S. military command, as the Joint Chiefs and Congress demanded, while coordinating their role with that of other UN forces.

The U.S. view, implied under Bush and stated under Clinton, was that the follow-on UN operation should draw on the UNITAF example. It would have enforcement authority under Chapter VII of the UN Charter, with the mandate, military means, and rules of engagement to use that authority effectively if necessary. The United States would not only support the

United Nations in this new, more "muscular" approach to conflict resolution, but also be prepared for the first time to allow U.S. combat as well as support forces to participate under UN command in certain situations.[4]

At the same time, both Washington and New York gave less attention to the fundamental issues confronting Somalia—the nature, prospects, and timing of reconciliation, what would be needed to rebuild Somalia's institutions, how to disarm and demobilize the militias, the best approach to the faction leaders, and a definition of success and the "endgame."

The United States had hoped that the transition to UNOSOM II would be so imperceptible as not to invite serious challenge by Aideed or the other factions. At one point this seemed possible not only because Somalia was relatively calm but because UNOSOM II's rules of engagement and many of its headquarters staff were holdovers from UNITAF, and because of the large number of forces remaining.[5]

But the transition was far from smooth. Although the United States felt that UNOSOM II was well prepared, its commanders, its main component units, and the UN Secretariat were not so sure. Their uncertainty was easily picked up by the Somalis, who also perceived a falling-off in military power, readiness, and will. The political approach followed by UNITAF, which emphasized dialogue with all and persuasion backed by firmness, was replaced by a more peremptory, intrusive attitude. UNOSOM II quickly reached judgments on the avenues of political reconstruction it considered appropriate for Somalia, backed the factions that supported them, and asserted its readiness to employ coercion if thwarted.

U.S. forces supporting UNOSOM II, including the QRF, were ordered to make the UN mission a success, at the same time keeping U.S. involvement and profile low. Yet there was no plan for providing additional U.S. forces should things go wrong, no worry that the pull-out of the Marines with their tanks and APCs would be seen by Somalis as a serious weakening and make some UNOSOM units nervous about their own safety. The other members of the Security Council and the secretary-general

---

[4]This concept was endorsed for UNOSOM II by the Bush administration, as mentioned in the Cheney-Powell press conference of December 4, 1992. It was reaffirmed by Ambassador Albright's vote for Security Council Resolution 814 and her statement at that time. Several speeches by high-level administration officials also validated the concept. It was included in earlier drafts of PDD 25, which favored the development of at least a standby UN military force, ready for rapid deployment.

[5]Significantly, however, small yet vitally important parts of UNITAF were not replaced, most notably the psychological operations unit which ran the *Rajo* radio station and newspaper, the engineers, the civil affairs unit, and other force multipliers.

seemed to assume that the United States could be counted on to provide increased support in the event of real need, because of the investment it had already made in Somalia. The UN special representative, Admiral Howe, was in constant communication with the secretary-general as well as unofficially with the Clinton administration.[6] Howe apparently saw no signs of serious trouble brewing. Thus the transition was completed, with a much broader and potentially explosive mandate, an uneasy situation on the ground, and no plans for the additional force which might be required to achieve success.

Failures of foresight and planning, and the persistence of unresolved differences between the United States and the United Nations, were nowhere more manifest, nor their consequences more serious, than in the area of disarmament. There is little doubt that most heavy weapons could have been removed from control of the factional militias and organized "bandits" throughout Somalia by UNITAF, probably with minimal combat, had it maintained momentum.[7] Tactical assistance, retraining, and other assistance could have been set up to support the voluntary program of demobilization, disarmament, and reintegration of militias as had been agreed by the Somali factions at Addis Ababa. Such an approach would have laid an excellent foundation, though it would have required a substantial increase in military and financial resources, an indefinite time commitment, an expansion of the original mandate beyond humanitarian aid for south Somalia, and willingness to confront and overcome armed resistance (at least at the local level). Both the Bush and Clinton

---

[6]Several of those interviewed for this book, both civilian and military, observed that Admiral Howe spent as much time on the telephone with officials in the Pentagon and the National Security Council as he did with those in UN headquarters, and that the Clinton administration was in agreement not only with the general thrust of policy guidance communicated to Howe by the United Nations but also with several of the most important actions undertaken by Howe, UNOSOM II force commander Bir, and U.S. forces commander Montgomery. In *On the Edge: The Clinton Presidency* (New York: Simon and Schuster, 1994), Elizabeth Drew mentions two such episodes: the arrest order for Aideed and the July 12 helicopter raid on the senior SNA and Habr Gidr leadership. According to Drew, National Security Advisor Anthony Lake asked Clinton on July 11 for approval for "a sensitive operation that was about to go forward in Somalia . . . the operation was a helicopter raid on Aideed's command center" (p. 274). Drew also reports that on July 2, at a White House lunch for journalists, Clinton had told his guests that Aideed would "continue to cause problems until and unless we arrest him" (p. 243).

[7]Walter Clarke's unpublished "Report to the Commandant of the U.S. Army War College," August 3, 1993, states: "It is hard to escape the conclusion now that the U.S. portion of the Restore Hope operation left a serious law and order situation with which the United Nations still has little capability to deal. One should not necessarily fault the United States for the defects of the United Nations but we should have taken the limitations of the United Nations into account when planning our initial role."

administrations decided against the United States' assuming responsibility for such a policy, which Congress almost certainly would have opposed. The U.S. stance on disarmament was clearly and repeatedly communicated to Boutros-Ghali, the Security Council, and the other UNITAF troop contributors.

During the period when UNITAF might have accepted a disarmament initiative in support of UNOSOM II, the United Nations was not willing to assume the responsibility. (Nor were the resources available for supporting militias during the demobilization phase and then creating jobs or at least the hope of alternative employment.) After the departure of U.S. and other UNITAF forces, the Security Council and the Secretariat failed to develop plans or mobilize the political support and resources required to implement an effective disarmament program.[8] Instead, the issue was left primarily to the field leadership of UNOSOM II without adequate planning or resources. Moreover, the emphasis of Resolution 814 was on coercive disarmament rather than on a more comprehensive and politically viable plan for demobilization and reintegration.

COORDINATION AND EXECUTION

The problems created by lack of clarity, foresight, and consistency at the highest political levels in Washington and New York encouraged, and were compounded by, misjudgments in the coordination, management, and execution of policies on the ground during UNOSOM II. During the previous phase, when policies were clearer, operations proceeded much more smoothly.

The U.S. military and civilian leadership in Somalia under UNITAF benefited from experience gained in earlier interventions in Vietnam and Lebanon. Oakley and Johnston had been involved in both, as had many of the officers under Johnston's command. Zinni had been in Vietnam when the U.S. buildup began in 1965, and watched it slowly bog down and lose steam. Oakley and Johnston had both served in Lebanon, Johnston during the disastrous 1982–83 period, and were determined to avoid the mistakes of those earlier conflicts. In Vietnam, for example, the U.S. effort had inadvertently evolved into virtually running the country. This

---

[8]This was done for some other UN peacekeeping operations—in Angola, for example, where it was ineffectual, and Mozambique, where it was moderately successful. It was a major part of U.S. planning for the Haiti operation in 1994.

progressively alienated and sidelined the South Vietnamese, turning them into onlookers in their own country as the U.S. civilian and military presence grew and its activities increased. When the United States departed, the military and civilian programs and initiatives it had introduced collapsed, greatly facilitating the North Vietnamese takeover.

Oakley and Johnston agreed that this approach would not be repeated in Somalia. The United States and UNITAF would take responsibility neither for administering Somalia nor for prescribing solutions to its profound social, economic, and political problems. UNITAF would seek to stop the civil war and provide security for relief efforts, as well as provide the chance for the Somalis to begin sorting out their own political future, with the prospect of long-term UN help. UNITAF's limited disarmament program had the collateral objective of helping open up the political process. It went hand in hand with political and humanitarian efforts to breathe new life into civil society and move away from a quarter-century of authoritarian rule.

In the Lebanon intervention of the early 1980s, the United States had intended to act as a neutral and friendly agent to bring an end to the fighting between Christians and Muslims in Beirut, as part of the larger effort to broker an Arab-Israeli settlement. When policy changed and U.S. Navy battleships and aircraft carriers were ordered to attack Syrian and Lebanese Muslim targets, the U.S. Marines on shore suddenly found themselves regarded as enemies rather than applauded as peacekeepers. Misunderstanding and mismanagement of the underlying political situation turned the U.S. intervention, in the eyes of virtually the entire Arab world, from neutrality to partisanship in support of Israel and their Maronite allies. The response was not long in coming—despite overwhelming U.S. superiority in weapons and firepower, a suicide mission took the lives of 241 Marines in their barracks near Beirut airport. Pressure from Congress and public opinion caused the Reagan administration to reverse policy and withdraw U.S. forces.

For the U.S. political and military leadership in Somalia, the lesson of Lebanon was loud and clear: "Don't take sides, and proceed carefully"— the traditional axiom of UN peacekeeping. If anything, the message was even more pertinent for Somalia, with its complex clan rivalries, struggles among an assortment of faction leaders, and the great pride and prickly independence of the Somali people. UNITAF, it was agreed, would not "pick a winner," would try hard not to play favorites, and would deemphasize coercion. Instead it planned to maintain a dialogue with all, remaining vigilant and ready to respond if attacked but pushing the factions to turn gradually away from the use of force and toward pursuing more peaceful political paths to power.

The purpose of UNITAF's and USLO's maintaining dialogue with all the faction leaders was not to legitimize them or their actions but to seek nonviolent solutions. A peacekeeping or peace enforcement operation may involve a strong military presence, with authority to use force if necessary, but it has of necessity been a maxim of peacekeeping that every effort must be made not to make enemies, or to be seen as taking sides in an internal confrontation. Even if some immediate military reaction should be necessary—for example, in response to an attack on peacekeepers—it should not lead to long-term hostility with any group.

UNITAF was able to avoid the ally-enemy pitfall, even though there were some occasions when it was obliged to use force. In Bosnia, UNPROFOR has also been guided by this precept, resisting numerous attacks and provocations and withstanding outside pressures that might vitiate the pursuit of its humanitarian mandate and put the United Nations in a position of permanently alienating one side or the other. The UN Transitional Authority in Cambodia (UNTAC) displayed similar wisdom in dealing with the provocations of the Khmer Rouge; it modified its mandate when necessary, to allow a successful completion of its basic mission to carry out elections.

It is debatable whether a slightly prolonged UNITAF presence would have substantially altered the military situation on the ground in summer 1993. What UNOSOM II needed more than temporary backup was the correct strategy and tactics, equipment, numbers of personnel, and special-skill units (e.g., intelligence, engineering, civil affairs, military police, special forces, and psychological operations), plus the proper military doctrine, training of forces, and cohesive command and control. All would have been necessary to protect a mission that had changed without an understanding of the immense consequences of the change or the necessity for substantially increased military forces to carry out a more prescriptive, broader set of policies.

In Somalia, as elsewhere, understanding the local political dynamic was imperative in order to avoid unnecessary pitfalls and maximize both popular and factional support. It was clear to UNITAF, for example, that constant dialogue and close vigilance over a tough adversary such as Aideed were essential, as was maintaining contact with all the faction leaders even after the transfer. It was also evident that nationbuilding could succeed only if it were pursued with a maximum of discussion, persuasion, and patience. Instead, UNOSOM II's awkwardness in pursuing fundamentally acceptable ends exacerbated the Somali perception that the United Nations was behaving as an almost neocolonial power, with the predictable result.

Additionally, to sustain the public interest and international support necessary to complete its task, it was important that UNOSOM clearly articulate and explain its goals. UNITAF commanders at the handoff and at USLO in Mogadishu conveyed this forcefully to the UNOSOM II military and political leadership, as the State and Defense departments had earlier to UN headquarters. However, given the difference in UNOSOM II's overall approach to Somalia, the arguments were not considered persuasive enough to ensure that needed actions were taken. Although the Italians, and also the Belgians and French, expressed differences of view with UNOSOM II from June through September, this was primarily done on the ground and with the Secretariat, and the new policy direction, devised and strongly supported by the United States and the secretary-general, was not challenged in the Security Council.

POLITICAL SUPPORT

The damage caused by the October 3 battle might have been less had the Clinton administration heeded the lessons of Vietnam and Lebanon about the absolute necessity of public and congressional support for any use of U.S. military force. Only a clearly articulated, pragmatic approach to a precisely defined objective, maximizing U.S. military effectiveness and minimizing the likelihood of casualties, would be acceptable. In Lebanon, this lesson had not been applied, and the unhappy result ensured that it was not overlooked again during the Reagan and Bush administrations. This was particularly evident in the Grenada and Panama operations, and also in protecting Persian Gulf shipping and in Operation Desert Storm. Obtaining regional and international participation, in part to enhance domestic support, became an essential requirement during the Bush administration, which prepared the way for Operation Restore Hope through consultation with Congress and public statements.

Unfortunately, as the situation on the ground became more complicated, and the missions of UNOSOM II and U.S. forces changed from humanitarian to military ends, the Clinton administration provided little explanation to the public or Congress. Public and congressional confusion increased and skepticism grew. Still there was no serious discussion of how the U.S. military had become the primary force engaged with Aideed's SNA, under whose command these forces were operating, or how long they would remain, despite sharply increased concern. Public information activities of UNOSOM II were of little help, since they took a simplistic anti-Aideed line to justify their operations.

Thus it is unsurprising that the October 3 events generated an immediate political explosion, obliging Clinton to change Somalia policy rapidly and precipitating a general loss of support for peacekeeping.[9] Soon afterwards, Congress defeated several requests for additional peacekeeping funds, and there was increased reluctance for the United Nations to act in Bosnia. The draft administration policy paper on peacekeeping (later PDD 25) was revised to include many more caveats on U.S. approval, financing, or participation in UN peacekeeping operations. The policy change was widely perceived in the international community as a failure of U.S. leadership and reluctance to engage in the resolution of world problems, as well as an indication that the Clinton administration would not stand up to a challenge, even though other countries were making a similar turnabout on peacekeeping.

The United States remained ready to use airpower under NATO command to support the United Nations in Bosnia, but participation of U.S. ground forces was categorically ruled out in the absence of a prior peace agreement, despite the worsening situation on the ground and appeals by the United Nations for more forces.[10] For a long period, the fear of U.S. casualties in peacekeeping inhibited administration thinking about how to oust the military regime in Haiti as some Republicans insisted that returning Jean-Bertrand Aristide to power was not worth the life of a single

---

[9]Events in Lebanon in 1982–83 had followed a very similar course, in good part because there was little or no appreciation by the administration of the dangers of lack of consultation with Congress and little public explanation to prepare for the possibility of casualties and to explore why the price might be acceptable.

[10]This substantially reduced the influence of the Clinton administration when it argued for a much more muscular military response to Bosnian Serb provocations, and for lifting the embargo on arms for the Bosnian army. The French and British stated flatly that they would withdraw their ground forces if U.S. policies on the use of NATO airpower and lifting the arms embargo were generally adopted, as their forces would be placed in excessive danger. UN special representative for Bosnia Yasushi Akashi remarked that U.S. reluctance reflected the Somalia syndrome. This clear implication that the United States had lost its nerve was sharply challenged by UN ambassador Albright, but Akashi had only stated publicly what most UN members were thinking. *The Economist* reported that it was being said at the United Nations that U.S. policy toward peacekeeping could best be characterized as "not one soldier, not one cent."

American soldier, and a number of Democrats seemed to agree. This, in turn, reinforced the Cédras regime's conviction, bolstered by the retreat of the *Harlan County*, that a firm stand would fend off U.S. military action. Later, when genocide swept Rwanda, both Congress and the administration were initially reluctant even to support, much less participate in, a UN peacekeeping operation.

When massacres began in Rwanda in April 1994, the United States and the rest of the Security Council decided to scale down UNMIR, the UN Mission in Rwanda, to around 250 peacekeepers, and resisted appeals from Boutros-Ghali to reinforce the mission until May, when the Security Council voted approval of a primarily African force of 5,500 troops. Even then, the United States was very reluctant to provide logistical and equipment support, much as it had been in Somalia early on. The UN plan for intervention was modified at the behest of the United States in late May to provide for establishing several safe havens inside Rwanda. This could have saved hundreds of thousands of lives but it was never implemented, in part because neither the United States nor any other major power gave it political, logistical, or financial support.

When the genocide caused a flood of refugees into terrible conditions, and increased TV coverage began to sensitize American public and congressional opinion on Rwanda, the administration responded with $500 million in relief support for the UNHCR and other relief organizations and another all-out commitment of U.S. military logistics and humanitarian capacity. From July 31 until September 1, some 300 U.S. Air Force and charter flights of supplies and equipment were flown in by the United States. U.S. forces were cautiously deployed to Uganda, eastern Zaire, and Rwanda for this purpose, though policy kept them from participating in or working directly with UNMIR. As soon as possible, key functions were handed over to civilians. By October 1, all U.S. forces had been withdrawn; appropriations were requested, and granted, to pay for these operations.[11]

In the wake of Somalia, NATO military establishments formed a consensus that the United Nations was incapable of directing a sizable military

---

[11] In an interview with administration officials published in the *Washington Post* on October 3, 1994, Thomas W. Lippman wrote that they admitted that differences between the United States and other UN Security Council members delayed deployment of a UN peacekeeping mission, and that they had spent countless hours wrangling over peripheral issues. Lippman argues that Rwanda was the first test of how the United States would respond to a war-induced humanitarian disaster after the ill-fated 1992–93 deployment to Somalia. Unfortunately for Rwanda, officials said, it did not meet the new, tougher test of importance to U.S. interests that the Clinton administration had set down following Somalia.

operation, especially where there might be combat. In Bosnia, this attitude aggravated relations between UNPROFOR and NATO to the point that Boutros-Ghali suggested in a July 25 report to the Security Council that the time might be coming for UN forces to withdraw, leaving peacekeeping operations entirely to NATO forces which advocated a more aggressive use of airpower to protect UN-established enclaves and to enforce weapons-free zones. The precedent set by the United States in organizing and commanding multilateral forces for the Gulf War and Somalia, with Security Council approval, was echoed by the French deployment to Rwanda in June 1994 and U.S. deployment to Haiti in October.[12]

LESSONS FROM SOMALIA FOR THE FUTURE OF PEACEKEEPING

Whatever lessons may be learned from the Somalia experience, it is important to recognize that the mission was by no means an unmitigated disaster. Recent negative publicity asserting that peacekeeping operations and the combined use of force, humanitarian relief, and political involvement in Somalia have been a huge failure is wide of the mark. We do not contend that Operation Restore Hope was a total success, a cure for Somalia's woes, or a model for future peacekeeping. However, it achieved an important humanitarian objective, showed that coordination of critical elements can be achieved, and produced a positive result. UNOSOM II carried forward much of the good work done in the humanitarian area, and in its second, cooperative phase had by spring 1994 restored some of the political momentum that had existed a year earlier. However, this was dissipated by the later resurgence of violence as Somali factions struggled for political advantage.[13] One can only hope that at some time in the future, the clan leaders, or new, more sober political leaders, will chart a different course of true reconciliation. The great majority of Somalis neither wish for nor deserve the fate which factional rivalry and violence has bequeathed them.

---

[12]Oakley and Johnston conceived the idea of "subcontracting," which has since become an accepted term of reference for peacekeeping operations authorized by the United Nations but carried out under the overall direction of a member state rather than from the UN Secretariat. For further discussion, see Giandomenico Picco, "The UN and the Use of Force," *Foreign Affairs*, September/October 1994, and "Weaknesses in the UN Secretariat," p. 163.

[13]This caused the Security Council to decide to terminate UNOSOM II no later than March 31, 1995—one year after the termination date for U.S. forces in Somalia.

Peace Enforcement

Once a crisis has gone beyond preventive diplomacy or small-scale conventional peacekeeping, the distinction between peacekeeping and peace enforcement cannot easily be maintained. As events evolved in Somalia, the theoretically clear distinction between peacekeeping under Chapter VI of the UN Charter and peace enforcement under Chapter VII became very badly blurred. In effect, UNITAF commanders and forces operated with a Chapter VI approach in some parts of the country, Chapter VII in others, changing in some sectors over time in response to the local political situation. (Similar situations, it may be noted, have occurred in Cambodia and Bosnia, underscoring the need to take the possibility of such shifts into account when defining mandates, rules of engagement, and force needs for future peacekeeping operations.)

The initial success of UNITAF accelerated UN rethinking regarding its traditional practices regarding sovereignty issues and seeking local permission to intervene. Faced with a country where there were no local authorities, the United Nations decided to embark on its first experiment in forceful humanitarian intervention, UNOSOM II. The events of summer 1993 have cast too great a shadow on the whole concept of Chapter VII enforcement. It would be wrong to conclude that such efforts cannot succeed under other circumstances, or if managed more carefully. For the moment, however, there is precious little enthusiasm for another venture akin to UNOSOM II.

The Use of Force

At the height of UNITAF's apparent success, it became clear that a severely minimalist approach to the use of force was far more likely to hamper a peacekeeping operation, inviting challenge by appearing weak, rather than inspiring cooperation by demonstrating both strength and peaceful intent. There was growing recognition that in many situations the United Nations must be perceived as having military capability, the will to use it, and the decisiveness to win armed confrontations, even while working hard to avoid them and remain neutral.

The will and ability to use overwhelming force to back a peacekeeping operation—as the Weinberger-Powell doctrine recommends—offers the greatest possibility of successfully completing a peacekeeping mission and minimizing casualties on all sides. Had a combat-ready force been sent to Haiti, for example, with the *Harlan County,* it is arguable that the hostile mob that met the ship would quickly have faded away[14] as did the hostility of Aideed's militia when confronted with the U.S. Marine Corps during UNITAF. A similar argument can be made that deploying a sufficiently powerful force to protect the Bosnian safe havens when they were established by the Security Council in August 1993, backed with the will to use it, could have persuaded the Serbs not to attack, avoiding the tragedy played out at Gorazde in spring 1994.

At the same time, however, decisions regarding when to use force, how much to use, and how to coordinate it with political considerations are by no means clear-cut, as the disagreements between the United Nations, NATO, and the troop contributors to UNPROFOR amply demonstrate. Where UN political and military commanders were hesitant to call for the use of airpower from fear that it could escalate into major confrontation and jeopardize humanitarian objectives, U.S. and NATO commanders believed that the loss of credibility from unfulfilled threats was more dangerous to the success of the mission. This clash of cultures is fairly typical. A high level of combined political and military experience and close personal relations between military and political commanders on the ground are required to find the correct overall approach.

No less essential to the judicious use of force is advance understanding of the local political situation and how it relates to peacekeeping objectives. Provision must be made for ongoing high-level political consultation and flexibility so that the mandate can be modified if need be, as UNTAC did when it encountered powerful opposition from the Khmer Rouge. UNTAC's decision against direct confrontation stands in marked contrast to UNOSOM II's approach to the SNA, and meant the difference between success and failure in Cambodia.

Weaknesses in the UN Secretariat

Flaws in the complex UN bureaucracy in New York have long been seen as substantially inhibiting the efficiency of peacekeeping operations.[15] There has been improvement over the last two years, in part because of lessons learned from UNITAF and UNOSOM. The offices of three under

---

[14]When the United States did intervene in Haiti in October 1994, it did so with overwhelming force and only after diplomatic preparations by former president Jimmy Carter, General Colin Powell, and Senator Sam Nunn had persuaded the Haitian military rulers not to resist.

[15]Among many studies of this problem, see *The Professionalization of Peacekeeping*, a study group report published by the United States Institute of Peace in 1993.

secretaries-general, which oversee different aspects of peacekeeping operations, continue to have difficulty coordinating, but the transfer of the field operations division of the peacekeeping office and the strengthened role of the military advisor to the secretary-general in working with the under secretary for peacekeeping have been significant improvements. Serious problems of military, operational, and logistics planning and supervision remain, as do problems of communication and authority between the field and the Secretariat.

The Secretariat must be further strengthened to organize, manage, and support peacekeeping and humanitarian operations, and UN missions in the field must be able to coordinate and lead multifaceted civil-military operations. The right combination of command structure, personnel, and logistic support is needed both at UN headquarters and in the field. This means that member states must contribute more funds, people, and equipment as well as cooperating more closely with the United Nations, regional governments, and nongovernmental agencies.

·Presently, budgetary and political constraints imposed by member states continue to make the Secretariat's task very difficult, as UN headquarters must mobilize each peacekeeping operation independently. The huge arrears owed by member states, as well as competition among them for representation on the Secretariat staff, prevent it from developing adequate staff, planning, and logistic capability.

The Secretariat continues to make efforts at improvement, though they move slowly because of inadequate support by member states as well as the cumbersome structure of the UN. For example, the Secretariat has been working to improve its communications with the field and other technical capabilities.[16] It has also been working for more than a year with member states to compile a list of earmarked military units and equipment so that they can be much more rapidly mobilized for future peacekeeping operations. The goal is a modest 100,000 from which a much smaller actual force would be selected.[17] The United States has been reluctant to respond, apparently nervous about a negative political reaction from Congress, and the Joint Chiefs and Department of Defense

---

[16]A requested $10 million U.S. contribution to assist in this process was rejected by Congress after the October 3–4 events in Somalia. Some improvements have been made, however. Round the clock communications with the field are in place for all operations; the military advisor has a staff of over one hundred experienced officers, seconded from member states.

[17]As of November 1, 1994, some twenty-five governments had committed approximately 40,000 personnel.

are opposed to earmarking particular units as peacekeeping units, preferring to select units at the time requirements for a mission become clear.[18]

One way of remedying the deficiencies of UN management of peacekeeping operations is through a form of subcontracting, mounting operations through non-UN multinational groups pursuant to certain types of consultation with the United Nations. The approach may prove particularly well suited for military operations involving large numbers of personnel. Operation Desert Storm was a huge multinational military operation with no direct UN involvement, which could not have been managed except by the U.S. military establishment. Similarly, UNITAF could have been mounted rapidly and successfully only by the United States.

UNITAF's effectiveness arose largely from the U.S. military's organizational and managerial strengths, enabling 28,000 U.S. troops and 10,000 troops from twenty other countries to be deployed very rapidly to one of the remotest locations in the world. Command and control were clearly established from the outset with all U.S. and foreign contingents under General Johnston's overall command. Planning at CENTCOM and Camp Pendleton enabled UNITAF to get off to a fast start, and the Cheney-Powell elaboration of the mission provided precision on its objectives and the support needed to accomplish them. The unique logistic capabilities of U.S. forces, including pre-positioning of equipment in the Indian Ocean, the rapid availability of suitable ships, and quick access to worldwide Air Force and commercial charter transport, enabled UNITAF to overcome the many infrastructure shortcomings in Somalia.

From the outset, however, UNITAF was seen as leading to a follow-on UN peacekeeping operation and requiring coordination with the UN Secretariat. The work UNITAF did to prepare the situation on the ground and the continuation of strong U.S. support enabled UNOSOM II to get off to a good start, notwithstanding the problems of assuming command in such a complex and volatile situation. Only afterward did difficulties develop.

Securing Agreement Among Troop Contributors

The experience of UNOSOM II and other peacekeeping operations shows the need for detailed advance agreement among troop-contributing

---

[18]Nevertheless the United States has earmarked regular units from the 82nd, 101st and other divisions, which have rotated duty for a decade with the U.S.-led multinational observer force in the Sinai.

nations on clear mandates, rules of engagement, and command and control procedures. The widely experienced and highly respected U.S. leadership of UNITAF was able to obtain agreement from all the other national units on these essentials, but it was not easy. A degree of autonomy and flexibility was accorded the forces responsible for each HRS, enabling Johnston and his staff to maintain effective control, even when there were difficulties with the Italians. It also impressed the Somalis, including potential opponents who tested but refrained from seriously challenging UNITAF forces. Admiral Howe and UNOSOM II, however, did not have the benefits of continuous on-site dialogue and support from the five permanent members of the Security Council and other key governments, and the lack of dialogue and support contributed to operational disagreements that might well have been avoided.

The Security Council, the troop contributors, and the UN Secretariat have taken action to begin to remedy this situation. As a direct result of the problems encountered by the troop contributors to UNOSOM II at the height of the Aideed crisis, the Malaysians took the lead early in 1994 in insisting on full consultation in the formulation of UNOSOM II's revised mandate and urged that the practice be extended to other peacekeeping operations.[19] The Secretariat has now established an informal working group of troop contributors, Security Council members, and other interested parties, which meets periodically to develop mandates before they are codified in Security Council resolutions. This is an important step toward ensuring that those who are taking the risks are involved in formulating the terms of reference for their missions.

The Mutual Nature of Multifaceted Operations

The political, military, and humanitarian elements of many peacekeeping operations cannot be logically separated. Peacekeeping operations, certainly under Chapter VII, are essentially political operations carried out by military means. Political preparation and continuing dialogue can reduce casualties and increase the chances of military success. The converse is also true: The leverage of political efforts to broker peace agreements is bolstered by sufficient military strength. In Somalia, for example,

---

[19]See Letter from Malaysian chargé d'affaires to the President of the Security Council, S/1994/120, February 4, 1994.

UNITAF had adequate strength; the second UN Angola Verification Mission (UNAVEM II) did not.

Humanitarian and economic actions complement and reinforce political-military goals if used in concert, but can undermine them if not used properly. Humanitarian relief and rehabilitation; repatriating refugees and displaced persons; rebuilding infrastructure; and helping with such political functions as elections and government institutions—each of these elements may be vital for the success or failure of the overall mission. Each must be carefully measured, and constantly revisited in the context of the local political situation and the willingness of the local political and military forces to accept UN activities in such areas. The capacity of UN forces to carry out their mandates, and the continued willingness of member states to support the operation, must also be clear. This will determine whether the mandate needs to be modified or terminated.

The interrelated issues of disarmament, demobilization, and reintegration of militias and armies are likewise often central to success, as is the creation of reliable, responsible police and security forces. Given their tremendous importance to peacekeeping and long-term stability, an ad hoc approach is inexcusable. Moreover, it is unnecessary, since there is more than a decade of experience developed in dealing with these issues elsewhere. The UN Secretariat and interested member states should identify a core of experienced personnel to work full-time on these issues, with others on call when a new peacekeeping operation is to be established.

The lessons Somalia taught about the importance of close coordination of the political, humanitarian, and security facets of an operation appear to have been put to good effect in the October 1994 U.S.-led intervention in Haiti. According to Defense Department and State Department officials, several critical concepts of the planning for Haiti are similar to those that arose in Somalia: early formation of a neutral police force, assisted by U.S. military police and by U.S. and international police training; coordination of security, political, and humanitarian activities in a Civilian-Military Operations Center (CMOC); widespread use of Special Forces, psychological operations, and civil affairs units; advance coordination with NGOs; and plans for disarmament, starting with heavy weapons and major caches in the cities along with demobilization and retraining. Obviously, planning is one thing, successful implementation in a very difficult politico-military environment another. However, the lessons learned in Somalia have been thoroughly studied. The planned transition from the U.S.-led phase to the UN-led one has been carefully reviewed by both the United States and the UN Secretariat; within a month after U.S. forces landed, future UN headquarters staff had begun working together with U.S. military and civilian officials to prepare for assuming command in a coordinated manner.

The Unique Role of the U.S. Military

Notwithstanding the present widespread erosion of confidence in peacekeeping, it is clear the United States and its military forces will be called upon in the future to participate in a variety of humanitarian peacekeeping operations, contributing the expertise, resources, and capabilities that only the U.S. military possesses at the present. Thus it is encouraging to note that a great deal of practical effort in humanitarian operations is being expended by the U.S. Army, often with NGO participation. The U.S. military has been rapidly expanding the teaching of peacekeeping at the Army's Joint Readiness Training Center in Louisiana and the Combat Maneuver Training Center in Germany. A Peacekeeping Institute has been established at the Army War College, and peacekeeping doctrine, training, and exercise are part of the curriculum for Marine Corps training at Quantico and elsewhere. More needs to be done, but the progress achieved in only a few years has been enormous. Until President Bush's approval of UNITAF and direct U.S. military participation in UNOSOM II, peacekeeping was not explicitly included in U.S. military doctrine, standard training, or contingency planning. Though U.S. military personnel have performed well with only basic training, supplemental peacekeeping training will prove invaluable.[20]

The United States needs to extend and expand training and preparedness programs including multinational cooperation in training and exercises, as well as planning to standardize equipment in certain key

---

[20]The United States military uses the terms "peace operations," "peace support operations," or "operations other than war" to describe the broad range of peacekeeping and humanitarian operations short of war—e.g. the missions in Somalia, Bosnia, and Rwanda as well as more traditional missions such as UNFICYP (Cyprus) and UNIFIL (Lebanon)—and including actions under both Chapters VI and VII of the UN Charter. The new U.S. Army manual draws heavily on experiences in Somalia as well as in Bosnia, Cambodia, and other countries. The United Kingdom uses the term "wider peacekeeping" for the same range of operations except for warlike actions taken under Chapter VII and termed peace enforcement. Its *Army Field Manual* includes a very useful summary and schematic outline placing much more emphasis than the U.S. Army manual on the principle of consent. This has obviously governed British actions and policy in UNPROFOR in Bosnia. Most of the specific ideas and actions contained in the British summary were practiced by UNITAF during Operation Restore Hope, without benefit of a manual, doctrine, or special training.

categories such as communications. It should be possible, for example, to identify some standard, widely used equipment from both NATO and Warsaw Pact inventories and have it stored on behalf of the United Nations. Creating a designated cadre of topflight officers and senior non-coms with demonstrated peacekeeping skills, ready for participation in an operation or for training and exercises with other countries, would be another valuable step. Individual units might be identified and trained specifically for various peacekeeping contingencies. Units for special functions such as psychological operations and civil affairs, special forces, and engineers might be less available, since many are in the reserves. However, these are precisely the units which have proven so valuable in peacekeeping operations, and special efforts are being made to facilitate their call-up.

The usefulness of flexibility, as demonstrated by the ability of U.S. military units and personnel to adapt quickly and effectively, even without special training, is an important but overlooked lesson of UNITAF. Another is the demonstrated capability of the United States to lead and inspire other national units in a coalition peacekeeping force. This leadership is not necessarily dependent on the United States' deploying large numbers of ground combat forces, but it does require commitment of at least a minimal number of officers and men for headquarters positions as well as for various specialty functions such as intelligence, special forces, psychological operations, civil affairs, engineering and logistics, and liaison. There is no mistaking the force-multiplier effect of these special highly skilled units; in a peacekeeping operation they take on even greater importance.

In contrast, a policy of committing no U.S. ground units and almost no other operational personnel for potentially dangerous operations would be an abandonment of U.S. leadership generally and of its valuable peacekeeping role in particular.[21] This would significantly diminish not only the UN's peacekeeping capabilities but also U.S. influence in many parts of the world. Clearly, for example, by refusing to put any U.S. ground forces in Bosnia, the U.S. administration reduced its leverage to urge a more muscular UN and NATO response to the Bosnian Serbs' violations of UN safehavens and convoy routes. The political fallout from this refusal to commit U.S. ground troops may extend well beyond the Balkans, in the process imperiling a number of key U.S. interests.

---

[21]PDD 25 does make an exception if the United States is seen to have a special, direct national interest.

Preventive Diplomacy

The difficulties encountered by the international community in alleviating the crisis in Somalia, as well as in Bosnia and Rwanda, have brought to the fore once again the issue of preventive diplomacy. Clearly there would have been much less suffering, death, and destruction had it been possible to ward off the utter collapse of the Somali state, and the international effort ultimately expended would have been much smaller. Though warning signs of collapse were clearly evident for years before the arrival of UNOSOM I, several opportunities for preventive diplomacy were allowed to pass. Mohamed Sahnoun has identified several such instances—the uprising in Hargeisa in 1988, the appeal of the Manifesto Group in May 1990, and Siad Barre's fall in January 1991—but none were seized before Somalia collapsed into chaos.

More complex, however, is the issue of who could have undertaken the task of prevention when problems arose. Neither the United Nations nor the United States was ready to do so. The UN Secretariat and Security Council were already engaged in more issues than they could handle, still troubled by sovereignty issues and reluctant to engage in internal disputes without a governmental request, and unable to foresee the immensity of the human tragedy. In the United States, presidential elections were coming up, and major changes in the USSR, Eastern Europe, and Germany commanded much attention. The United States saw no strategic reason to take the lead in mobilizing international action for remote Somalia, much less to act unilaterally. No other major power was ready to intervene, and overtures from Italy and Egypt were doomed because of their historical relationships with Somalia. In theory, the OAU or the regional states might have become involved. But Ethiopia was just coming out of its own transition from a decade of Marxist rule and civil war, Eritrea was barely establishing itself as an independent state; and neither Sudan nor Kenya had the requisite influence. The OAU lacked the capacity, will, and focus, as did the Arab League and the Organization of Islamic Countries. None of these regional organizations had given much thought to or undertaken serious efforts at preventive diplomacy.[22]

---

[22]The OAU had been active and occasionally effective in diplomatic initiatives related to interstate disputes during the 1960s, but this role gradually faded as member states opposed any intervention in their internal affairs. The OAU took no serious role in dealing with the building Somali tragedy. Ethiopia, Djibouti, and Uganda undertook limited efforts to resolve the conflict but had very few resources of their own and little outside support.

Effective preventive diplomacy is hardly a matter of happenstance. It requires a delicate mix of timing, negotiating strategies, and the right personalities for effective mediation, as well as encouragement and properly applied pressure and persuasion from outside parties. Improving the ability to identify potential humanitarian crises earlier, as well as devising strategies to minimize their impact, requires developing a cadre of qualified people, in government and international organizations, with the skills and credentials to take on such sensitive tasks. It also requires the early generation of international will to take such low-cost action as mediation and conflict prevention and to engage in crisis management and conflict resolution. Combined political and humanitarian action should be taken from the outset, with the possibility of early sanctions and even the use of appropriate small-scale military support for political action. The United States must be a full partner when it joins peacekeeping operations, prepared to commit a reasonable store of forces of all kinds from the outset, using the policy guidelines in PDD 25 as factors to be carefully considered before making a decision, not as rigid preconditions.[23] A number of policy institutes and NGOs as well as governments are devoting attention to the important issues of early warning and preventive diplomacy. The experience of Somalia can help them come to more realistic conclusions.

THE FUTURE OF PEACEKEEPING

In years to come the United States, the United Nations, and the international community will continue to face tough dilemmas of where to intervene with peacekeeping operations. The most effective approach will be to act sooner, before crises develop to the stage where large expenditures and forces are required.

---

[23]The criteria enumerated in PDD 25 as the basis for U.S. support, financing, or participation in a UN peacekeeping force can be interpreted as preconditions or guidelines. The initially negative U.S. reaction to a proposed UN peacekeeping force for Rwanda was widely seen as due to the operation's not meeting PDD 25 requirements. As international and domestic concern mounted, the United States advised the UN Secretariat on how to improve the plan for the operation and softened its application of PDD 25 so that U.S. approval of the resolution empowering a UN force was possible, as well as the provision of some military equipment. However, no U.S. ground forces were to be allowed to participate. Ultimately, the United States did provide air transport and 2,350 troops to facilitate delivery of relief supplies to camps in Zaire. The revised UN-U.S. plan to establish safe havens along the border, however, was never implemented. See Thomas Lippman, "U.S. Troop Withdrawal Ends Frustrating Mission to Save Rwanda Lives," *Washington Post*, October 3, 1994.

Even if there is an improvement in preventive diplomacy, however, the future will certainly see more peacekeeping operations. There are too many people competing for too few resources in a world where national and international institutions inspire diminishing respect. Ethnicity, religion, clan and tribal differences, and other potentially divisive forces are increasingly becoming sources of identity, means for mobilizing political support, and causes of conflict in a world seen by many as humiliating and hostile. Media pressures exacerbate the potential discontent and instability. In some cases, crises may elicit an international response for strategic reasons, in others for humanitarian reasons. In some cases the world may try to ignore crises. The United Nations and regional organizations will often be involved in efforts at prevention or mitigation, as will NGOs and international organizations, because no one nation will wish to take on the burden alone.

In situations where the international community chooses not to respond through existing channels, individual countries may take the lead as the United States did for Somalia, the Russians for Georgia, and the French for Rwanda. In these cases there can still be UN involvement by means of a Security Council endorsement and by associating separate UN operations with an intervention outside the formal UN framework.

Following the unresponsiveness of member states to the secretary-general's efforts to rapidly mobilize a peacekeeping force for Rwanda, numerous discussions began to address prospects for establishing a standing UN peace force. In theory, it would be able to deploy much more rapidly than is the case with the present ad hoc system. In practice, there would be a number of very difficult issues to resolve before it could be implemented. What would be the relative authorities of the Security Council, the secretary-general, and troop contributing countries? The sources of financial, material, and logistics support? How would command and control issues be resolved? Though the idea bears further examination and exploration, it would be premature to expect it to take shape in the present climate, until member states are persuaded that it is doable and such issues as the Secretariat's managerial capacities are resolved.

Continued movement to strengthen the military support capability of the Secretariat could increase member states' willingness to participate, especially as it made peacekeeping operations more efficient in the field. A larger, more professional military staff and a more influential military advisor to the secretary-general, as well as greater consultation and dialogue with member states and regional organizations regarding training and equipment, would also enhance prospects for improvement.

The United States must face the necessity of being an active international leader, willing to commit financial, humanitarian, military, and political resources to international peacekeeping, whether in a formal UN operation or through some form of subcontracting. This does not necessarily mean a large number of U.S. forces, but U.S. nonparticipation will have a debilitating effect on the reputation and international leadership potential of the U.S. military, as well as on the influence and position of the United States as a respected superpower. The experience of Operation Restore Hope showed that the right combination of the United States' unique military capabilities and a considered political strategy can be effective in humanitarian missions, as Operation Restore Democracy in Haiti seems to indicate. The United States does not have to bear the burden alone, but it must remain engaged.

Appendixes

A. UN Security Council Resolution 794

December 3, 1992

The Security Council,

Reaffirming its resolutions 733 (1992) of 23 January 1992, 746 (1992) of 17 March 1992, 751 (1992) of 24 April 1992, 767 (1992) of 27 July 1992 and 775 (1992) of 28 August 1992,

Recognizing the unique character of the present situation in Somalia and mindful of its deteriorating, complex and extraordinary nature, requiring an immediate and exceptional response,

Determining that the magnitude of the human tragedy caused by the conflict in Somalia, further exacerbated by the obstacles being created to the distribution of humanitarian assistance, constitutes a threat to international peace and security,

Gravely alarmed by the deterioration of the humanitarian situation in Somalia and underlining the urgent need for the quick delivery of humanitarian assistance in the whole country,

Noting the efforts of the League of Arab States, the Organization of African Unity, and in particular the proposal made by its Chairman at the forty-seventh regular session of the General Assembly for the organization of an international conference on Somalia, and the Organization of the Islamic Conference and other regional agencies and arrangements to promote reconciliation and political settlement in Somalia and to address the humanitarian needs of the people of that country,

Commending the ongoing efforts of the United Nations, its specialized agencies and humanitarian organizations and of non-governmental organizations and of States to ensure delivery of humanitarian assistance in Somalia,

Responding to the urgent calls from Somalia for the international community to take measures to ensure the delivery of humanitarian assistance in Somalia,

<u>Expressing grave alarm</u> at continuing reports of widespread violations of international humanitarian law occurring in Somalia, including reports of violence and threats of violence against personnel participating lawfully in impartial humanitarian relief activities; deliberate attacks on noncombatants, relief consignments and vehicles, and medical and relief facilities; and impeding the delivery of food and medical supplies essential for the survival of the civilian population,

<u>Dismayed</u> by the continuation of conditions that impede the delivery of humanitarian supplies to destinations within Somalia, and in particular reports of looting of relief supplies destined for starving people, attacks on aircraft and ships bringing in humanitarian relief supplies, and attacks on the Pakistani UNOSOM contingent in Mogadishu,

<u>Taking note</u> with appreciation of the letters of the Secretary-General of 24 November 1992 (S/24859) and of 29 November 1992 (S/24868),

<u>Sharing</u> the Secretary-General's assessment that the situation in Somalia is intolerable and that it has become necessary to review the basic premises and principles of the United Nations effort in Somalia, and that UNOSOM's existing course would not in present circumstances be an adequate response to the tragedy in Somalia,

<u>Determined</u> to establish as soon as possible the necessary conditions for the delivery of humanitarian assistance wherever needed in Somalia, in conformity with resolutions 751 (1992) and 767 (1992),

<u>Noting</u> the offer by Member States aimed at establishing a secure environment for humanitarian relief operations in Somalia as soon as possible,

<u>Determined further</u> to restore peace, stability and law and order with a view to facilitating the process of a political settlement under the auspices of the United Nations, aimed at national reconciliation in Somalia, and <u>encouraging</u> the Secretary-General and his Special Representative to continue and intensify their work at the national and regional levels to promote these objectives,

<u>Recognizing</u> that the people of Somalia bear ultimate responsibility for national reconciliation and the reconstruction of their own country,

1. <u>Reaffirms</u> its demand that all parties, movements and factions in Somalia immediately cease hostilities, maintain a cease-fire throughout the country, and cooperate with the Special Representative of the

Secretary-General as well as with the military forces to be established pursuant to the authorization given in paragraph 10 below in order to promote the process of relief distribution, reconciliation and political settlement in Somalia;

2. Demands that all parties, movements and factions in Somalia take all measures necessary to facilitate the efforts of the United Nations, its specialized agencies and humanitarian organizations to provide urgent humanitarian assistance to the affected population in Somalia;

3. Also demands that all parties, movements and factions in Somalia take all measures necessary to ensure the safety of United Nations and all other personnel engaged in the delivery of humanitarian assistance, including the military forces to be established pursuant to the authorization given in paragraph 10 below;

4. Further demands that all parties, movements and factions in Somalia immediately cease and desist from all breaches of international humanitarian law including from actions such as those described above;

5. Strongly condemns all violations of international humanitarian law occurring in Somalia, including in particular the deliberate impeding of the delivery of food and medical supplies essential for the survival of the civilian population, and affirms that those who commit or order the commission of such acts will be held individually responsible in respect of such acts;

6. Decides that the operations and the further deployment of the 3,500 personnel of the United Nations Operation in Somalia (UNOSOM) authorized by paragraph 3 of resolution 775 (1992) should proceed at the discretion of the Secretary-General in the light of his assessment of conditions on the ground; and requests him to keep the Council informed and to make such recommendations as may be appropriate for the fulfillment of its mandate where conditions permit;

7. Endorses the recommendation by the Secretary-General in his letter of 29 November 1992 (S/24868) that action under Chapter VII of the Charter of the United Nations should be taken in order to establish a secure environment for humanitarian relief operations in Somalia as soon as possible;

8. <u>Welcomes</u> the offer by a Member State described in the Secretary-General's letter to the Council of 29 November 1992 (S/24868) concerning the establishment of an operation to create such a secure environment;

9. <u>Welcomes also</u> offers by other Member States to participate in that operation;

10. <u>Acting</u> under Chapter VII of the Charter of the United Nations, <u>authorizes</u> the Secretary-General and Member States cooperating to implement the offer referred to in paragraph 8 above to use all necessary means to establish as soon as possible a secure environment for humanitarian relief operations in Somalia;

11. <u>Calls</u> on all Member States which are in a position to do so to provide military forces and to make additional contributions, in cash or in kind, in accordance with paragraph 10 above and <u>requests</u> the Secretary-General to establish a fund through which the contributions, where appropriate, could be channelled to the States or operations concerned;

12. <u>Authorizes</u> the Secretary-General and the Member States concerned to make the necessary arrangements for the unified command and control of the forces involved, which will reflect the offer referred to in paragraph 8 above;

13. <u>Requests</u> the Secretary-General and the Member States acting under paragraph 10 above to establish appropriate mechanisms for coordination between the United Nations and their military forces;

14. <u>Decides</u> to appoint an ad hoc commission composed of members of the Security Council to report to the Council on the implementation of this resolution;

15. <u>Invites</u> the Secretary-General to attach a small UNOSOM liaison staff to the Field Headquarters of the unified command;

16. Acting under Chapters VII and VIII of the Charter, <u>calls upon</u> States, nationally or through regional agencies or arrangements, to use such measures as may be necessary to ensure strict implementation of paragraph 5 of resolution 733 (1992);

17. Requests all States, in particular those in the region, to provide appropriate support for the actions undertaken by States, nationally or through regional agencies or arrangements, pursuant to this and other relevant resolutions;

18. Requests the Secretary-General and, as appropriate, the States concerned to report to the Council on a regular basis, the first such report to be made no later than fifteen days after the adoption of this resolution, on the implementation of this resolution and the attainment of the objective of establishing a secure environment so as to enable the Council to make the necessary decision for a prompt transition to continued peace-keeping operations;

19. Requests the Secretary-General to submit a plan to the Council initially within fifteen days after the adoption of this resolution to ensure that UNOSOM will be able to fulfil its mandate upon the withdrawal of the unified command;

20. Invites the Secretary-General and his Special Representative to continue their efforts to achieve a political settlement in Somalia;

21. Decides to remain actively seized of the matter.

B. Seven Point Agreement Signed by Mohamed Farah Aideed and Ali Mahdi Mohamed

December 11, 1992

1. Immediate and total cessation of hostilities and restoration of unity of the U.S.C.

2. Immediate and total cessation of all negative propaganda.

3. To break the artificial lines in the capital city of Mogadishu.

4. All the forces and their technicals should report to their respective designated locations outside the city within the next 48 hours, and be controlled by the joint committee.

5. The already established reconciliation committee of the U.S.C. should convene their meetings within the next 24 hours.

6. We call upon all Somalis throughout the country to seriously engage on cessation of all hostilities and join with us for peace and unity of Somalia.

7. We express our deep appreciation to the international community for its efforts to assist Somalia and appeal to it to extend and expand its assistance including not only humanitarian relief aid but also reconstruction and rehabilitation as well as a national reconciliation conference.

Source: John Hirsch

C. General Agreement and Supplement Signed in Addis Ababa

January 8, 1993

We, the undersigned Somali political leaders, meeting at the United Nations Economic Commission for Africa in Addis Ababa, Ethiopia, from 4 January 1993 at the Informal Preparatory Meeting on National Reconciliation in Somalia, would like to thank the Secretary-General of the United Nations, H.E. Boutros Boutros-Ghali, who has facilitated this meeting in collaboration with the Organization of African Unity, the League of Arab States, the Organization of the Islamic Conference and the Standing Committee of the Horn of Africa.

We also thank the Government and people of Ethiopia, and H.E. Meles Zenawi, President of the Transitional Government of Ethiopia, for hosting the Meeting and for his personal engagement in assisting our efforts to reach the following agreement.

We, the Somali participants, further express our deep appreciation for the concern of the international community for the humanitarian crisis in our country and recognize their wish for us to reach a peaceful solution to our country's severe problems.

After discussing our problems and considering all options, we have agreed on the following points:

1. The convening of a National Reconciliation Conference in Addis Ababa on 15 March 1993;

2. The declaration of an immediate and binding cease-fire in all parts of the country under the control of the concerned warring factions, subject to paragraph (a) below;

3. The immediate cessation of all hostile propaganda against each other and the creation of an atmosphere conducive to reconciliation and peace;

4. The United Nations Operation in Somalia (UNOSOM), in consultation with the relevant regional and subregional organizations, will be responsible for the logistical preparations of the National Reconciliation Conference;

5. The establishment of further mechanisms for the continuation of free dialogue amongst all political factions and leaders in Somalia in preparation for the National Reconciliation Conference;

6. To continue and enhance our full and unrestrained cooperation with all international organizations working inside and outside Somalia to distribute humanitarian relief to our people;

7. To commit ourselves, without reservation, to facilitating the free movement of Somali people throughout the entire country as a measure of confidence-building before the National Reconciliation Conference.

This agreement shall be valid upon completion and adoption by consensus on the following three points, and a separate communiqué will be issued before leaving Addis Ababa:

a. The establishment of the modalities for implementing the cease-fire amongst all warring parties and the creation of a mechanism for disarmament;

b. The agenda of the National Reconciliation Conference;

c. The criteria for participation in the National Reconciliation Conference.

This agreement, signed in Addis Ababa on 8 January 1993, shall be considered binding on all the undersigned parties henceforth and all signatories shall be obliged to secure the support and implementation of this agreement amongst their movements and followers.

1. Somali Africans Muki Organization (SAMO)
   Mr. Mohamed Ramadan Arbow, Chairman

2. Somali Democratic Alliance (SDA)
   Mr. Mohamed Farah Abdullahi, Chairman

3. Somali Democratic Movement (SDM)
   Abdi Muse Mayo, Chairman
   Col. Mohamed Nur Aliyou, Chairman (SNA)

4. Somali National Democratic Union (SNDU)
   Mr. Ali Ismael Abdi, Chairman

5. Somali National Front (SNF)
   General Omar Hagi Mohamed Hersi, Chairman

6. Somali National Union (SNU)
   Dr. Mohamed Ragis Mohamed, Chairman

7. Somali Patriotic Movement (SPM)
   General Aden Abdillahi Noor, Chairman

8. Somali Patriotic Movement (SPM) (sna)
   Col. Ahmed Omar Jess, Chairman

9. Somali Salvation Democratic Front (SSDF)
   General Mohamed Abshir Musse, Chairman

10. Southern Somali National Movement (SSNM) (sna)
    Col. Abdi Warsame Isaaq, Chairman

11. United Somali Congress (USC) (sna)
    General Mohamed Farah Aidid, Chairman

12. United Somali Congress (USC)
    Mr. Mohamed Qanyare Afrah, Chairman

13. United Somali Front (USF)
    Mr. Abdurahman Dualeh Ali, Chairman

14. United Somali Party (USP)
    Mohamed Abdi Hashi, Chairman

January 8, 1993
Addis Ababa, ETHIOPIA
Africa Hall

**AGREEMENT ON IMPLEMENTING THE CEASE-FIRE AND
ON MODALITIES OF DISARMAMENT**

*(Supplement to the General Agreement signed in Addis Ababa
on 8 January 1993)*

We, the undersigned Somali political leaders, meeting in Addis Ababa, Ethiopia, on 15 January 1993 at the Informal Preparatory Meeting on National Reconciliation in Somalia;

Having agreed on the need for a viable and verifiable cease-fire to promote the peace process in Somalia;

Recognizing that such cease-fire is intricately linked to questions of disarmament;

Further recognizing that disarmament cannot be accomplished in a single event but through a sustained process;

Hereby agree on the following:

I. Disarmament

1.1 All heavy weaponry under the control of political movements shall be handed over to a cease-fire monitoring group for safe-keeping until such time as a legitimate Somali Government can take them over. This process shall commence immediately and be completed in March 1993.

1.2 The militias of all political movements shall be encamped in appropriate areas outside major towns where the encampment will not pose difficulties for peace. The encamped militias shall be disarmed following a process which will commence as soon as possible. This action shall be carried out simultaneously throughout Somalia. The international community will be requested to provide the encamped militias with upkeep.

1.3 The future status of the encamped militia shall be decided at the time of the final political settlement in Somalia. Meanwhile, the international community will be requested to assist in training them for civilian skills in preparation for possible demobilization.

1.4 All other armed elements, including bandits, shall be disarmed immediately and assisted through rehabilitation and integration into civil society.

II. Cease-fire monitoring group

2.1 A cease-fire monitoring group comprising UNITAF/United Nations troops shall be established immediately. There shall also be a committee composed of representatives of the warring factions to interlocute with the monitoring group and observe the implementation of the agreement by UNITAF/United Nations troops.

III. All sides agree in principle that properties unlawfully taken during the fighting shall be returned to the lawful owners. This shall be implemented as and when the situation allows.

IV. All POWs shall be freed and handed over to the International Committee of the Red Cross and/or UNITAF. This process shall commence immediately and be completed by 1 March 1993.

The present agreement shall enter into effect on 15 January 1993.

Source: "The Situation in Somalia," UN Document S/25168, January 26, 1993

D. Addis Ababa Agreement of the First Session of the Conference on National Reconciliation in Somalia

March 27, 1993

After long and costly years of civil war that ravaged our country, plunged it into famine, and caused acute suffering and loss of life among our people, there is the light of hope at last: progress has been made towards the restoration of peace, security and reconciliation in Somalia.

We, the Somali political leaders, recognize how vital it is that this process continue. It has our full commitment.

By our attendance at this historic Conference, we have resolved to put an end to armed conflict and to reconcile our differences through peaceful means. We pledge to consolidate and carry forward advances in peace, security and dialogue made since the beginning of this year. National reconciliation is now the most fervent wish of the Somali people.

We commit ourselves to continuing the peace process under the auspices of the United Nations and in cooperation with the Regional Organizations and the Standing Committee of the Horn as well as with our neighbors in the Horn of Africa.

After an era of pain, destruction and bloodshed that turned Somalis against Somalis, we have confronted our responsibility. We now pledge to work toward the rebirth of Somalia, to restore its dignity as a country and rightful place in the community of nations. At the close of the Holy Month of Ramadan, we believe this is the most precious gift we can give to our people.

The serenity and shade of a tree, which according to our Somali tradition is a place of reverence and rapprochement, has been replaced by the conference hall. Yet the promises made here are no less sacred or binding.

Therefore, we, the undersigned Somali political leaders, meeting at Africa Hall in Addis Ababa, Ethiopia between 15 and 27 March 1993, hereby reaffirm our commitment to the agreements signed during the Informal Preparatory Meeting on National Reconciliation in January 1993.

In concord to end hostilities, and to build on the foundation of peace for reconstruction and rehabilitation in Somalia, we agree to proceed within the framework of the following provisions and decisions:

I. Disarmament and Security

1. Affirm that uprooting of banditry and crime is necessary for peace, stability, security, reconciliation, reconstruction and development in Somalia;

2. Further affirm that disarmament must and shall be comprehensive, impartial and transparent;

3. Commit ourselves to complete, and simultaneous disarmament throughout the entire country in accordance with the disarmament concept and timeframe set by the Cease-fire Agreement of January 1993; and request that UNITAF/UNOSOM assist these efforts so as to achieve a substantial completion of the disarmament within 90 days;

4. Further reiterate our commitment to the strict, effective and expeditious implementation of the Cease-fire/Disarmament Agreement signed on 8 and 15 January 1993;

5. Reaffirm our commitment to comply with the requirements of the Cease-fire Agreement signed in January of 1993, including the total and complete handover of weapons to UNITAF/UNOSOM;

6. Urge UNITAF/UNOSOM to apply strong and effective sanctions against those responsible for any violation of the Cease-fire Agreement of January 1993;

7. Stress the need for the air, sea and land borders of Somalia to be closely guarded by UNITAF/UNOSOM in order to prevent any flow of arms into the country and to prevent violation of the territorial waters of Somalia;

8. Further stress the need for maximum cooperation by neighboring countries to assure that their common borders with Somalia are not used for the movement of weapons in Somalia, in keeping with the United Nations arms embargo against Somalia;

9. Agree on the need to establish an impartial National and Regional Somali Police Force in all regions of the country on an urgent basis through the reinstatement of the former Somali Police Force and recruitment and training of young Somalis from all regions, and request the assistance of the international community in this regard.

II. Rehabilitation and Reconstruction

1. Affirm the need to accelerate the supply and operation of relief, reconstruction and rehabilitation programs in Somalia;

2. Welcome the conclusion of the Third Coordination Meeting on Humanitarian Assistance to Somalia;

3. Express our appreciation to donor countries for their continued humanitarian assistance to Somalia and, in particular, for the generous pledge, made at the Third Coordination Meeting, to mobilize $142 million for relief and rehabilitation efforts in Somalia;

4. Call upon UNOSOM, aid agencies and donor countries to immediately assist in the rehabilitation of essential public and social services, and of necessary infrastructure, on a priority basis by the end of June 1993;

5. Assure the international community of the full desire of Somali leaders to reestablish, with the assistance of UNOSOM, a secure environment for relief, reconstruction and rehabilitation operations and the protection of relief and rehabilitation workers and supplies;

6. Condemn the acts of violence committed against relief workers and all forms of extortion regarding humanitarian operations;

7. Urge the organizations within the UN system and NGOs to effectively utilize Somali human resources in the rehabilitation and reconstruction process in Somalia.

III. Restoration of Property and Settlement of Disputes

1. Affirm that all disputes must henceforth be settled by dialogue, negotiations and other peaceful and legal means;

2. <u>Further affirm</u> that all private or public properties that were illegally confiscated, robbed, stolen, seized, embezzled or taken by other fraudulent means must be returned to their rightful owners;

3. <u>Decide </u>to deal with this matter within the framework specified in the report of the committee on the peaceful settlement of disputes.

IV. <u>Transitional Mechanisms</u>

The Somali people believe that there is concurrence among the people of Somalia that Somalia must retain its rightful place in the community of nations and that they must express their political views and make the decisions that affect them. This is an essential component of the search for peace.

To achieve this, political and administrative structures in Somalia need to be rebuilt to provide the people as a whole with an opportunity to participate in shaping the future of the country.

In this context, the establishment of transitional mechanisms which prepare the country for a stable and democratic future is absolutely essential. During the transitional period, which will last for a period of <u>two years</u> effective from the date of signature to this agreement, the emphasis will be upon the provision of essential services, complete disarmament, restoration of peace and domestic tranquility and on the attainment of the reconciliation of the Somali people. Emphasis will also be put on the rehabilitation and reconstruction of basic infrastructure and on the building of democratic institutions. All of this will prepare the country to enter a constitutional phase in which the institutions of democratic governance, rule of law, decentralization of power, protection of human rights and individual liberties, and the safeguarding of the integrity of the Somali Republic are all in place.

Therefore, we have agreed to a broad outline of a framework for a transitional system of governance to allow for the provision of essential services, the creation of a basis for long-term planning, and for the resumption of greater administrative responsibility by Somalis. In general terms, this system will be composed of four basic administrative components that will be mandated to function during the transitional period.

Taking into account the reality of the situation in Somalia today and the need for stability, we hereby agree to the establishment of the following four basic transitional organs of authority:

1. <u>The Transitional National Council (TNC)</u>

The TNC will:

a) be the repository of Somali sovereignty;

b) be the prime political authority having legislative functions during the period in question;

c) interact, as appropriate, with the international community, including UNOSOM;

d) appoint various committees, including the Transitional Charter Drafting Committee, as required;

e) appoint Officers for its various functions;

f) appoint the heads of administrative departments;

g) oversee the performance of the departments created; and

h) establish an independent Judiciary.

The TNC shall be composed of:

a) Three representatives from each of the 18 regions currently recognized, including one woman from each region;

b) Five additional seats for Mogadishu;

c) One nominee from each of the political factions currently participating in the First session of the National Reconciliation Conference;

2. <u>The Central Administrative Departments (CADs)</u>

The TNC will appoint the heads of the Central Administrative Departments, whose prime function will be to re-establish and operate the departments of civil administration, social affairs, economic affairs and humanitarian affairs, paving the way for the re-establishment and operation of a formal government. The CADs shall comprise skilled professionals having the ability to reinstate, gradually, the administrative functions of national public administration. The performance of these departments will be overseen by the TNC.

3. Regional Council (RCs)

Regional Councils shall be established in all the existing 18 regions of Somalia. The present 18 regions shall be maintained during the transitional period. The Regional Councils shall be entrusted primarily with the task of implementing humanitarian, social and economic programs in coordination with the TNC and will also assist in the conducting of the internationally-supervised census. The Regional Councils will liaise with UNOSOM II, UN specialized agencies, NGOs and other relevant organizations directly and through the Central Administrative Departments and Transitional National Council. The Regional Councils shall also be responsible for law and order at the regional level. In this regard, the law enforcement institution will be a regional police force and a regional judiciary. The District Councils (see below) in each region shall send representatives who will constitute the Regional Councils.

4. District Councils

District Councils shall be established in the present districts in every region. District council members shall be appointed through election or through consensus-based selection in accordance with Somali traditions. The District Councils shall be responsible for managing the affairs of the district including public safety, health, education and reconstruction.

V. Conclusion

The Conference agreed on the appointment, by the TNC, of a Transitional Charter Drafting Committee referred to in section IV 1 (d) above. In drafting the Transitional Charter, the Committee shall be guided by the basic principles of the Universal Declaration of Human Rights and by the Somali traditional ethics.

The Conference agreed that the TNC shall appoint a "Peace Delegation" composed of political movements and other social elements to travel to all parts of the country for the purpose of advancing the peace and reconciliation process as well as to explain the agreements reached in Addis Ababa.

We further agree that the TNC shall appoint a National Committee to bring about reconciliation and seek solutions to outstanding political problems with the SNM.

The Conference also calls upon the international community and in particular on the neighboring states to facilitate the noble effort at reconciliation by providing moral and material support.

In conclusion, we the undersigned, in agreeing to the above, resolve that never again will Somalia suffer the tragedy of the recent past. Emerging from the darkness of catastrophe and war, we Somalis herald the beginning of a new era of peace, of healing and rebuilding, in which cooperation and trust will overcome hatred and suspicion. It is a message we must pass on to our children and our grandchildren so that the proud Somali family, as we knew it, can once again become whole.

We, the undersigned, hereby pledge to abandon the logic of force for the ethic of dialogue. We will pursue the process of national reconciliation with vigor and sincerity, in accordance with this declaration and with the cooperation of the people of Somalia as a whole.

Recognizing the tragic and painful recent history of problems in our country, we pledge to achieve comprehensive national reconciliation through peaceful means. We also pledge to adopt, in all parts of Somalia, transitional measures that will contribute to harmony and healing of wounds among all the people of Somalia.

We invite the Secretary-General of the United Nations and his Special Representative in Somalia, in accordance with the mandate entrusted to them by the UN Security Council, to extend all necessary assistance to the people of Somalia for the implementation of this agreement.

SIGNATORIES

1. SAMO   Mohamed R. Arbow
2. SDA   Mohamed F. Abdullahi
3. SDM   Abdi Musse Mayow
4. SDM (SNA) Mohamed Nur Alio
5. SNDU   Ali Ismail Abdi
6. SNF   Gen. Omar Haji Mohamed

7. SNU   Mohamed Rajis Mohamed

8. SPM   Gen. Aden Abdullahi Nur

9. SPM (SNA)   Ahmed Hashi Mahmmud

10. SSDF   Gen. Mohammed Abshir Mussa

11. SSNM   Abdi Warsame Isaq

12. USC (SNA)   Gen. Mohammed Farah H. Aidid

13. USC   Mohammed Qanyare Afrah

14. USF   Abdurahman Dualeh Ali

15. USP   Mohamed Abdi Hashi

Before proceeding to adopt the Agreement, I should also like to confirm to the participants that at the meeting of all political leaders yesterday, prior to the signing of the document they unanimously agreed that one of the five additional seats for Mogadishu would be reserved for Mr. Ali Mahdi. This understanding remains binding.

Source: John Hirsch

E. UN Security Council Resolution 814

March 26, 1993

The Security Council,

Reaffirming its resolutions 733 (1992) of 23 January 1992, 746 (1992) of 17 March 1992, 751 (1992) of 24 April 1992, 767 (1992) of 27 July 1992, 775 (1992) of 28 August 1992 and 794 (1992) of 3 December 1992,

Bearing in mind General Assembly resolution 47/167 of 18 December 1992,

Commending the efforts of Member States acting pursuant to resolution 794 (1992) to establish a secure environment for humanitarian relief operations in Somalia,

Acknowledging the need for a prompt, smooth and phased transition from the Unified Task Force (UNITAF) to the expanded United Nations Operation in Somalia (UNOSOM II),

Regretting the continuing incidents of violence in Somalia and the threat they pose to the reconciliation process,

Deploring the acts of violence against persons engaging in humanitarian efforts on behalf of the United Nations, States, and non-governmental organizations,

Noting with deep regret and concern the continuing reports of widespread violations of international humanitarian law and the general absence of the rule of law in Somalia,

Recognizing that the people of Somalia bear the ultimate responsibility for national reconciliation and reconstruction of their own country,

Acknowledging the fundamental importance of a comprehensive and effective programme for disarming Somali parties, including movements and factions,

Noting the need for continued humanitarian relief assistance and for the rehabilitation of Somalia's political institutions and economy,

Concerned that the crippling famine and drought in Somalia, compounded by the civil strife, have caused massive destruction to the means of production and the natural and human resources of that country,

Expressing its appreciation to the Organization of African Unity, the League of Arab States, the Organization of the Islamic Conference and the Non-Aligned Movement for their cooperation with, and support of, the efforts of the United Nations in Somalia,

Further expressing its appreciation to all Member States which have made contributions to the Fund established pursuant to paragraph 11 of resolution 794 (1992) and to all those who have provided humanitarian assistance to Somalia,

Commending the efforts, in difficult circumstances, of the initial United Nations Operation in Somalia (UNOSOM) established pursuant to resolution 751 (1992),

Expressing its appreciation for the invaluable assistance the neighbouring countries have been providing to the international community in its efforts to restore peace and security in Somalia and to host large numbers of refugees displaced by the conflict and taking note of the difficulties caused to them due to the presence of refugees in their territories,

Convinced that the restoration of law and order throughout Somalia would contribute to humanitarian relief operations, reconciliation and political settlement, as well as to the rehabilitation of Somalia's political institutions and economy,

Convinced also of the need for broad-based consultations and deliberations to achieve reconciliation, agreement on the setting up of transitional government institutions and consensus on basic principles and steps leading to the establishment of representative democratic institutions,

Recognizing that the re-establishment of local and regional administrative institutions is essential to the restoration of domestic tranquillity,

Encouraging the Secretary-General and his Special Representative to continue and intensify their work at the national, regional and local levels, including and encouraging broad participation by all sectors of Somali society, to promote the process of political settlement and national reconciliation and to assist the people of Somalia in rehabilitating their political institutions and economy,

Expressing its readiness to assist the people of Somalia, as appropriate, on a local, regional or national level, to participate in free and fair elections, with a view towards achieving and implementing a political settlement,

Welcoming the progress made at the United Nations-sponsored Informal Preparatory Meeting on Somali Political Reconciliation in Addis Ababa from 4 to 15 January 1993, in particular the conclusion at that meeting of three agreements by the Somali parties, including movements and factions, and welcoming also any progress made at the Conference on National Reconciliation which began in Addis Ababa on 15 March 1993,

Emphasizing the need for the Somali people, including movements and factions, to show the political will to achieve security, reconciliation and peace,

Noting the reports of States concerned of 17 December 1992 (S/24976) and 19 January 1993 (S/25126) and of the Secretary-General of 19 December 1992 (S/24992) and 26 January 1993 (S/25168) on the implementation of resolution 794 (1992),

Having examined the report of the Secretary-General of 3 March 1993 (S/25354 and Add.1 and 2),

Welcoming the intention of the Secretary-General to seek maximum economy and efficiency and to keep the size of the United Nations presence, both military and civilian, to the minimum necessary to fulfil its mandate,

Determining that the situation in Somalia continues to threaten peace and security in the region,

A

1. Approves the report of the Secretary-General of 3 March 1993;

2. Expresses its appreciation to the Secretary-General for convening the Conference on National Reconciliation for Somalia in accordance with the agreements reached during the Informal Preparatory Meeting on Somali Political Reconciliation in Addis Ababa in January 1993

and for the progress achieved towards political reconciliation in Somalia, and also for his efforts to ensure that, as appropriate, all Somalis, including movements, factions, community leaders, women, professionals, intellectuals, elders and other representative groups are suitably represented at such conferences;

3. <u>Welcomes</u> the convening of the Third United Nations Coordination Meeting for Humanitarian Assistance for Somalia in Addis Ababa from 11 to 13 March 1993 and the willingness expressed by Governments through this process to contribute to relief and rehabilitation efforts in Somalia, where and when possible;

4. <u>Requests</u> the Secretary-General, through his Special Representative, and with assistance, as appropriate, from all relevant United Nations entities, offices and specialized agencies, to provide humanitarian and other assistance to the people of Somalia in rehabilitating their political institutions and economy and promoting political settlement and national reconciliation, in accordance with the recommendations contained in his report of 3 March 1993, including in particular:

   (a) To assist in the provision of relief and in the economic rehabilitation of Somalia, based on an assessment of clear, prioritized needs, and taking into account, as appropriate, the 1993 Relief and Rehabilitation Programme for Somalia prepared by the United Nations Department of Humanitarian Affairs;

   (b) To assist in the repatriation of refugees and displaced persons within Somalia;

   (c) To assist the people of Somalia to promote and advance political reconciliation, through broad participation by all sectors of Somali society, and the re-establishment of national and regional institutions and civil administration in the entire country;

   (d) To assist in the re-establishment of Somali police, as appropriate at the local, regional or national level, to assist in the restoration and maintenance of peace, stability and law and order, including in the investigation and facilitating the prosecution of serious violations of international humanitarian law;

   (e) To assist the people of Somalia in the development of a coherent and integrated programme for the removal of mines throughout Somalia;

(f) To develop appropriate public information activities in support of the United Nations activities in Somalia;

(g) To create conditions under which Somali civil society may have a role, at every level, in the process of political reconciliation and in the formulation and realization of rehabilitation and reconstruction programmes;

B

Acting under Chapter VII of the Charter of the United Nations,

5. Decides to expand the size of the UNOSOM force and its mandate in accordance with the recommendations contained in paragraphs 56-88 of the report of the Secretary-General of 3 March 1993, and the provisions of this resolution;

6. Authorizes the mandate for the expanded UNOSOM (UNOSOM II) for an initial period through 31 October 1993, unless previously renewed by the Security Council;

7. Emphasizes the crucial importance of disarmament and the urgent need to build on the efforts of UNITAF in accordance with paragraphs 59-69 of the report of the Secretary-General of 3 March 1993;

8. Demands that all Somali parties, including movements and factions, comply fully with the commitments they have undertaken in the agreements they concluded at the Informal Preparatory Meeting on Somali Political Reconciliation in Addis Ababa, and in particular with their Agreement on Implementing the Cease-fire and on Modalities of Disarmament (S/25168, annex III);

9. Further demands that all Somali parties, including movements and factions, take all measures to ensure the safety of the personnel of the United Nations and its agencies as well as the staff of the International Committee of the Red Cross (ICRC), intergovernmental organizations and non-governmental organizations engaged in providing humanitarian and other assistance to the people of Somalia in rehabilitating their political institutions and economy and promoting political settlement and national reconciliation;

10. Requests the Secretary-General to support from within Somalia the implementation of the arms embargo established by resolution 733 (1992), utilizing as available and appropriate the UNOSOM II forces authorized by this resolution, and to report on this subject, with any recommendations regarding more effective measures if necessary, to the Security Council;

11. Calls upon all States, in particular neighbouring States, to cooperate in the implementation of the arms embargo established by resolution 733 (1992);

12. Requests the Secretary-General to provide security, as appropriate, to assist in the repatriation of refugees and the assisted resettlement of displaced persons, utilizing UNOSOM II forces, paying particular attention to those areas where major instability continues to threaten peace and security in the region;

13. Reiterates its demand that all Somali parties, including movements and factions, immediately cease and desist from all breaches of international humanitarian law and reaffirms that those responsible for such acts be held individually accountable;

14. Requests the Secretary-General, through his Special Representative, to direct the Force Commander of UNOSOM II to assume responsibility for the consolidation, expansion and maintenance of a secure environment throughout Somalia, taking account of the particular circumstances in each locality, on an expedited basis in accordance with the recommendations contained in his report of 3 March 1993, and in this regard to organize a prompt, smooth and phased transition from UNITAF to UNOSOM II;

15. Requests the Secretary-General to maintain the fund established pursuant to resolution 794 (1992) for the additional purpose of receiving contributions for maintenance of UNOSOM II forces following the departure of UNITAF forces and for the establishment of Somali police, and calls on Member States to make contributions to this fund, in addition to their assessed contributions;

16. Expresses appreciation to the United Nations agencies, intergovernmental and non-governmental organizations and the ICRC for their contributions and assistance and requests the Secretary-General to

ask them to continue to extend financial, material and technical support to the Somali people in all regions of the country;

17. Requests the Secretary-General to seek, as appropriate, pledges and contributions from States and others to assist in financing the rehabilitation of the political institutions and economy of Somalia;

18. Requests the Secretary-General to keep the Security Council fully informed on action taken to implement the present resolution, in particular to submit as soon as possible a report to the Council containing recommendations for establishment of Somali police forces and thereafter to report no later than every ninety days on the progress achieved in accomplishing the objectives set out in the present resolution;

19. Decides to conduct a formal review of the progress towards accomplishing the purposes of the present resolution no later than 31 October 1993;

20. Decides to remain actively seized of the matter.

F. UN Security Council Resolution 837

June 6, 1993

The Security Council,

Reaffirming its resolutions 733 (1992) of 23 January 1992, 746 (1992) of 17 March 1992, 751 (1992) of 24 April 1992, 767 (1992) of 27 July 1992, 775 (1992) of 28 August 1992, 794 (1992) of 3 December 1992 and 814 (1993) of 26 March 1993,

Bearing in mind General Assembly resolution 47/167 of 18 December 1992,

Gravely alarmed at the premeditated armed attacks launched by forces apparently belonging to the United Somali Congress (USC/SNA) against the personnel of the United Nations Operation in Somalia (UNOSOM II) on 5 June 1993,

Strongly condemning such actions, which directly undermine international efforts aimed at the restoration of peace and normalcy in Somalia,

Expressing outrage at the loss of life as a result of these criminal attacks,

Reaffirming its commitment to assist the people of Somalia in reestablishing conditions of normal life,

Stressing that the international community is involved in Somalia in order to help the people of Somalia who have suffered untold miseries due to years of civil strife in that country,

Acknowledging the fundamental importance of completing the comprehensive and effective programme for disarming all Somali parties, including movements and factions,

Convinced that the restoration of law and order throughout Somali would contribute to humanitarian relief operations, reconciliation and political settlement, as well as to the rehabilitation of Somalia's political institutions and economy,

Condemning strongly the use of radio broadcasts, in particular by the USC/SNA, to incite attacks against United Nations personnel,

Recalling the statement made by its president on 31 March 1993 (S/25493) concerning the safety of United Nations forces and personnel deployed in conditions of strife and committed to consider promptly measures appropriate to the particular circumstances to ensure that persons responsible for attacks and other acts of violence against United Nations forces and personnel are held to account for their actions,

Taking note of the information provided to the Council by the Secretary-General on 6 June 1993,

Determining that the situation in Somalia continues to threaten peace and security in the region,

Acting under Chapter VII of the Charter of the United Nations,

1. Strongly condemns the unprovoked armed attacks against the personnel of UNOSOM II on 5 June 1993, which appear to have been part of a calculated and premeditated series of cease-fire violations to prevent by intimidation UNOSOM II from carrying out its mandate as provided for in resolution 814 (1993);

2. Expresses its condolences to the Government and people of Pakistan and the families of the UNOSOM II personnel who have lost their lives;

3. Reemphasizes the crucial importance of the early implementation of the disarmament of all Somali parties, including movements and factions, in accordance with paragraphs 56–69 of the report of the Secretary-General of 3 March 1993 (S/25354), and of neutralizing radio broadcasting systems that contribute to the violence and attacks directed against UNOSOM II;

4. Demands once again that all Somali parties, including movements and factions, comply fully with the commitments they have undertaken in the agreements they concluded at the informal Preparatory Meeting on Somali Political Reconciliation in Addis Ababa, and in particular with their Agreement on Implementing the Cease-fire and on Modalities of Disarmament (S/25168, annex III);

5. Reaffirms that the Secretary-General is authorized under resolution 814 (1993) to take all necessary measures against all those responsible for the armed attacks referred to in paragraph 1 above, including against those responsible for publicly inciting such attacks, to establish the effective authority of UNOSOM II throughout Somalia, including to secure the investigation of their actions and their arrest and detention for prosecution, trial and punishment;

6. Requests the Secretary-General urgently to inquire into the incident, with particular emphasis on the role of those factional leaders involved;

7. Encourages the rapid and accelerated deployment of all UNOSOM II contingents to meet the full requirements of 28,000 men, all ranks, as well as equipment, as indicated in the Secretary-General's report of 3 March 1993 (S/25354);

8. Urges Member States to contribute, on an emergency basis, military support and transportation, including armored personnel carriers, tanks and attack helicopters, to provide UNOSOM II the capability appropriately to confront and deter armed attacks directed against it in the accomplishment of its mandate;

9. Further requests the Secretary-General to submit a report to the Council on the implementation of the present resolution, if possible within seven days from the date of its adoption;

10. Decides to remain actively seized of the matter.

G. Radio Address by Mohamed Farah Aideed (excerpts)
March 10, 1994

In the name of Allah, the gracious, the merciful

Allahu akbar allahu akbar allahu akbar

Ladies and gentlemen,
Brothers and sisters

First of all accept my warmest greetings with great love and affection. I am congratulating you for the holy month of Ramadhan wishing all of you to fast and celebrate the iid-al-fitr in joy and happiness.

Brothers and sisters,

As you may all be aware of, I have been away from the country for a relatively long period of time and this is due to extraordinarily heavy duties relating to the current difficulties facing our country.

To give you brief details of these heavy tasks, we have been addressing two extremely important issues, namely;

1. a) to create and nurture mutual understanding among the Somali people in order to achieve a lasting peace settlement in Somalia.

   b) to pave the way for the formation of an all inclusive broad based government of national unity.

2. To convey and brief the world governments and the international community at large on the political, social and economic realities in Somalia, and the SNA's general principles, policies, strategies and views to approach the national issues of our country.

We have temporarily established our base here in Nairobi since many Somali political organizations and a large number of Somali people in all walks of life are stationed here. During this period we had an opportunity to have constant contacts with many Somali political organizations and their supporters.

Since this was a rare opportunity which we could not have secured in the last several years, we have deemed it necessary to sacrifice much time and effort to conduct a series of informal meetings, sessions, consultations, exchange of views and ideas, and profound mutual briefings with Somali political organizations and their supporters all of which are intended to get rid of suspicion, mistrust and all ill feelings which resulted from the civil war.

The fruitful results of these efforts include among other things that most of the Somali people and organizations we met have demonstrated mutual understanding, cordial and brotherly feelings, and their readiness in cooperation to bring a lasting peace in all parts of the country and to work for the reconstruction of Somalia.

Another good result of those meetings and sessions is that it is agreed to make peace in all parts of the country where hostilities still persist. It is also agreed to make Kismayo and its related environment a zone of peace following the pattern of peace-making in the central and north-eastern regions.

As for the general political issues tremendous achievements were made when many Somali people and organizations have taken a common political stand with the SNA on the basis of the national interests, and these common political views paved the way for the formation of a broad based national government in the near future. It is also a great pleasure for us that during our stay here in Nairobi the fifth organization—the Somali Peace Loving Union (SPLU)—has joined the Somali National Alliance (SNA) while other organizations have applied to join in the SNA.

Major successes have also been achieved on the issue of foreign policy during our stay in Nairobi. We had an opportunity to visit in their countries four eastern and horn of Africa presidents with whom we had exchanged our ideas and views.

We have also met with senior envoys and delegates from the U.S., Russia, Italy, Zimbabwe, Eritrea, Ethiopia, Uganda, Sudan, representatives from the donor countries, the deputy OAU secretary general, ambassadors and diplomats all of whom were interested in the Somali issue. We learned from all these governments and organizations that the world fully agreed and supports the SNA position to leave the Somalis to solve their problems. The intrusion on the lives and properties of the Somali people was a serious mistake; and as a result of these the world has agreed to change the mistaken policies pursued by UNOSOM. This change was demonstrated in the UN Security Council resolutions 855 and 879. It was also manifested in the formation of the new independent organ to direct and coordinate rehabilitation and the reconstruction programs for Somalia. The transfer and the replacement of UNOSOM officials involved in UNOSOM's misguided policies and the resulting destruction is an unmistakable indication that the world has recognized the serious mistakes committed by UNOSOM.

Therefore in responding to these positive changes we had an opportunity to meet with the new UNOSOM administrators, who agreed with us that the Somali people have the exclusive right to decide the future of their country and to solve their political problems while UNOSOM provides the necessary assistance, and UNOSOM troops will be confined to protect the relief aid and the security of the aid workers.

So that, it is necessary for us to take advantage of the assistance provided by the international community, to overcome our current difficulties. It is necessary for us to join our hands and to work together for peace and to rebuild our country since we are now left alone to decide our destiny. We also have the heavy responsibilities to protect and ensure the safety of the foreign aid workers who came from distant places for the purpose of helping our suffering people.

I would like to remind you that the assistance provided by the international community is limited in time, and in quantity. Therefore, it is the responsibility of all Somalis to facilitate the smooth operation of the aid programs to make it possible for all Somalis wherever they are to derive the maximum benefits possible.

We have the obligation to provide the necessary security for the withdrawing UN troops to enable them to have a safe withdrawal.

Finally we would like to express our gratitude to the UN Security Council, the donor countries, the governments in the eastern and horn of Africa and to all those who contributed to the change of the mistaken policies by UNOSOM.

Our special thanks are due to the government and the people of the United States for their courageous decision to change its policy when they fully understood the realities in Somalia.

We are also grateful to the transitional government of Ethiopia for its great contribution to bring about the above mentioned changes and their key role in mediating between the SNA and the new administration of UNOSOM.

Source: Bureau of African Affairs, U.S. Department of State, Washington, D.C.

Select Bibliography

BOOKS

Drew, Elizabeth. *On the Edge: The Clinton Presidency*. New York: Simon and Schuster, 1994.

Drysdale, John. *Whatever Happened to Somalia*. London: Haan Associates, 1994.

Laitin, David, and Said Samatar. *Somalia: Nation in Search of a State*. Boulder: Westview Press, 1987.

Lewis, I. M. *Understanding Somalia: Guide to Culture, History, and Social Institutions*. London: Haan Associates, 1993.

Makinda, Samuel M. *Seeking Peace from Chaos: Humanitarian Intervention in Somalia*. Boulder: Lynne Rienner Publishers, 1993.

Metz, Helen Chapin, ed. *Somalia: A Country Study*. Washington, D.C.: Congressional Research Service, 1993.

Righter, Rosemary. *Utopia Lost: The United Nations and World Order*. New York: Twentieth Century Fund Press, 1995.

Sahnoun, Mohamed. *Somalia: The Missed Opportunities*. Washington, D.C.: United States Institute of Peace Press, 1994.

ARTICLES AND REPORTS

Adam, Hussein M. "Rethinking the Somali Political Experience." U.S. Institute of Peace symposium, Washington, D.C., October 16, 1992.

——. "A Terrible Beauty Being Born?" In I. William Zartman, ed., *Collapsed States*. Boulder: Lynne Rienner Publishers, forthcoming.

Bolton, John R. "Wrong Turn in Somalia." *Foreign Affairs*, January–February 1994.

Callahan, Thomas J. "Some Observations on Somalia's Past and Future." *CSIS Africa Notes*, March 1994.

Clarke, Walter J. "Testing the World's Resolve in Somalia." *Parameters*, U.S. Army War College Quarterly, vol. 23, no. 4, Winter 1993–94.

Cohen, Herman J. "Intervention in Somalia." In Allan Goodman, ed., *The Diplomatic Record 1992–1993*. Boulder: Westview Press, forthcoming.

"Country Reports on Human Rights Practice for 1993." Washington, D.C.: U.S. Government Printing Office, February 1994.

Farer, Tom. "A Paradigm of Legitimate Intervention." In *Enforcing Restraint: Collective Intervention in Internal Conflicts*. New York: Council on Foreign Relations, 1993.

Hall, Brian. "Blue Helmets." *New York Times Magazine*, January 2, 1994.

Hamrick, S. J. "Aideed It My Way." *New Republic*, August 9, 1993.

Hoar, Joseph P. "Humanitarian Assistance Operations Challenges: The CENTCOM Perspective on Somalia." *Joint Forces Quarterly*, vol. 1, no. 2, November 1993.

Natsios, Andrew. "Food Through Force: Humanitarian Intervention and US Policy." *Washington Quarterly*, vol. 17, no. 1, Winter 1994.

Oakley, Robert B. "An Envoy's Perspective." *Joint Forces Quarterly*, Autumn 1993.

"Peacemaking and Peacekeeping: Implications for the United States Military." Washington, D.C.: United States Institute of Peace, 1993.

"The Professionalization of Peacekeeping." Washington, D.C.: United States Institute of Peace, 1993.

Rawson, David. "The Somali State and Foreign Aid: Development and Disintegration," unpublished.

"A Report on the Second Annual Peacekeeping Mission," November 2–16, 1993. New York: United Nations Association of the USA, 1994.

"Report to the Congress on U.S. Policy in Somalia." Office of the President, Washington, D.C., October 13, 1993.

Rikhye, Indar Jit. "Strengthening UN Peacekeeping: New Challenges and Proposals." Washington, D.C.: United States Institute of Peace, 1993.

Rivlin, Benjamin. "The Problematic Role of Regionalism in Peacekeeping." New York: Ralph Bunche Institute on the United Nations, May 19, 1994.

Ruggie, John Gerard. "Peacekeeping and U.S. Interests." *Washington Quarterly*, Autumn 1994.

Samatar, Said. "Somalia: A Nation in Turmoil." London: Minority Rights Group, 1991.

Schraeder, Peter J. "The Horn of Africa: U.S. Foreign Policy in an Altered Cold War Environment." *Middle East Journal*, vol. 46, no. 4, Autumn 1992.

"Somalia and Operation Restore Hope: A Preliminary Assessment." London: African Rights, May 1993.

Stevenson, Jonathan. "Hope Restored in Somalia?" *Foreign Policy*, no. 91, Summer 1993.

Urquhart, Brian. "Needed: A U.N. Volunteer Military Force." *New York Review of Books*, June 10, 1993.

——."Who Can Police the World?" *New York Review of Books*, May 12, 1994.

United States Institute of Peace

The United States Institute of Peace is an independent, nonpartisan federal institution created and funded by Congress to strengthen the nation's capacity to promote the peaceful resolution of international conflict. Established in 1984, the Institute meets its congressional mandate through an array of programs, including grants, fellowships, conferences and workshops, library services, publications, and other educational activities. The Institute's Board of Directors is appointed by the President of the United States and confirmed by the Senate.